**BY UNITED MEN OF HONOR**

UNSTOPPABLE LEADERS

PRESSING FORWARD WITH POWER

VISIONARY AUTHORS

BRETT DABE & KEN A. HOBBS II

CONTENTS

Introduction v

Embracing Advertunity, Ken A. Hobbs II 1

Chasing Shadows, Christopher Simpson 17

When the Wounded Rise, Jim Beaulne 29

Living Under His Watchful Eye, Bob Tardell 45

The Refiner's Fire, Brian Wheeler 57

The Narrow Way That Leads to Life, Rob McLaughlin 73

Keeping the Ground You've Gained, Jeribai Tascoe 85

A Journey of Faith, Marriage, and Grace, Jon Maples 101

From Darkness to His Marvelous Light,
Antonio Fernandez Saavedra 113

From Death to Life, Eric Bucher 129

Led by THE Unstoppable Leader, Joshua P. Clark 141

From Self to Servant, Joshua Ajini 157

Our God Can, David S. Stroup 167

Strength in Surrender, Sanul Corrielus 183

The Thrill of Being a Godly Leader, Dwight W. Bell 195

From 467 to Freedom, Tim May 209

On the Team, In the Game, Ryan Otto 221

From Broken to Blessed, Greg Coury 235

Discovering Whose You Are, Nick Reyes 247

The Search for Serenity, George Mercado 261

Finding the Warrior in Me, Stanley VanHorn 271

God's Perfect Plan, Tyler Carroll 287

From Fear to Love, Brett Dabe 299

Afterword 311

INTRODUCTION

When it storms in Yellowstone National Park, not surprisingly, most animals flee. But the mighty bison does something extraordinary—it charges directly into the approaching storm, which minimizes its time in hardship and helps it emerge stronger.

What if, as followers of Christ, we were to lead like bison, with the same counterintuitive courage?

We live in a world that whispers, "Avoid conflict. Dodge difficulty. Wait for safer conditions." But Jesus calls us to something radically different. He calls us to courageous and unstoppable leadership. And although leading on God's terms may not take us down a comfortable path, with His direction and provision, we can lead our followers through the storms of life and emerge stronger.

When Jesus walked on water toward His terrified disciples, He didn't calm the storm first and then safely approach the boat; He stepped through the chaos of the wind and waves. When Peter asked to join Him, Jesus didn't say, "Wait for calmer seas." He said one word: *"Come"* (Matthew 14:29 NIV).

That same invitation echoes through Scripture and into our lives today.

Jesus modeled a leadership that confounded worldly wisdom. He touched lepers when others maintained distance, ate with tax collectors when religious leaders demanded separation, and spoke truth when silence would have been safer. Our Lord and Savior chose a cross when a crown was within His reach.

Jesus' own life is the blueprint for the type of leadership He is calling you to. Our Savior didn't promise us a life free from hardship. Instead, He promised something better: His presence in the middle of every trial.

*"In this world you will have trouble, but take heart!
I have overcome the world"* (John 16:33 NIV).

Jesus doesn't always offer those who lead for Him an escape route from difficulties. But He always provides us with the power to be resilient, influential, authentic, persistent, and purposeful, allowing us to lead those He has entrusted us with through the storms of life and emerge triumphant.

Every parable Jesus told, every miracle He performed, and every confrontation He encountered revealed this truth: God's kingdom operates by different principles than the world's systems. Where the world sees impossibility, our all-powerful God sees opportunity. So where others might retreat, kingdom leaders will have the courage necessary to decisively advance into a future that God has given them the vision to see.

Jesus spent forty days in the wilderness facing temptations, not avoiding them. He wept over Jerusalem's rebellion, not ignoring it. He sweat blood as He faced the cross, not bypassing it. At every crucial moment, Jesus moved toward the challenge, not away from it.

This is your inheritance as His follower.

You are called to be a leader in all circumstances—not just the comfortable ones. God has commissioned you to be an unstoppable leader who influences earth's problems using heaven's solutions. To be salt that preserves and light that exposes. To be a man who doesn't just survive storms but learns to dance in the rain.

Jesus invested three years developing ordinary men into world-changing leaders. He did not do this by protecting them from hardship, but by preparing them, teaching them, and guiding them. He sent them out with minimal resources and maximum faith, and promised to send the Holy Spirit to accompany them on their journey of leadership.

Under the apostles' leadership, the early church exploded across the Roman Empire. These weren't men with advanced degrees or political connections. They were ordinary guys who had learned to think like their Master. They understood that what looks like defeat can become victory, what seems like an end can become a beginning.

However, Jesus also shared the vision that though the harvest would be plentiful, the workers would be few. Today, He is offering you the Holy Spirit and calling you to be His worker—His world-changing leader.

The principles Christ demonstrated in the Bible aren't outdated religious concepts. They're timeless leadership truths that work in boardrooms and living rooms, in churches and communities. When you lead as Jesus led, people don't just follow your instructions; they catch your vision. They don't just complete tasks; they embrace transformation.

That same Spirit who raised Christ from the dead lives in His people today. If you have invited Him into your life, the same authority that calmed storms and healed sickness flows through you, and the same love that drew tax collectors and transformed prostitutes beats in your heart. And if you haven't yet invited Him into your life, keep reading! An adventure greater than you could ever imagine awaits you!

Jesus doesn't offer you His power to make your life easier, however. He gives it to make your life matter more. He's calling you to leadership that goes beyond managing your comfort. Leadership that creates, rather than consumes, builds up rather than breaks down, and serves rather than demands service.

This kind of leadership doesn't wait for perfect preparation or ideal circumstances. It acts in accordance with divine instruction even when human logic argues otherwise. It trusts God's promises more than present problems and believes that we can overcome natural challenges with supernatural solutions.

The world desperately needs men to lead as Jesus led. Men who combine strength with gentleness, truth with grace, and conviction with compassion. Men who aren't afraid to disrupt the status quo when the status quo dishonors God or hurts people.

Your community, your workplace, your family—they're all waiting for the leader you've been called to be—not perfect, but obedient to our heavenly Father. Not fearless, but faithful to God's call. You are not destined to be a leader who has all the answers, but one who knows God, *the* answer-giver, personally.

Storms are coming. They always do. Economic pressures, cultural shifts, and personal crises are all part of living in a fallen world. But with God in your corner, you will never have to face them alone. The One who walked on water walks with you. The One who multiplied loaves will multiply your efforts. The One who conquered death will conquer your fears.

Jesus didn't build His church on men who avoided storms; he built it on men who learned to trust Him in the middle of the storms. Men who discovered that His strength really is made perfect in weakness and His grace truly is sufficient for every need.

This is your moment to step into that inheritance.

The question Jesus asks hasn't changed in two thousand years: "Who do you say that I am?" Your answer to that question will determine everything about how you lead. If you say that He's just a good teacher, you'll lead with good advice. If you believe that He's merely a good moral example, you'll lead with noble intentions.

But if your response is that Jesus Christ is truly Lord, the risen Christ who holds all authority in heaven and earth, then you have the power to lead with supernatural confidence, knowing that He who began a good work in you will complete it.

Unstoppable Leaders: Pressing Forward with Power

The storm clouds are gathering. While others seek shelter, Jesus is calling you to walk on water.

Will you step out of the boat? Will you strive to be an *Unstoppable Leader*? Your future awaits.

Ken A. Hobbs II

Ken A. Hobbs II is a Christ follower devoted to impacting others in para-church ministries, missions, and business, where he leads a marketplace ministry. Ken is the Founder of United Men of Honor—leading, coaching, and empowering men to lead with integrity and faith in their homes, businesses, and communities. www.unitedmenofhonor.com. His previous three books, *United Men of Honor: Overcoming Adversity Through Faith, Navigating Your Storm,* and *Fit 2 Fight,* are #1 Amazon best-sellers.

Ken is an executive team leader and serves on the Leadership Team of Band of Brothers. He is passionate about the bootcamps, which prevent men from fighting their struggles alone. www.GreatLakesBootcamp.com and www.BandofBrothersFL.com

A a Senior Vice President/Financial Coach/Multiple Brokerage owner and operator for www.primerica.com/kenhobbs2, Ken has impacted communities nationwide with business-building, coaching/training, personal financial coaching, and services for over 30 years. Visit www.TheRealHowMoneyWorks.com/us/Kenhobbs2 for your free book on How Money Works.

Ken supports his wife, Kimberly, in Women World Leaders and World Publishing and Productions. www.WomenWorldLeaders.com. He also supports Kerus Global Education, African Orphan Care Project, and anti-trafficking/trauma training as an Advisory Board member. www.kerusglobal.org

Ken is a husband, father, stepfather, brother, and uncle who passionately loves his family and friends.

EMBRACING ADVERTUNITY

By Ken A. Hobbs II

When adversity creates an opportunity, it is what I call an Advertunity!

Advertunity is the word I use to describe my life. From my earliest memories until today, it has defined my decision-making and my hope for the future. We all face challenges and adversity; it is just a part of growing up and living in this broken world. But how we respond or react to those challenges and adversities defines our character. Ultimately, our response can catapult us into becoming an unstoppable leader, for we know that when our faith is tested, it stirs up in us the power of endurance.

My story is filled with poor choices, broken pieces, hurt, and significant setbacks. But it is also filled with major comebacks, grace that saved my life, and a Savior who restored everything exceedingly, abundantly, and beyond.

Now to Him who is able to do exceedingly abundantly beyond all that we ask or imagine, according to the power that works in us (Ephesians 3:20 MEV).

In the Bible, some people who made the most egregious decisions also made the most positive impacts. Why? Because they didn't allow their stories to end with their mistakes, they pushed through to their comebacks. You might feel like you are defeated, but your story is not over. Your victory is coming. God changes labels and rewrites stories. And when He changes yours, don't be afraid to share your testimony—it could be the key that unlocks someone else's prison.

In the book *United Men of Honor*, I wrote about the four men who helped shape me and led me through many adversities, creating opportunities that have changed my life. In *Navigating Your Storm*, I wrote about my lighthouse moments, when I either saw God's light directly or saw it reflected through people. In *Fit 2 Fight*, I shared the battle I walked through with my dad when he was diagnosed with dementia and Alzheimer's disease. In all those stories, resilience was the key to being an unstoppable leader. Resilience comes naturally when we learn to accept grace, mercy, and forgiveness from our Lord and offer it to ourselves. Let me share some highlights of my Advertunities.

BLINDSIDED

In 2005, I turned 40. What a milestone year that was—my business was growing, and my wife and I enjoyed seeing our son excel in school and sports. He played in two sports on three teams, including a travel basketball team I managed. I was loving being a dad, team manager, and business owner, and I thought I had an unstoppable marriage. My son's mom and I had gotten through some tragedies and challenges that would have taken out most marriages, including losing three of my grandmothers in the same year.

The first part of the year went by amazingly. In our business, we promoted a vice president and opened a new office. My wife and I celebrated our 19th wedding anniversary. And, despite being shocked by 220 volts of electricity while repairing a pool pump, I suffered no permanent injuries. I had a fantastic time at a surprise 40th birthday party thrown for me at my home, earned company trips, and received recognition for achievements. To top it off, my son was invited to join a top college prep school and play for its state champion football team.

However, what seemed like incredible successes soon gave way to some of the most challenging adversities of my life.

Running a travel basketball team and supporting my son as a new driver who was participating in a high school summer camp and training program added to my already stretched financial obligations. Despite the bills piling up from paying the office staff, rent, two car payments, maintaining a large home, a mortgage, and private prep school tuition, I was so excited for the once-in-a-lifetime opportunities my son was receiving that I looked past all the financial pressure.

In late August, we were preparing to travel with my son's football team to Tyler, Texas, for their season kickoff game when Hurricane Katrina came through South Florida, where we lived, as a Category 1 hurricane. We boarded up my mom's home and our home before leaving, and, thank God, only some of our trees were damaged. Although my son's team lost the game, we had an incredible experience—in Texas, high school football is like pro football. I returned home filled with excitement for the fall season. Little did I know that some of the worst days of my life were just ahead of me.

In October, we were hit with another hurricane. Hurricane Wilma, a Category 3, caused extensive damage to our home. We, however, received a sizable insurance settlement in our joint account to make repairs.

But then, BOOM! Suddenly, all the money was gone from the account. My wife had taken the funds. It was the beginning of the end.

After 20 years, our marriage crumbled. For the next two years, I tried everything I could to save it, to no avail. I could not fix this! The following year, my wife filed for divorce and hired what I call a "man-hater" attorney who requested lifetime alimony. There was no light in sight. Rocks and waves were everywhere. *Why God??*

DOWNWARD SPIRAL

My business began to crumble, I gained 30 lbs., and my son was affected terribly. Our divorce was finalized, incurring legal bills of over $50k. And I accepted the alimony agreement. I took a second mortgage, got a contract to sell the house, and moved everything into storage. I rented an apartment in Ponce Inlet (Daytona Beach) for five months. The plan was for my son to play football, graduate early, and start college.

Then, the house sale fell through, and just as quickly as the economy began to crumble at the end of 2007, so did my business. To top it off, my son made some bad decisions and ended up in the hospital. I was at my office three hours away from him when it happened. I traveled back as quickly as possible and stayed with him through serious issues that required prayer, counseling, and 24-hour support.

I was on the verge of losing my home, business, mental health, and nearly my son. Although I worked my business the best I could, I refused to leave my son alone. Through it all, I couldn't help but wonder, *Where is my guiding light? Is this the end?* Still, I knew I needed to be strong for my son.

As I look back, I now recognize that God was using me for my son's Advertunity.

TRUSTING GOD

Our condominium was right next to the Big Red Lighthouse of Ponce Inlet. As the morning sun rose each day, I listened to the waves crash while taking walks on the beach. The walks to the lighthouse became my healing time. My son and I found a local church, and together we worshiped, prayed, went to counseling, and refocused on our new beginnings.

When my son graduated, we moved back to our house, which had not sold. He decided not to go to college and began working jobs as a nightclub bouncer and restaurant server, essentially enjoying two years of spring break. I started online dating, and had 50 first dates! Unable to afford alimony, business expenses, and a big house payment, I rented out our home and we moved into a small duplex as we waited for the economy to recover after hitting bottom. But then the house went into foreclosure, and then modification. We moved back in, taking in vagabond roommates to help make ends meet. All the while, I wondered, *Where is my light in the darkness?*

My family, business partners, and church family supported me through this turbulent time. I cried out to God, praying Psalm 23 through it all.

> *The Lord is my Shepherd; I shall not want... He leads me beside the still waters. He restores my soul... though I walk through the valley of the shadow of death, I WILL FEAR NO EVIL [!!!]... Your rod and Your staff, they comfort me (Psalm 23:1-4 NKJV emphasis added).*

After four years of wandering and a short-lived relationship that ended abruptly, my son decided to go into the Navy Special Operations for four years and three deployments on aircraft carriers.

As I write, I am immensely proud of my son's service and resilience to become the man he is today. He has just started his own business and owns a beautiful home. God is working in his life daily.

EXCEEDINGLY AND ABUNDANTLY

During one of my son's deployments, while alone after a rebound relationship, I met the woman of my prayers. She found me on Christian Mingle. My 3-page profile and a 100% personality match made me stand out. We met at Starbucks, and sparks flew. The day after we met, she traveled to visit her mom and family. We talked on the phone for ten days straight, sometimes all day and all night. We fell in love with each other's stories and what we had learned through our trials. She is now my "heartmate." If I had still been with my son's mom, I would never have served in the ministries we participate in and run today. Advertunity!

Though Kimberly and I have vastly different personalities, we share the same heart goals for the Lord, family, and the rest of our journey here on earth. We married in three months and merged our lives, intent on serving the Lord and each other. We have now been married for 13 years and serve in five ministries together, including United Men of Honor and Women World Leaders, which we founded, and work with Kerus Global Education with my aunt, Jennie Cerullo. We have traveled and served on orphan care missions, led life groups, authored books, organized Band of Brothers bootcamps and women's events, and appeared on TV shows and podcasts. Currently, we are working on producing movies and developing many more ideas together for God's kingdom. Our businesses have grown as we've walked hand in hand. Kimberly reflects God's light to me, and God uses people and situations to guide us through the adversities of life.

From every adversity I've faced since childhood, I can see now the opportunities they created. Advertunities!

LEANING INTO ADVERTUNITIES

Sometimes, God shines His light directly, and sometimes indirectly, allowing it to reflect through others. I am, and am becoming, the man God wants me to be because His light was always present through all my hardships. I encourage you to reflect on your own life. I pray that as you do, it will become crystal clear that God has always been with you, too, turning your adversities into Advertunities. Jesus is the director who creates opportunities through every adversity.

God also positions us to reflect His light and provide Advertunity moments for others. May you step out and be a guide for your family, at your job or business, in your community, and in your world. Look to Him, acknowledge the adversity, and then redirect opportunities with others.

Jesus spoke to the people...and said, "I am the light of the world. If you follow me, you will not have to walk in darkness, because you will have the light that leads to life" (John 8:12 NLT).

Scripture is full of examples of God transforming adversity into opportunity, revealing His power, purpose, and grace. Here are several passages and examples that demonstrate this concept:

Genesis 50:20 (NIV):
"You intended to harm me, but God intended it for good to accomplish what is now being done, the saving of many lives."
Joseph speaks to his brothers, stating that their betrayal and his suffering led to his rise in Egypt and the preservation of God's people.

Romans 8:28 (NIV):
And we know that in all things God works for the good of those who love him, who have been called according to his purpose.
This is an encouraging promise, reminding us that God can redeem any situation for His divine plan.

2 Corinthians 12:9 (NLT):
"My grace is all you need. My power works best in weakness."
The thorn in Paul's flesh became a source of spiritual strength and humility.

Philippians 1:12 (TPT):
I want you to know, dear ones, what has happened to me has not hindered, but helped my ministry of preaching the gospel, causing it to expand and spread to many people.
Paul, writing from prison, saw his suffering as a platform for spreading the

message of Christ. Chained to a Roman centurion, Paul wrote Philippians, arguably the most positive, encouraging book in the Bible. Advertunity.

James 1:2–4 (NLT):
Dear brothers and sisters, when troubles of any kind come your way, consider it an opportunity for great joy. For you know that when your faith is tested, your endurance has a chance to grow. So let it grow, for when your endurance is fully developed, you will be perfect and complete, needing nothing.
When trials are experienced rather than merely endured, they can become transformative, creating Advertunities.

Becoming and empowering unstoppable leaders is not about holding a title or position; it is about influence, resilience, and the ability to inspire others toward a shared vision. Unstoppable leaders are not born; with God's help, they are forged in the fires of adversity, refined by purpose, and propelled by a relentless commitment to growth.

Whether you are stepping into leadership or mentoring others to do so, the journey to becoming unstoppable begins with intentionality, courage, faith, perseverance, and a reliance on brothers to see you through. Unstoppable leaders know where they are going. They have a compelling vision that transcends personal ambition and see adversity as an opportunity. This vision becomes a spiritual GPS, guiding decisions and energizing other leaders to keep the faith.

Resilience is built through adversity. Everyone faces setbacks, but what sets unstoppable leaders apart is their ability to rise stronger. They do not avoid adversity; they transform it into opportunity, reframing challenges. Instead of asking, "Why is this happening to me, God?" ask, "What is this teaching me, Lord?" When someone is struggling, do not just offer them solutions or try to fix it; offer your presence, guidance, and wisdom to show them what God is developing in them through their struggles. Reflect God's light so others can see the strength within their faith.

Unstoppable leaders speak truth and listen to others with grace. Their words build trust, ignite action, and are real, not perfect. They listen deeply, communicate clearly, and connect emotionally. Authenticity breeds connection, so they know to share their journey, doubts, and dreams. Authentic leadership is not about being in charge—it is about caring for those in your charge. Unstoppable leaders serve others, asking, "How can I help you succeed?" They put others' needs first and elevate their potential. Leadership multiplies when we invest in others—so make it a point to mentor, coach, and celebrate others' growth. My dad taught me that you can use math to determine what kind of person someone is and how to lead them. You can either add and multiply, or subtract and divide. You choose.

Ego seeks recognition, while mission seeks impact. Unstoppable leaders stay grounded in their purpose and resist distractions that dilute their focus. They detach from applause and don't lead for likes, follows, or recognition, but for legacy and impact. Unstoppable leaders let their mission be louder than their ego. They know that pride goes before the fall, so they are intent on helping others find meaning and guiding people to discover what truly matters: God, family, work, or business. Purpose-driven individuals become powerful leaders; they make values their compass. In turbulent times, values are the anchor. As a leader, make decisions rooted in integrity, courage, compassion, and the promises that are written in God's Word.

Unstoppable leaders live their values. They don't just talk about them, they embody them, letting their actions reflect their faith, beliefs, and principles. They create a values-driven culture, helping others define and live by their values, which builds trust and unity. They inspire action through passion. Passion is contagious. When leaders are lit with the Holy Spirit from within, they ignite others. Unstoppable leaders do not just manage, they mobilize, inspire, and empower, leading with energy and showing up with enthusiasm. A leader's passion and faith can be the spark that lights someone else's fire and gives them hope—fanning another's flames. As an unstoppable leader, recognize what excites and motivates those around you and help them pursue what sets their soul on fire. And share your story, allowing others to use what you have learned as a survival guide, helping them recognize their Advertunity.

Leadership is not a solo sport; it is a relay. As you grow as an unstoppable leader, remember to be ready to pass the baton. Help others rise by leading and coaching intentionally. Share your wisdom, but also your wounds. Let others learn from your journey. Acknowledge small wins. Encouragement fuels momentum—challenge with love. Push people to grow, but do it with compassion. Believe in the God-given potential placed in each of us, even when those you are leading doubt it. Create opportunities. Empower others to step into leadership, letting them take risks, make decisions, and learn through experience.

My story is not about being fearless; it is about being faithful to the promises of God and looking to Him for strength, never losing hope. You, too, can stay faithful to His purpose, His people, His principles, and most importantly, to our Lord. When you lead with heart, humility, and hope, you not only become unstoppable, you help others become unstoppable, too. I have learned through all my adversities to love God, love people, and keep pressing forward no matter what.

Philippians 3:14 (NIV) states: *I press on toward the goal to win the prize for which God has called me heavenward in Christ Jesus.* In this verse, Paul uses the analogy of a runner who focuses on the goal ahead of him, preventing him from being overtaken by distractions. Paul plainly states his own spiritual goal: the prize of the upward call of God in Christ Jesus.

May Christ Jesus also be our prize as we strive to become unstoppable leaders. Rise. Lead boldly. Lift others even as you fight through adversity.

Choose to be unstoppable every day, seeing every adversity as an Advertunity.

An Unstoppable Leader Is...
RESILIENT

Turning Setbacks Into Comebacks

By Brett Dabe

Count it all joy, my brothers, when you fall into various temptations, knowing that the testing of your faith produces endurance (James 1:2-3 WEB).

Here's what I've learned about getting knocked down: It's not the fall that defines you as a man; it's what you do while you're getting back up.

Job understood this better than anyone. This guy lost everything in one day. His wealth, his children, and his health. His friends told him to curse God and give up. His wife suggested he just die and get it over with. But Job knew something they didn't: Trials aren't punishment; they're preparation.

In the middle of his worst nightmare, Job declared his loyalty to God, saying, *"Though he slay me, yet will I trust Him"* (Job 13:15 NKJV). That's not denial or blind optimism; that's resilience rooted in faith. Job didn't just survive his trials; he emerged from them twice as blessed.

Most men think resilient leaders are just tougher than everyone else. That's not true—they're actually more flexible. Think about Joseph facing years of betrayal and false accusations. His brothers sold him into slavery,

Potiphar's wife lied about him, and he spent years in prison for crimes he didn't commit. But Joseph stayed flexible through it all. He didn't become bitter or give up on God's plan. He served excellently wherever God placed him, from slave quarters to prison cells to Pharaoh's palace. That's biblical resilience: bending without breaking, trusting God's timing even when it doesn't make sense.

When Daniel was thrown into the lion's den, he didn't spend the night complaining about being treated unfairly. Instead, he trusted God's protection, slept soundly, and woke up surrounded by sleeping lions. When his enemies checked on him the next morning, expecting to find bones, they found a man ready for breakfast.

The difference between men who bounce back and men who stay down isn't talent or circumstances; it's perspective. When something goes wrong, most guys ask, "Why me, God?" Resilient leaders ask, "What are You preparing me for through this?"

Scripture says trials produce patience, and patience produces character, and character produces hope (Romans 5:3-5). That's not just spiritual encouragement; it's a practical process. Your faith gets stronger the same way your muscles do: through resistance.

Consider Jeremiah. God called him to preach to people who didn't want to hear his message. For forty years, Jeremiah faced rejection, persecution, and even imprisonment. His own people threw him in a muddy cistern and left him to die. But Jeremiah kept preaching because he trusted God's calling more than people's approval. Jeremiah could have quit after the first year of opposition. Instead, he stayed faithful for four decades. His resilience came from knowing that God's Word doesn't return empty, even when it seems like nobody's listening.

Taking care of your body also matters in this process. Paul wrote that our bodies are temples of the Holy Spirit (1 Corinthians 6:19-20). You can't lead your family or serve God's purposes when you're running on empty. Even Jesus Himself withdrew to pray and rest when the crowds pressed in on Him. Sleeping isn't lazy. Exercising isn't selfish. Taking breaks isn't weak. And these aren't luxuries, either; they're stewardship of what God has given you. When you're well-rested and healthy, you can think through problems instead of just reacting to them.

But here's the key thing about biblical resilience: It's not about getting back to where you were; it's about letting God use the setback to position you for something better. Elijah faced deep depression after his victory over the prophets of Baal. Instead of pushing through the darkness alone, he rested, ate, and listened for God's still small voice. God didn't scold Elijah for his weakness; He strengthened him and gave him new assignments. Sometimes resilience means admitting you need help and receiving what God provides through rest, relationships, and renewed purpose.

Ezra faced the overwhelming task of rebuilding Jerusalem's spiritual foundation after the exile. The people had intermarried with pagans and abandoned God's law. Instead of giving up on the situation, Ezra wept, prayed, and then took decisive action to restore holiness among God's people.

Resilience isn't about being superhuman; it's about trusting that God can work through anything, learning from it, and then getting back to the work He's called you to do. It's about having a short memory for pain and a long memory for God's faithfulness.

Scripture reminds us that *all things work together for good to those who love God, to those who are called according to His purpose* (Romans 8:28 NKJV). That includes your failures, your setbacks, and your biggest mistakes. God specializes in turning messes into messages and tests into testimonies.

You don't build resilience by avoiding problems; you build it by walking through your problems with God. Every challenge you overcome with His help makes you more convinced of His faithfulness for the next one.

The kingdom doesn't need more men who never fall down. It needs more men who know how to lean on God to get back up and then use their comeback story to encourage others. Peter denied Jesus three times, but Jesus restored him and made him the foundation of the early church.

Resilient Christian leaders don't avoid the storms; they learn to be resilient as they trust God in the middle of the storm and emerge with a testimony that can strengthen someone else's faith.

. . . .

CHRISTOPHER SIMPSON

Christopher C. Simpson serves as the President & CEO of CBMC International, an organization that transforms the global marketplace with the gospel of Jesus Christ.

A former U.S. Marine Corps Officer and retired Special Agent with the United States Secret Service, Chris spent 28 years in public service, leading in high-stakes environments around the world. As a Marine Corps Commanding Officer, he developed frontline leadership while serving alongside the nation's most capable personnel. In 1999, he joined the Secret Service, protecting seven U.S. presidents and leading elite teams on complex international missions. From 2003 to 2008, he served as Diplomatic Attaché to Colombia during a period of intense geopolitical conflict.

Today, Chris speaks and writes internationally on gospel-centered leadership, identity, and purpose—calling Christian professionals to live faithfully in every sphere of influence. He holds a Bachelor's in Operational Leadership and History from Tulane University and a Master's in Christian Ministry from Liberty Theological Seminary. He and his wife Ana live in Florida.

You can reach Chris at csimpson@cbmcint.org.

Chasing Shadows

By Christopher Simpson

As I grew up in a blink-and-you'll-miss-it town in West Tennessee—two stoplights and a Dairy Queen. That was the epicenter. If you were under forty, that's where you were. Bell-bottoms, bad hair, and big dreams— all crowded around dipped cones, chili dogs, and a kind of small-town simplicity that felt like the whole world. Life was unpolished. Real. And looking back, I wouldn't change a thing.

My family wasn't wealthy. More than once, dinner was bologna on Saltines with hot sauce—because sometimes, you just had to make do. But we weren't poor; we had family.

My biological father walked out when I was two. Just up and left. That should've left a hole. But it didn't. Because I was surrounded. Raised by women who didn't just survive hardship, they stared it down and outlasted it. A mother, a grandmother, a great-grandmother, aunts, cousins—each making sure I knew I had a place at the table.

My stepdad was a truck driver. He was hardworking, steady, and the kind of guy who didn't waste words. But he was there. He showed up. And in a world where so many people say one thing and do another, *showing up matters.*

Back then, we didn't need social media to tell us who we were supposed to be. We just were. Childhood was forts in the woods, scraped knees, and launching off homemade bike ramps. We drank from the hose, stayed outside until the streetlights flickered on, and ran wild.

Boys were boys—no confusion about it. And girls? Well, they were annoying… until suddenly, they weren't. Life was simple, reckless, and good.

And church? That wasn't up for debate. It was just part of life, like Friday night football and sweet tea. I was a "churchian," the default setting for most everybody in the South. My grandmother led the choir. My great-grandmother played the organ. I was the kid who mowed the church lawn every Saturday.

I knew the stories. I had all the right answers in Sunday school. But looking back, I can see what I was missing. I knew *about* Jesus—but I didn't *know* Him. My faith wasn't personal. It was cultural, inherited, expected—just another box checked.

I had dreams—big ones, at least from my limited perspective. And in my mind, those dreams were far beyond the city limits. Step one: Get this dirt-poor kid to college. I didn't have a safety net. I had work ethic and hustle, and that was about it. So I went all in. I studied and played every sport I could. Because dreams don't pay tuition.

And then I saw it: The U.S. Marine Corps—still looking for "a few good men." I mean, these guys recruited by saying, "We never promised you a rose garden." So naturally, who in their right mind signs up for that? Apparently, this guy.

Seventeen-year-old me—big dreams, zero dollars, and a can-do attitude a mile wide. I applied for the Marine Option NROTC national scholarship: four years of tuition and books in exchange for active-duty service as a Marine Corps Officer. And somehow I won it.

For a kid like me with plenty of drive and no money, this wasn't just an opportunity. It was oxygen. Soon after, Tulane University came knocking with free room and board. When you're broke, an offer like that is a spiritual experience. So I packed my bags for New Orleans, a city built for sin.

THE CLIMB

Tulane was a different world—money, pedigree, privilege. I was a first-gen kid from small-town Tennessee; no legacy, no connections. But I didn't flinch. I showed up, leaned in, and rose fast—#1 in the nation's largest officer training program, Dean's List, leadership awards. I didn't just survive. I thrived.

Then came Marine Corps Officer Candidate School. Unlike enlisted boot camp, where they break you down and rebuild you, OCS tests something different. What they want to know is—can you lead when everything in you is screaming to quit? Can you take charge when you're sleep-deprived, beaten down, and exhausted?

I found out the answer. I left as an honor graduate.

The climb got steep fast. I graduated from Tulane, was commissioned as a Second Lieutenant, and four years later—I was a Captain. At twenty-six, I was a Commanding Officer with 130 Marines and civilians under my charge.

Here's the thing about climbing—you never really feel like you've arrived. You just start asking: "What's next?"

THE BADGE, THE GUN, AND SERVICE

I applied for the Secret Service, thinking, *There's no way.* Black suits. Earpieces. Standing between a president and a bullet? It felt out of my league. But it wasn't. Six months later—record time—I was in. Then came the Academy. High pressure, no margin for error. I didn't just survive it. I crushed it. Turns out, I was built for this. The mission, the intensity, the weight—it fit like it had my name on it.

They sent me to the Miami Field Office—the Wild West of federal law enforcement. Miami was fast. Ruthless. Dangerous. The place was crawling with criminal activity, and our squad was setting records for arrests.

The job was relentless. If you were a threat to the President, we were coming for you. If you were running counterfeits or trafficking stolen identities, we were kicking in your door. We faced hardened criminals from across the U.S. and Latin America who were sophisticated and violent.

On 9/11/2001, I was in Sarasota, Florida, on protection for President George W. Bush.

The first plane hit. Then the second.

The entire world shifted.

Secure the President. Get him to Air Force One. Get those wheels up. Everything moved at hyper-speed. We had no idea what was next, but we knew one thing: Get the leader of the free world into the sky where he would be out of reach.

Once AF1 was airborne, the Marine in me roared to life. I called my wife. "I'm going back in the Corps."

But my wife knew something too. "No, you're not."

"Yes, I am."

"Well, mister, you're going by yourself."

Cooler heads prevailed. Looking back, that was the right call. Because the fight was already in front of me—I just didn't see it yet.

INTO THE FIRE

After that, everything hit warp speed. I became second-in-command for the Secret Service's International Squad. I taught myself Spanish and built relationships where trust is earned. I learned how things really work in places most Americans never see.

Within four years, I was named Diplomatic Attaché to Colombia. If you know anything about Colombia in the early 2000s, you know this wasn't a vacation destination. Colombia was the epicenter of counterfeit currency production, producing more fake U.S. dollars than any other country in the world. By the time I left, that wasn't the case anymore. Our teams seized over $100 million in counterfeit—the most in Secret Service history. We shut down operations and put entire networks out of business.

I had my picture hanging at Headquarters, and a medal from a grateful Colombian nation hanging on my chest. But success came at a cost. My brake lines were cut in Medellín. I was chased through jungles by narco-terrorists. The more damage we did, the more people got angry.

But somehow, I kept getting out. And at the time, I chalked it up to training. To instincts. To just being good at what I did. I didn't yet realize that I wasn't the one writing the story.

After Colombia, I had my pick of protection assignments. I chose the G.W. Bush Protective Division in Dallas. Shift Leader. Top Foreign Advance Agent. If there was a high-risk trip, a volatile region, a location that made everyone else hesitate—I was the one they called.

Venezuela. Haiti. Mumbai. The Arctic Circle. I ran more foreign lead advances than anyone else on my detail. It wasn't even close. I was the guy, almost to the point of embarrassment.

The dream job. The badge. The gun. The earpiece. The sunglasses. Top Gun, but in a blacked-out armored Suburban. Listen, my Facebook life was on point.

But here's the thing about illusions—they don't hold up forever.

THE MIRAGE

Now that you've seen the polished surface, let's rewind to 1994—Marine Corps Officer Candidate School. I was filthy, exhausted, and sitting through a mandatory chapel service. That's when it happened. The Gospel didn't just hit my ears. It hit my soul.

I had known the language—Sunday school, verses, prayers. But this time, it broke me.

You'd think that was the turning point. The breakthrough. But it wasn't.

Instead of surrender, I suited up. Seventeen more years of fighting God for control. Convicted but not converted. Moved but still in charge.

Because I liked the idea of Jesus—just not the cost of following Him.

I wasn't about to step off the throne.

"Lord, You can have this part of my life, but my sex life? Off-limits."

"Lord, I'll give You this, but my money? That stays with me."

"Lord, You can call the shots, but this next move? I'll take the lead on this one."

I spent 17 years white-knuckling my own kingdom while paying lip service to His. Why would I surrender? *I was winning.* Every goal I set—I crushed. I was the guy people pointed to and thought, "That's the man I want to be like."

But here's what they didn't see—I was skipping across the surface of life like a rock on water, never sinking in, never finding depth. I was chasing one achievement after another, one shallow relationship after the next, one thrill after the last.

And from the outside? I looked like I had it all together. People would say, "Man, you've made it." But on the inside? There was this hollow space in me that nothing could fill. There was no joy. Not the real kind.

And here's the thing—if you've never had real joy, you don't even know what you're missing. Everybody rides the roller coaster of temporary happiness, *but joy?* That's something entirely different.

Didn't matter how high I climbed—every win left me wanting. I had what the world promised would satisfy, but my soul stayed hungry. That's the lie, isn't it? That success will settle us. But it doesn't. We chase because we're hollow—grabbing titles, trophies, pleasures—hoping something sticks. But the applause fades. The gold gets heavy. And the ache? Still there.

One day, in His mercy, God took the gloves off. "Enough. Kid, get off My throne."

THE DAY MY WORLD CHANGED

I married a good woman—a strong, steady, faithful woman. But she, like me, had never seen what a truly surrendered life looked like.

I had been sprinting through life—head down, heart numb, chasing wins like they could save me. Titles. Accolades. Control. I was good at it. Until God wrecked the whole thing—*in love.* Our son was born with autism, and suddenly, my playbook didn't work. I couldn't fix it. I couldn't lead my way out. I was undone. It was like God said, "You've been doing this your way long enough. Now, we do it Mine."

And that was the beginning of the breaking. The unraveling. The terrifying realization that all my strength had an expiration date. I had nothing left. I had spent years thinking I was powerful. Thinking I was in control. But there I was, standing in the middle of something I couldn't outrun, outthink, or outmuscle. For the first time in my life, I saw the truth: I had no power at all.

And so, alone in my living room in Dallas, Texas, in 2011, I dropped to my knees. I was done. Done performing, cycling through the same empty motions, and convincing myself it would all eventually click.

So I told God, "I'm done pretending. I've spent my life trying to look strong, trying to make it work—but I can't fix this. I can't heal my son. And the truth is, even with all You've given me, I've never found real joy. I've chased success, but I've come up empty. I need You to step in. I need You to do what I can't."

For years, I had played the part—authoritative, successful, put-together. But the truth? I had nothing figured out. That gnawing hunger that was never satisfied was proof of it. No achievement filled it. No title quieted it. No amount of success could make it go away.

What I needed was the God I had spent years keeping at arm's length. And that night, Christ met me. Not in a vague, abstract way. I felt Him. Hands on my shoulders. A presence so real I could barely breathe.

And He spoke. Not, "Now that I have you, life will be easy." No. He said, "Now that I have you, I am never letting you go."

That changed everything. Until that point, my entire life had been about proving something. Trying to climb, achieve, win. I had been stacking up accomplishments like bricks, trying to build up my throne. In the end, I was just chasing shadows. The light was behind me, and instead of turning to face Him, I had spent my life staring at my own shade. What I needed wasn't another milestone. I needed real life. I needed Jesus. Because belonging to Him is the most real "real" there is.

A NEW MISSION

So I started charting a new course. Except this time I wasn't the one at the helm. God was. He was writing the story now.

For most of my life, I had been climbing. Hustling. Strategizing. Executing. Leadership was my rhythm. But now? I was learning to follow.

While serving as a Senior Special Agent on the Trump Protective Division, God called me to seminary. The Word stopped being something I heard about and started being something I stood on, truth I carried into the field, even in body armor and an earpiece.

This was different. For the first time in my life, I wasn't trying to prove anything. I wasn't clawing for position or striving to earn worth. I was finally resting—really resting—in the reality that Jesus had already secured my spot. Do you have any idea how freeing that is?

I wasn't chasing ambition. I wasn't reaching for status. I was stepping into calling—etched into my DNA before I ever took my first breath.

And when I looked back, I could see it. God had been shaping me the whole way. The discipline of a Marine. The calm under pressure. The strategy. The logistics. The weight of responsibility. None of it wasted.

This was a season of surrender. And that's where the real impact begins.

After 28 years of combined service, I retired from the federal government. And now? I serve as the President & CEO of CBMC International, a century-old global movement of professional men and women connecting business and the marketplace to Christ. *I went from the Secret Service to the Sacred Service.*

SAME ENEMY, SAME CALLING

Here's what I've learned since stepping out of the public sector and into kingdom work full-time: *It's the same enemy.* The same darkness that fuels wars, crime, and corruption is after our homes, whispers lies to our children, sabotages our marriages, and numbs men into apathy.

I used to think the battle was visible—terrorists, threats, enemies you could see. But the real war was always spiritual. I was standing in the gap, unaware of the darkness behind the curtain. Now I see it.

And here's the truth: the fight hasn't changed—but I have. God didn't call me to spectate. He called me to suit up. No more waiting for someone "more qualified." If you're breathing and surrendered, you're in. God's kingdom doesn't need fans. It needs fighters.

Somewhere along the way, we got sold a lie. The illusion of success is an arrow in the enemy's quiver. He doesn't need to break you with some catastrophic failure—Satan just needs to keep you distracted, lulled to sleep by a nice little life, where you've convinced yourself that keeping your head down is the wise thing to do.

As long as success is about your name, your grind, your comfort—you're no threat. Hell doesn't flinch at self-made men chasing shadows. But the second you drop the hustle, toss your paper crown, and step into the life God actually called you to? That's when the gates of hell feel pressure. That's when you realize it was never about climbing ladders or building platforms.

It was always about surrender. Always about His name. His mission. His kingdom. And when that clicks—you don't just show up differently. You fight differently. With joy. With fire. With scars that preach.

So let me ask you: Are you still chasing shadows? Still running after that mirage of success? Still convinced that if you just land the right job, stack up the right number in your bank account, slap the right title next to your name, then—finally—you'll be satisfied?

Brother, hear me—because I've been there. Chasing shadows. Gripping crowns I was never meant to wear. Thinking success would satisfy, that applause would heal. But it won't. It never does. It just drains you—grinds you down until you're a shell with a résumé. We make lousy gods. So lay it down.

That weight you're carrying? It's not yours to bear. You weren't made to build your brand. You were made to bow low and rise up in a better kingdom—one that doesn't collapse under pressure. The only one that lasts.

> *For what will it profit a man if he gains the whole world and forfeits his soul? Or what shall a man give in return for his soul (Matthew 16:26 ESV)?*

It's time.

Jim Beaulne

Jim Beaulne is a seasoned leader in the financial industry with over 35 years of experience. Based in Ottawa, Canada's capital city, he oversees a network of 50 offices throughout Eastern Canada, helping families create financial independence and build a better future. Jim is married to his incredible wife Trish, and together they've raised four amazing adult children: Eric, Christina, Brock, and Cassandra.

Behind Jim's business success is a man who knows what it means to hurt. Abandoned at birth, abused in childhood, and left to survive on his own by age 16, Jim's early life was marked by trauma, loneliness, and shame. Even after achieving material success, he found himself empty—until a near-fatal snowmobile accident became the wake-up call that led him to surrender his life to Jesus Christ.

Through God's grace, wise mentors, and a community of godly men, Jim experienced deep healing and identity restoration. Today, his life is a testimony that no past is too broken, and no man is too far gone for God to redeem. Jim now inspires others to rise, lead, and walk in their God-given calling as unstoppable leaders.

WHEN THE WOUNDED RISE

By Jim Beaulne

We all have a story. And behind every story is a wound. But what if we leverage our wounds to help us rise? My story is one of deep abandonment, inner pain, false validation, and ultimately, transformation.

It's not just a story about where I came from, but who I've become by the grace of God. You see, the enemy tried to write a narrative over my life, a narrative that said I wasn't wanted, wasn't good enough, and would never amount to anything. But God...God had a different plan.

My journey is one of coming to understand God's grace, goodness, and faithfulness. It's about how God takes wounded men and turns them into unstoppable leaders.

THE WOUNDING

I was born 56 years ago in Ottawa, Canada, in a home for teenage mothers. My wound began right there, with physical abandonment from my birth mother. From foster homes to eventual adoption, my first year was marked by instability. I was adopted in Sudbury and raised in Timmins, but my wound only deepened.

My adoptive mother emotionally abandoned me. My father, a violent alcoholic, brought physical and mental abuse. If I didn't meet my mother's demands, she would manipulate stories to my father that led to beatings. I learned early: Home isn't safe. You're not wanted.

When I was in the 7th grade, my mother said, "The only reason we adopted you is because no one else wanted you."

Another time, after mom and dad had a phone conversation, my dad told me, "When I get home, I'm going to kill you or cripple you."

At 16, I left. I had to. I ended up in a rundown house, renting an 8x3-foot room... completely alone.

And that kind of loneliness? It lasts. It becomes a breeding ground for false identities.

The wounds of abandonment go deep—deeper than most people realize. When you're unwanted from the beginning, something happens to your core identity. The enemy plants lies early, and mine were: "You're not wanted." "You're too much trouble." "You're not worth fighting for." These weren't just thoughts; they became the foundation of who I believed I was.

But Ephesians 2:10 says, *For we are God's handiwork, created in Christ Jesus to do good works, which God prepared in advance for us to do* (NIV). For years, I couldn't see myself as God's handiwork, only as someone's mistake. The truth is, God had been preparing good works for me even while I was convinced I was worthless.

As a young child, I learned to survive by recognizing danger, making myself small when tension rose, and disappearing emotionally when I couldn't physically escape. Children aren't supposed to live in survival mode, but when home isn't safe, you adapt.

It wasn't just the emotional toll that wore me down; It was the physical hardship, too. At age 16, I knew what it meant to be hungry, to go without. I remember waking up on a Tuesday morning with nothing but a bag of chips, knowing that was my food for the next two days. At other times, it was a cold package of uncooked wieners, just something to get by on. I know what it's like to have too much month left after the money is gone.

And I know the depth of loneliness. When I was 17, I woke up on Christmas morning alone in that tiny room I rented. No tree. No gifts. No family. Just silence. The silence screamed louder than any words of rejection I had ever heard. I wouldn't wish that kind of isolation on anyone.

But it didn't end there. Loneliness followed me into my senior year of high school. I remember graduation—the day every student is supposed to be celebrated. Parents were showing up with cameras, proud smiles, and hugs for their graduating children. But I had no one. When the teacher turned to me and said, "Let's get a picture with your family," I swallowed my pride and replied, "It's fine. I have no one here."

The pain and embarrassment of that moment are something I'll never forget.

And it raises a question some of you may be asking right now: Can someone with such a past become an unstoppable leader?

THE COUNTERFEIT LIFE

I became a poser, not wanting anyone to know the broken kid I was inside—the unloved, unwanted kid. So I went looking for validation, but vowed never to give my heart to a woman. Instead, I used women for validation through counterfeit intimacy. That became my drug of choice—others have used alcohol, gambling, food, or fighting. For me, it was sexual conquest.

The problem with the counterfeit? It never satisfies. It numbs you, but it doesn't heal you. It medicates, but it doesn't transform you. And when you're left empty again, you go looking for another hit.

The exhaustion of living a double life is something I wouldn't wish on anyone. By day, I was building success, pursuing achievement, driving nice cars. People looked at me and saw someone who had made it. But behind closed doors, I was dying inside.

I became a master of compartmentalization. I could pursue success during the day and destructive behaviors at night. I could attend church on Sunday and live in contradiction on Monday. The cognitive dissonance was crushing, but I didn't know how to stop. I was living as the apostle Paul once described: *I do not understand what I do. For what I want to do, I do not do, but what I hate I do* (Romans 7:15 NIV).

The worst part wasn't the sin itself. It was the shame that followed. Each time I compromised or betrayed my values, I promised myself it would be the last time. But without real transformation, without addressing the root wound, I was destined to repeat the cycle.

This is why willpower isn't enough. This is why "try harder" Christianity fails. You can't heal a heart wound with behavior modification. You need something deeper. You need what only God can provide.

THE INTERVENTION

In December 1990, I made a decision for Christ. But it wasn't yet a commitment. I wanted freedom, but I didn't know how to walk in it. I still had an unhealed wound, and it eventually led to infidelity in my first marriage, which ended painfully. The church at that time didn't know what to do with someone like me. I heard "try harder" Christianity. I heard "manage your sin." But I didn't hear grace.

Yet God never gave up on me. Even when I didn't believe I could be used, He kept pursuing me. His love was pursuing me even when I was running from it.

The Lord appeared to us..., saying, "I have loved you with an everlasting love; I have drawn you with unfailing kindness" (Jeremiah 31:3 NIV).

The emptiness I was carrying hit such depths that on February 3, 2000, my 2nd wife, Trish, and I had a conversation about separating. Looking back, I realize what was really happening: shame was speaking louder than hope. Wounds and lies were again threatening to tear apart my family.

But God had other plans. Because the very next day, on February 4, 2000, I was in a serious snowmobile accident. I hit a barbed wire fence at high speed. It was a crash that, by every natural account, should have decapitated me. I survived.

That was no coincidence. That was mercy. That was God intervening in my story with a loud and painful wake-up call.

I remember lying in the snow at -20 degrees, my leg mangled from a broken femur, unable to move. As I looked up into the winter sky, with nothing but pain and stillness around me, I had an impression in my spirit—a whisper I couldn't deny: "Jim, do I have your attention?"

That moment silenced everything. And through chattering teeth and shallow breaths, I whispered back to God: "If I get through this, I will seek to find who You are and what You are all about."

The physical pain was excruciating, but it was nothing compared to the spiritual awakening happening in that moment. As I lay there in the snow, unable to move, I realized this wasn't just an accident—this was an intervention. Sometimes God has to break something to get our attention, but He's always preparing to heal something deeper.

And that moment marked the beginning of a deeper surrender—one where

I knew God had spared me, not just for survival, but for transformation. For purpose. For leadership. When I finally reached the end of myself, I surrendered. Not with a religious mask, but with my real, broken self. And that's when He met me.

HEALING

Jesus didn't come for people who have it all together. He came for the wounded, the addicted, the ones who've made a mess of things. People like me.

> The Spirit of the Sovereign Lord is on me, because the Lord has anointed me to proclaim good news to the poor. He has sent me to bind up the brokenhearted, to proclaim freedom for the captives and release from darkness for the prisoners (Isaiah 61:1 NIV).

Many of us reading this book are high achievers. We're respected. We lead businesses, teams, even families. But can I be honest? Leadership doesn't protect you from shame—it often hides it. Jesus said in Matthew 23:27 (NIV): *"You are like whitewashed tombs, which look beautiful on the outside but on the inside are full of the bones of the dead and everything unclean."* That was me. I looked strong, but inside, I was dying.

I had to learn that God doesn't bless the image of you. He blesses the real you.

Sometimes the people closest to me—my wife, my kids, my closest friends— were the ones I hurt the most. I wasn't trying to hurt them. I was just... hurt. As they say, hurt people hurt people. But over time, through counseling and the Word of God, I began to understand what healing looks like.

James 5:16 (NIV) tells us: *Confess your sins to each other and pray for each other so that you may be healed.* That's what I've had to do. Confess, own it, and let God change me from the inside out.

One of the men God used in those early years of healing was Lyle Johnson. When I first sat down with him, I asked, "Can your God take away this deep void? This vacuum and emptiness that I've been trying to fill with everything else in this world?" I had tried it all—high six-figure income, material wealth, expensive cars, and travel. But the emptiness remained.

Lyle's demeanor wasn't religious. It was calm, full of love, like something I had never seen before. He didn't pressure me. He simply spoke with a quiet confidence and deep compassion. He told me that if I surrendered to God's plan, I wouldn't be giving up everything. I would be gaining everything.

See, the enemy had convinced me that following God meant losing all the fun, all the success, and all the ambition. I didn't realize then that the enemy always magnifies the cost and minimizes the reward. God was never trying to take something from me—He was trying to give me something better.

And I couldn't do it alone. I needed men in my life to walk this out with me—to do life together as I grew into a leader.

> Let us...not give up meeting together, as some are in
> the habit of doing, but encouraging one another—
> and all the more as you see the Day approaching
> (Hebrews 10:24-25 NIV).

Lyle showed me what grace looks like in action. He didn't preach at me. He didn't flinch at my story. He shepherded me through the process of understanding that the emptiness I felt wasn't my enemy—it was God's invitation. Ecclesiastes 3:11 says, *He has made everything beautiful in its time. He has also set eternity in the human heart.* That longing, that void, that desperate search for meaning—it was designed to lead me to God.

Lyle accepted me when I couldn't accept myself.

Another man God placed in my life who made a deep impact was Larry Brune, a former professional football player. Larry modeled what it looks like to walk with humility and strength, even in the midst of brokenness. He showed me that grace isn't just for the pulpit—it's for everyday living. Larry lived out how God can use us, not despite our brokenness. But through it. He didn't preach at me. He didn't flinch at my story. He shepherded me and modeled what grace looks like in action. He accepted me when I couldn't accept myself.

Another couple who played a powerful role was Kent and Karen Bandy from Ellel Ministries. I've blown it with my wife more times than I can count—but they've helped me understand the heart of a woman. They taught me that masculinity is not about domination or performance, but about servanthood and protection.

I've also been fortunate enough to work in a company with many excellent, balanced, and unstoppable leaders. Men and women who lead passionately in their businesses and homes, and serve faithfully in their churches and communities. They're not perfect, but they are surrendered.

Some of you reading this book have built a successful business, but you haven't yet built a healed heart. You're a great provider, but you're still haunted by shame. You're leading others, but no one's truly leading you.

> *What good is it for someone to gain the whole world,*
> *yet forfeit their soul?* (Mark 8:36 NIV).

Leadership is not just about influence—it's about wholeness. I had to let Jesus lead me before I could truly lead others.

Looking back, I realize now that God was always pursuing me. For years,

I didn't believe I was the kind of person God would ever use. Someone with a past like mine? Someone who struggled with temptation? With an inappropriate thought life? With actions I wish I could undo? Someone who—at times—hurt the very people who were closest to me?

But God doesn't see you through the lens of your failures. He sees you through the blood of His Son. His specialty is using wounded, imperfect people to show off His perfect grace.

My sacrifice, O God, is a broken spirit; a broken and contrite heart you, God, will not despise (Psalm 51:17 NIV).

I longed for a life of meaning and impact, but I didn't believe that was possible—I thought God overlooked people like me. But I was wrong. God wasn't overlooking me—He was waiting for me. Waiting for me to stop running, stop hiding, and finally surrender.

And when I did, He didn't meet me with condemnation. He met me with restoration. He didn't just clean up my past—He redefined my future.

For though the righteous fall seven times, they rise again (Proverbs 24:16 NIV).

Life is not about perfection—it's about perseverance. It's about being the kind of man who knows he's failed, but keeps getting up. Keeps fighting. Keeps growing.

And that's me. I'm not sinless. But I can stand here today and say that, by God's grace, I sin less. I'm not perfect, but I'm progressing. I'm not who I used to be—and I'm not yet who I'll become. But I am—by the mercy of God—an unstoppable leader.

LEADING FROM YOUR SCARS

Being an unstoppable leader doesn't mean being invulnerable; it means being authentic.

In business, ministry, and my family, I've learned to lead *from* my scars, not *in spite* of them.

The apostle Paul understood this. God told him, *"My grace is sufficient for you, for my power is made perfect in weakness."* Paul's response? *Therefore, I will boast all the more gladly about my weaknesses, so that Christ's power may rest on me* (2 Corinthians 2:9 NIV).

This is the paradox of kingdom leadership: Your greatest strength comes from owning your greatest weakness. When people see that you've walked through fire and have emerged refined rather than consumed, they trust you to lead them through their valleys.

That's what 2 Corinthians 1:3-4 means: *Praise be to the God and Father of our Lord Jesus Christ, the Father of compassion and the God of all comfort, who comforts us in all our troubles, so that we can comfort those in any trouble with the comfort we ourselves receive from God.*

The wounded healer isn't just a concept; it's a calling. And it's the most powerful form of leadership there is. Isaiah 61:3 (NIV) says God gives us: *"a crown of beauty instead of ashes, the oil of joy instead of mourning, and a garment of praise instead of a spirit of despair."*

So here's my heart for you today: If you've ever doubted that God could use you or thought your past disqualified you, or if you've fallen more times than you can count, congratulations! You're exactly the kind of person God loves to use.

If God can turn my story around, He can turn yours around. Don't stay stuck. Don't let shame define you. The same God who raised me up wants to raise you up, too.

Let Him do it. Your story isn't over. In fact, it's just getting started. If you will surrender, He'll make you more than just a man who survives. He'll make you an unstoppable leader.

As we close, I encourage you to pause, spend some time with God, and reflect on the following questions:

- When have I felt disqualified by my past?

- What counterfeit sources of validation have I turned to instead of Christ?

- Who are the people God might be calling me to shepherd?

AN UNSTOPPABLE LEADER IS...
COURAGEOUS

Stepping Into Fear to Unlock a Breakthrough

By Ken A. Hobbs II

Courage is not the absence of fear; courage is the decision to move forward despite fear. For the Christian leader, courage is not rooted in self-confidence but in "Godfidence"—the unwavering belief that the One who calls you is faithful and equips those He sends. Courage is the fuel that propels the unstoppable leader into uncharted territory, through adversity, and toward a breakthrough.

Meet Keith... A man whose life exemplifies what it means to lead courageously. A former youth pastor turned nonprofit founder, Keith didn't set out to be a trailblazer; he simply wanted to serve. But God had bigger plans. When Keith felt the call to launch a community center in one of the most crime-ridden neighborhoods in his city, fear gripped him. He had no funding, no building, and no guarantee of safety. What he did have was a word from God: "Go."

Keith wrestled with the call. He prayed, fasted, and sought counsel. Every logical voice told him to wait, to plan more, to be cautious. But the Spirit whispered, "Step out." And so he did. With trembling hands and a heart pounding with uncertainty, Keith signed a lease on a dilapidated building and began the work. That decision—made in the face of fear—unlocked a wave of transformation. Today, the resulting community center serves hundreds of families. It offers job training and has become a beacon of hope in Miami. Courage was the key.

Christian leadership often demands making tough decisions when circumstances are uncertain. Shadrach, Meshach, and Abednego faced King Nebuchadnezzar's golden image and had to choose: bow down and live, or stand firm and potentially die. Their response revealed true courage: *"The God we serve is able to deliver us from it [the burning fiery furnace]... But even if he does not, we want you to know, Your Majesty, that we will not serve your gods"* (Daniel 3:17-19 NIV). Courageous leaders don't wait for perfect conditions; they move when God speaks.

- Comfort is the enemy of God's calling. Staying safe may preserve your reputation, but it rarely advances the kingdom.

- Fear is a liar. It exaggerates risk and minimizes God's power.

- Faith is the antidote. When fear says, "You can't," faith declares, "God can, and God will!"

Being an unstoppable leader reminds us that courage isn't flashy—it's often quiet, gritty, and persistent. It's the decision to show up when quitting seems easier. It's the choice to speak truth when silence seems safer. It's the resolve to lead with integrity when compromise seems more convenient.

When a leader steps into fear with faith, he inspires others to do the same—courage multiplies. As we keep pressing forward, we raise up other leaders, leading those who once doubted their worth to find new purpose. Young men who once feared failure discover strength. Courage creates a ripple effect.

Consider Joshua. When Moses died, Joshua was tasked with leading Israel into the Promised Land. God's repeated words to him weren't strategic instructions—they were a command: *"Be strong and courageous"* (Joshua 1 NIV). Why did God stress this? Because courage is the prerequisite for breakthrough, and God knew that Joshua's courage would lead an entire nation to its destiny.

- Courageous leadership creates courageous followers.

- Breakthrough begins with bold obedience.

- Your courage may unlock someone else's calling.

Unstoppable leaders develop godly courage in the secret place—spending time in prayer, seeking the Holy Spirit's wisdom while reading Scripture, and communing daily with God our Father. Courage isn't manufactured—it's imparted. When David faced Goliath, he didn't rely on armor or strategy. He relied on the God who had delivered him from lions and bears. David's courage was born in the fields of solitude, not on the battlefield. The same is true for us.

- Private victories precede public courage.

- The more you know God, the less you fear man.

- Intimacy breeds boldness.

If you want to lead courageously, cultivate your relationship with God. Let His voice be louder than your doubts. Let His promises drown out your insecurities. Let His presence be your anchor. When we make a decision to step into fear, it does not just change our life—it changes lives around us. That's the power of courageous leadership. It unlocks doors that fear tries to keep shut. It births movements that comfort would never allow. It ushers in miracles.

What breakthrough is waiting on your courage?

- Is there a conversation you've been avoiding?

- A vision you've been delaying?

- A risk you've been resisting?

God is not looking for perfect leaders; He's looking for courageous ones. Leaders who will say "yes," even when the road seems difficult, move forward when the future is uncertain, and trust Him, even when His instructions don't seem to make sense.

You are called to be an unstoppable leader—not because you're fearless, but because you're faithful. Courage is your inheritance; it's the mark of those who walk with God. So step into the fear. Lean into the unknown. Trust the One who goes before you.

Your courage may unlock a breakthrough that ripples through generations.

Be bold. Be brave. Be unstoppable!

. . . .

BOB TARDELL

Bob Tardell has come to realize and appreciate all the blessings in his life. He would like to express his eternal gratitude to Jesus for His presence, as nothing is possible without Him and everything is possible with Him. Bob is now 79 years old, and he came to our Lord and Savior just two years ago.

Bob was married to the greatest person he has ever known. Steffi was his guiding light, inspiration, and the love of his life. She passed in 2013 after they shared 44 years together. The unfilled void she left tormented his heart for years. Only Bob's surrender and commitment to God returned him to living purposefully.

For Bob, every day is a beautiful day. Each new day is an opportunity to do God's work, meet new people, and create positive energy to uplift others, so hopefully, they can know that they are not alone nor forgotten.

Bob's heartfelt chapter is dedicated to those whose love and kindness towards others made him the person he always hoped to become.

Today is the day the Lord has made; let us rejoice and be glad in it.

Living Under His Watchful Eye

By Bob Tardell

> *[You] are protected by the power of God through faith*
> *for a salvation* (1 Peter 1:5 WEBUS).

I felt honored when Kenny Hobbs approached me to write this chapter. In a previous book, *Navigating Your Storm,* I wrote in great depth about the many adversities I had confronted and overcome throughout my life. Kenny's insistence that I write, based on his awareness of a specific time in my life when I rose to become an *Unstoppable Leader,* helped me understand how impactful it would be for me to communicate this story to others.

The year is 2010. It is December. I'm driving to our offices in Fort Lauderdale, Florida, completely unaware that my life is about to change forever. As I pull into the driveway of Allied Vision Group, the company I built from scratch in my garage twenty-one years earlier, I notice nine black SUVs parked outside. People are running back and forth, each wearing jackets with "FBI" imprinted boldly on their backs.

They meet me at the door and immediately lead me into a room, which they lock behind me. My business partner, Jules, and our VP, Harvey, are already sequestered there. We are advised that Homeland Security has initiated this raid, and we are being charged with knowingly buying stolen goods. The charges are both criminal and civil. Initially, we are not permitted to make any outgoing calls; however, we prepare a priority list of who to contact, with an emphasis on seeking legal counsel immediately.

To underscore the severity of the situation, we later find out that before our arrival, the FBI entered the premises with guns drawn, forcing three of our employees to the ground with weapons pointed at the backs of their heads.

Yet even in this moment of absolute chaos, something extraordinary happens. A feeling rises up through the painful flashes of potentially losing everything—an inner strength of conviction I've never known before. Along with this comes clarity, endurance, and fearlessness that will carry me through the next six years.

It is as though something awakened in me that I cannot explain. As I write, I now believe it was the Pilot Light of God, and it truly led me to become an unstoppable leader.

THE FOUNDATION OF FAITH

Since the age of four, I had always been aware that there was a presence beyond my physical being. *How did I get in this body?* I asked that question often as I peered into the mirror. My inner sense was that I was always being watched over. There was no foundation in my youth for any spiritual faith or connection to God. Yet, I knew there was something or someone far greater that existed.

That belief triggered an unwavering resilience and determination, far beyond any abilities or skill set that I felt I possessed. Yet I did not fail! The question was never, *How did I wind up in all these stressful situations?* But, *How can I extricate myself from them?*

Incredibly, the answers did not reveal themselves to me until I was seventy-seven years of age! But I'm getting ahead of myself. Let me take you back to that December day and the crisis that would test every ounce of leadership within me.

THE CRISIS UNFOLDS

My company, Allied Vision Group, was created in 1989 with my business partner Jules. For the first eleven years, I worked out of my garage in New Jersey. In 2000, the business shifted to Florida, where we rented offices and warehouse space. We specialized in buying and selling contact lenses domestically and internationally. We were gray marketeers, which meant we customarily acquired our products through alternative sources, rather than directly from manufacturers.

We ran a family-oriented business, with Jules, Harvey, and I having our children work for us. The rest of the employees were all related to each other or close friends. The person who sold us the products in question had done so for five years without any "red flags" indicating theft—nothing suspicious signifying he ran a covert operation or obtained them illegally.

With full assurance, I can state that we were completely innocent, which made the entire matter much more distressful and painful.

At the time of the invasion, the perpetrator had already been incarcerated. He pled guilty and told authorities that we didn't know the product was stolen. Regardless, the government proceeded under the banner of "willful blindness"—believing we should have known the products were stolen without direct evidence. We were left to fight the charges.

We suddenly found ourselves in a nightmare. Our computers were seized and returned destroyed. The bank suspended our credit line, and the government seized all our funds, keeping 40% when the matter was resolved fifteen months later.

THE BATTLE BEGINS

We reacted quickly. By Friday, we retained a criminal attorney. With charges in Atlanta, we needed separate civil lawyers there. By Monday, we had hired five attorneys.

The bank placed us in "Workout and Recovery"—a liquidation process. At the critical meeting, three bank legal team members from New York joined three team members from Florida. Jules, Harvey, our attorney Michael, and I attended.

After ninety minutes of discussion, I realized I had to make the strongest argument for continuing operations. This was my moment to be an unstoppable leader.

My appeal was very forceful. It related to the inherent value of our large inventory and involved convincing the authorities, via logic, not to take control of our inventory for just ten cents on the dollar, thereby putting us out of business. Concisely and logically, I stated that under our—my—leadership, we could sell the product at cost plus a minimum of 15% profit, making the assets worth 115%, instead of ten cents on the dollar.

At that moment, I could gauge their positive reaction and realized that we were not going to be shut down. We would live to fight another day. However, the battle had just begun as we were forced to exist under the rule of Workout and Recovery while dealing with the charges leveled against us.

I envisioned a strategy that would raise funds quickly without vendors or customers ever becoming aware of the dire circumstances under which we had to function. In short order, our checking account rose from zero to $400,000 within seven days. As soon as the bank saw that significant amount in our account, they insisted we pay all of it toward the dormant line of credit. Previously, we had been told we had to pay $150,000 a month toward the debt. But now they had full control, and the $3.5 million debt was forcibly reduced to $3.1 million in the blink of an eye. We were back to square one.

On December 28, the company was closed for the holidays, but the bank called me and insisted that we pay down another $100,000, so the balance would be $3 million going into the new year. Luckily, I tracked down Vicki, our accounting manager, to see if we had any funds. She told me there were a few checks on her desk, but she wasn't certain if they added up to $100,000. I drove to the office that night to prepare a bank deposit. The total was $120,000.

On January 3, 2011, everyone returned to work. We had $20,000 left, and still had to cover our normal bills, pay vendors, and distribute salaries. The bank kept punching us in our gut, without relief, which only encouraged me more than ever to fight this injustice. Jules and I put as much as we could personally into the account just to survive. And Jules, Harvey, and I took huge salary cuts.

Despite the accountant's insistence that we fire personnel, reduce the number of days those who remained worked, and cut back on benefits, I refused. They all had families and responsibilities, and I could not allow this burden of ours to crush them. I never deviated. I listened to that Pilot Light of God.

THE PERSONAL TEST

Through this impossibly horrendous time, I was learning to know and accept my God-given strengths as an unstoppable leader. It became second nature for me to lead with determination and confidence in my abilities and decision-making.

In 2013, all of these skills and core values came to the forefront in the most personal way.

My life and happiness always centered around the love I shared with my devoted wife, Steffi, our daughter Ali, and our granddaughter Alannah. The love of my life, Steffi, stood beside me for over 40 years, with unwavering love, support, and trust. Through all our struggles, we walked in harmony and unison.

By early 2013, my wife had become seriously ill and was diagnosed with cancer. At the same time, the company was mired in a standstill, having never fully recovered from what transpired in 2010. The only way to turn the tide for the company was to access more funds, and those efforts were tireless. For literally months, I worked remotely, treasuring every second I could be with Steffi. I remained attentive to the business, as securing those funds was essential for the company to thrive once again.

In March, we found a community banker specializing in SBA loans. He became our advocate, initiating the lengthy paperwork process.

Steffi's cancer spread rapidly, and it was apparent there was no medical treatment that could change the outcome. For at least four months, we were inseparable, with far too many hospitalizations. Every second together was precious, and I was always by her side throughout each night at the hospital.

On Saturday, August 4, 2013, two bankers drove to our house. At the kitchen table, I signed off on the loan approval. In another room in our home, my wife was lying in a hospital bed with hospice care. It was only 48 hours before she passed, unaware of what was happening.

Early the following week, the funds were sent to us. I had a very clear vision of what needed to be done with the extra money. I laid out my plan to Jules; he deferred to me to lead the way. Harvey, on the other hand, believed in "controlled growth"—slow and steady. At that point, that was unacceptable to me. We had to recover quickly. Every extra dollar had to be allocated to build our inventory; this was the only means to increase sales. Harvey was instructed to buy as much as possible, and when done, to buy more, and then again. He asked what to do if he wound up ordering more than we had money for, and I assured him I would figure that out, but he was not to stop buying as much as possible.

My vision was infallible, and I never altered the plan of action. I was that unstoppable leader taking on the responsibility that I gladly accepted and adopted.

From 2014 to January 2017, the company's sales increased by over 200%. I know my instincts and insights came from a higher power. He made that possible, and the company rose from the ashes. Confidence and conviction came from beyond my logical mind—what I now know as faith and trust.

THE RESOLUTION

The summary of our legal battles tells the story of God's protection:

The criminal charges were dropped within thirty days.

Civil charges were dropped in March 2012—we were never allowed to testify, waive Fifth Amendment rights, and defend ourselves.

The company was placed back into the Commercial Loan Department after 15 months in Workout and Recovery.

Allied Vision Group was the first and ONLY company placed into Workout and Recovery that did not file for bankruptcy. We were the sole survivors!

In January 2017, with the company achieving its highest level of revenue ever, we were approached by two private equity gentlemen to undertake the sale of our company. We would be their very first client. I knew this was the right time and the right individuals to accomplish our goal, and God guided me to make that correct choice.

The process proceeded at an unusually rapid pace. The company was sold on August 28, 2017.

THE REVELATION

How could that be possible? How could I, with no specific skills from my prior training and education, rise to the levels I did? How could the company survive through the Homeland Security and banking crisis to accomplish the impossible?

The answers came to me at age seventy-seven, and they changed everything I understood about my life and leadership.

In September 2022, I sought out medical treatment and made an appointment for a colonic cleansing. My therapist was Janet Berrong. Our first session was very interesting. With each succeeding therapy, our conversations became extraordinary, and my inquisitiveness led her to share her faith and trust in Jesus.

Could this provide the answers I had sought for decades?

I began going to church with Janet, reading the Bible, and meeting the most kind, caring, and selfless community of Christian people. This all filled my life with incomparable joy. Janet introduced me to two of her good friends, Kimberly and Kenny Hobbs. They became an integral part of my life as well. With my newfound friends, I began to consider the possibility of being baptized to show my commitment, surrender, and faith in honoring our Lord and Savior.

I accepted the fact that my intentions were pure, and I asked Janet if she would baptize me in the pool at Kimberly and Kenny's home. They happily and joyfully accepted, and my baptism took place on June 11, 2023. Praise the Lord—the day of my salvation!

I had never tried to encourage or sway my daughter Ali regarding faith and spirituality. I don't think we ever discussed those topics, as I felt she should find her own way without any outside influence. When I shared with her that I had been baptized, she told me she had come to Jesus decades earlier and had also been baptized! Our wonderful relationship of love and respect for each other became elevated to the highest level possible. The beautiful connection we always had grew exponentially. It has been such a blessing for us to share in the glory of God together as I've found answers to those questions that plagued me for over seventy years!

He has indeed watched over me my entire life.

THE TRUTH ABOUT UNSTOPPABLE LEADERSHIP

Looking back on those six years of crisis, I now understand that the qualities that made me an unstoppable leader weren't my own—they were God's strength working through me. That "Pilot Light of God" I felt during the darkest moments was His presence, guiding every decision and giving me every strategy and every moment of courage, even when logic said to give up.

Here's what I learned about being an unstoppable leader under His watchful eye:

Trust the inner voice over external circumstances. When the FBI invaded our offices, when the bank threatened to shut us down, when my wife lay dying while I signed loan papers—in each impossible moment, there was a voice deeper than fear that said, "Keep going." That voice wasn't mine; it was His.

Protect those you lead, even when it costs you. Refusing to fire employees or cut their benefits when our accountant insisted wasn't just good leadership— it was following Christ's example of sacrificial love. An unstoppable leader leads with the heart of a servant.

Make decisions from vision, not fear. My strategy to buy inventory aggressively once we finally got funding defied conventional wisdom. Harvey wanted "controlled growth," but I knew we needed bold action. That vision came from above, not from business school.

Persevere when others would quit. We were the only company in Workout and Recovery that didn't file for bankruptcy. Why? Because unstoppable leaders draw their strength from an unshakeable source. But those who hope in the Lord will renew their strength. They will soar on wings like eagles; they will run and not grow weary, they will walk and not be faint (Isaiah 40:31 NIV).

Recognize that timing belongs to God. The sale of our company in 2017 at the peak of its value wasn't my brilliant planning—it was divine timing. An unstoppable leader learns to recognize and move with God's perfect timing.

I felt a sense of euphoria when the sale of the company was finalized, only to be accompanied by the most profound sadness as I was without my wife Steffi to celebrate that momentous occasion with me. She was my beloved who had faith in me throughout our journey together.

But even in that moment of mixed joy and sorrow, I knew the truth: I *am* that Unstoppable Leader. I remain humbled by all that had to be overcome. It was only through His guidance and under His watchful eye that everything came to pass—all because of Him.

I am eternally grateful to God for this and all the blessings that fill my life every day.

If you find yourself facing impossible circumstances, remember this: You are protected by God's power through faith. Trust that Pilot Light within you. Listen to His voice above the chaos. Lead with courage, knowing you are under His watchful eye.

That's what makes a leader truly unstoppable.

BRIAN WHEELER

 Brian Wheeler is the lead pastor of Kenmore Baptist Church (www.kenmorebaptistchurch. com), and co-founder of Rising Up Ministries (www.risingupministries.org), which operates in the USA and Ukunda, Kenya.

Brian is proud to have answered the call to be a husband, father, pastor, musicianary, writer, and business owner. He is also a licensed real estate agent in New York (www.bwheeler.kw.com), and a licensed financial coach. He has a burden and charge from the Lord to help families create and thrive in generational wealth and blessings.

Brian has had an eclectic work history, from restaurants to mental health, musician to entrepreneur. Every experience has given him tremendous tools for his ministry toolbox, and God uses them all!

Brian is married to the love of his life, Gia, and is the proud father of Abby and Zachariah, and bonus dad to JJ.

Brian can be found on most social networks under @bigwheel8.

THE REFINER'S FIRE

By Brian Wheeler

What happens when you are *finally* living the life that God created you for after decades of disobedience, and it comes crashing to a halt? What happens when you are forcibly and aggressively removed from not one, but two heavenly-appointed positions that are fulfilling the call on your life? Despite the adversity, anger, frustration, rejection, and confusion, you must stand firm on who God says you are and who He calls you to be. All of those negative feelings and worldly reactions are from the enemy, attempting to plant seeds of doubt in your heart.

This is part of my story, and I can tell you from experience that our heavenly Father will never take away the best to give you second best. So, *fix your eyes on Jesus, the founder and perfecter of our faith* (Hebrews 12:2 ESV).

In just over thirty years of management and leadership, the Lord has brought me through many trials and tribulations, lessons, and blessings. He has cultivated my heart and certainly thickened my skin! Despite all I grew through in those years, the real adversity began once I became a pastor. That's when I learned through experience that the heat of the Refiner's fire burns hottest through spiritual warfare.

FOUNDATION OF FAITH

I grew up in a Christian home as the first-generation child of a pastor. My parents did not grow up in church and were nearly divorced when I was a toddler. My mother was saved while separated from my dad, and shortly thereafter invited my father to church, which led him to salvation! All of our lives quickly became radically different, and the call on the Wheeler family was loud and clear.

My father became a pastor when I was in kindergarten, and my mother was a nurse. What a blessing to be raised by loving and nurturing parents! It's what they were made to do. My big brother has cerebral palsy, so in addition to my parents caring for others, there was extra care, love, and patience at home. Growing up in this environment, especially with a brother who has special needs, helped me mature quickly while developing the same loving and nurturing characteristics as my parents. Leadership and working through adversity became second nature to me because of the example my parents set.

My father's loving and teaching spirit taught me so much about life and ministry through the years. Now, as a pastor and leader myself, I often look back on the valuable lessons Dad taught me about spiritual warfare. Once we moved to Buffalo, New York, for my father to pastor a church on the city's west side, the Lord showed him the reality of the spiritual realm. God revealed its influence on our family and church, as well as the authority that King Jesus has given us over the enemy.

> *"Behold, I have given you authority to tread on serpents and scorpions, and over all the power of the enemy, and nothing shall hurt you"* (Luke 10:19 ESV).

My parents worked hard to break generational curses of brokenness, addiction, and poverty, ensuring that the Wheeler family would live in the blessings of the Lord from then on. Praise God! My dad also instilled deeply in me a warrior spirit, often referring to two powerful verses from the prophecies of Jeremiah. These verses were written to Babylon, yet they are powerful reminders for any member of the Kingdom of God:

> *"Cursed is he who does the work of the Lord with slackness, and cursed is he who keeps back his sword from bloodshed"*
> (Jeremiah 48:10 ESV).

> *"You are my hammer and weapon of war: with you I break nations in pieces; with you I destroy kingdoms"*
> (Jeremiah 51:20 ESV).

I was establishing this firm foundation of faith and strength around the same time I began working part-time jobs in high school. My natural, God-given leadership abilities began to shine. At sixteen, I accepted my first leadership role at the local supermarket. I was also helping lead worship and direct the choir at church, and for the first time in my life, I felt the call to ministry.

THE FIRST SETBACK

During my junior year in high school, my father's pastorate came to an abrupt halt when his heart and calling for spiritual warfare and the power of the Holy Spirit became too much for the conservative Baptist congregation. Back then, I was so upset and confused; now I can look back and see it was the work of the enemy. Oftentimes, when Satan can't get you off course, he will go after all the people in this world who will.

My parents' faith and dedication to the calling on our family never wavered, and we began attending a large Pentecostal church as we healed and Dad figured out his next steps in ministry. I met the first pastors and leaders, besides my father, who helped me advance in my calling, and I quickly found myself serving in the choir and on the worship team.

During my senior year, I received a partial scholarship to a Christian college in Missouri. I thrived initially, but as I grew in independence and began to taste what the world had to offer, I began to stray from all that I knew.

I got fed up with the hypocrisy of the church, and instead of leaning into my faith, I ran away from it. The final straw came when a professor dismissed my paper on spiritual warfare, giving me a failing grade because he didn't believe in it. Again, when the enemy can't get you, he'll do his best to use the people around you. This adversity got to me, and I checked out mentally, emotionally, and spiritually.

THE WILDERNESS YEARS

I began working two jobs, one at a psychiatric hospital and the other at my best friend's pizzeria. My leadership abilities were put to use at both places, and I excelled. Eventually, the pizzeria grew rapidly, and I became the district manager overseeing multiple locations. After a few years, I was on top of the world! I was making a great income, and at twenty-seven, I purchased my first home.

All the momentum came crashing down one morning while I was making pizza dough. I went to put the dough bowl back on the mixer and felt a tremendous POP in my lower back. I crumpled to the ground in excruciating pain and realized I had no use of my legs! An ambulance was called, and I learned that a disk in my lower spine had exploded, causing my vertebrae to crash together.

A month later, I had spinal fusion surgery. After months of physical therapy, including learning to walk and drive again, I knew I had to move back home to Buffalo, New York, to be near my family.

I sold my house and headed back to Buffalo. My parents welcomed me with open arms, and I continued to heal. Within a few months, I was working full-time and reunited with my high school sweetheart. She was finalizing a divorce; our romance rekindled, and we eventually married.

I was managing restaurants again, working long hours, but we made it work. We had two beautiful children together and purchased our home. Everything seemed to be going well.

So I thought.

Years of hard work apart, misaligned goals, and financial stress led to an unhappy marriage. After almost ten years, our marriage ended when I discovered that she was having an affair. I lived in the basement of our home for months until we had a custody agreement in place.

I still wasn't walking with the Lord; I remained in my "time in the desert," running from Him and what He called me to do. I continued to work hard and gained many "tools for my toolbox" through various leadership positions. Even through the heartbreak and divorce, I remained laser-focused on my work because it was my only sense of normal.

THE CALLING REKINDLED

I began searching for spirituality everywhere, except in God, and became deeply involved in the New Age movement. While seeking healing after my divorce, I reached out to a Facebook friend who had a unique worldview. Once we met in person, we fell deeply in love and delved further into New Age practices together.

Six months later, she had a near-death experience during an ayahuasca ceremony. She passed out and woke up in the spirit realm, hearing a great voice saying that although she'd been a "good person," she didn't know Jesus. After seeing a slideshow of her life, she heard the voice say, "If I send you back, you must help My children come home."

She came back—praise the Lord! Once we talked about it, I thought, *If God can do that to her, what am I waiting for? I already know the truth!* We went all in for King Jesus, together!

I was working full-time in sales, as well as running two of our own businesses; we shut them all down, got established in a local church, and I began Bible school to answer the call on my life after twenty years. We got married and were baptized together on the same day. We pursued the Lord with all our hearts. It was blissful and amazing!

I thought that surely the adversity and devastation would come to an end. I was finally living the life God called me to. There would be smooth sailing ahead!

Of course, that certainly was not the case. Now that I was pursuing all God had for me, the enemy dug in his heels and fought even harder.

FIRST MINISTRY REJECTION

Although my father was retired from work and ministry, he had been regularly filling the pulpit for a local church. He felt the prompting to apply for the pastor's position at that church on the condition that I could join him as assistant pastor and worship leader. He was hired, and we began to live out the dreams and prayers he'd had for many years of us serving the Lord together in ministry. At first, everything was incredible; it was a small church, but those in attendance responded well, and God was working powerfully among us. Instead of receiving a salary, my family and I lived in the parsonage on the property. I also held a full-time job as a manager at the city's largest homeless shelter.

Many members of the church did not attend services, yet they held considerable influence and power in the background. As things began to change, they pushed back against the things they didn't like. I was accused of stealing from the church through a fundraising raffle we did, and my family was aggressively attacked verbally. One night at a scheduled executive board meeting, the room quickly filled with former church members, most of whom we didn't recognize. They confronted us and insisted we be fired, told us to turn in our keys, and the police were called to escort us out!

I cried out to the Lord, "God, we are doing what You have asked! We are preaching Your Word; we are leading as You are directing us! Why is this happening?!"

Since we lived on the property and couldn't move immediately, we endured relentless harassment and intimidation.

When Satan can't get you off course, he will go after all the people in this world who will.

SECOND MINISTRY REJECTION

Meanwhile, at my full-time job, there were numerous problems and employee retention issues. The HR department hosted a town hall meeting to discuss what changes we all thought should be made to make it a better place to work. I didn't speak up at the meeting, but once I returned to my office, the Lord gave me a crystal clear vision of what the organization needed. I began to type and wrote out the entire job description for a Spiritual Director, which I submitted to the executive team and HR.

This was a Christian organization, but it had been decades since they had any pastoral leadership. The position the Lord gave me the vision for was exactly that. I even said that I didn't care if I got the position; I was just the messenger that God chose to speak what He was calling for.

Sure enough, a few months later, they decided to create the position, and I was blessed to be promoted to it! How INCREDIBLE to be living out not only the call on my life with the skills that God had given me, but to do it for a position that He created through me. I was blown away and so very grateful!

But once again, the enemy came, rearing his ugly head. The new position was not well received by much of the leadership of the organization, and the two members of the executive team responsible for adding the position soon left for other companies. I did my best to lead with love, strength, and courage, but was told by the executive team that I was in a "holding pattern" until they decided the next steps for the position.

Just two months later, those "next steps" became the elimination of my position and the end of my employment at an organization I loved with all my heart, where God had divinely placed me.

Once again, I cried, "God, I am doing exactly what You said... Why is this happening to me?! I just want to do what You're telling me to do!"

When Satan can't get you off course, he will find the people in this world who will.

THE REFINER'S FIRE REVEALED

But here is what I learned through this painful process: When the enemy destroys the plans God has for you through other people, God does NOT remove the calling or His mandate. He simply gives you something better than you could imagine and places you where you can thrive, live out your calling, and fulfill your dreams.

God never takes away the best to give you second best!

> *For though we walk in the flesh, we are not waging war according to the flesh. For the weapons of our warfare are not of the flesh but have divine power to destroy strongholds. We destroy arguments and every lofty opinion raised against the knowledge of God, and take every thought captive to obey Christ* (2 Corinthians 10:3-5 ESV).

The Refiner's fire burns hot, but it burns for a purpose. Every rejection, every setback, every attack was God preparing me for something greater. The fire didn't destroy me—it purified me! It removed the dross of my own expectations, my need for human approval, and my reliance on the ways of the world. The fire revealed that my calling wasn't dependent on any organization or group of people; it was only between me and God.

Through the fire, I learned that unstoppable leadership isn't about avoiding opposition—it's about moving forward despite it. When people reject you, when doors slam shut, when the enemy uses others to discourage you, that's often a sign you're moving in the right direction. The resistance confirms the calling!

I am now blessed to be the lead pastor of an incredible church, and I have founded an equally incredible ministry alongside my wife. God has also placed me alongside some exceptional leaders, taking ground for the Kingdom every day. Regardless of what this crazy world and our enemy send our way, we fight for our Lord, and we live out all He calls us to.

When the going gets tough, the tough get going—and you dig in your heels and FIGHT for the Kingdom of God. There is a power, hope, and purpose that we live in that is greater than anything we will find in this world! Our eternal glory with the Lord Almighty is the reason we persevere, endure, and remain UNSTOPPABLE in this world.

THE UNSTOPPABLE TRUTH

Here's what every leader facing opposition needs to understand: God's calling on your life is irrevocable. People can reject you, institutions can fire you, circumstances can seem to derail you—but they cannot cancel what God has ordained. The Refiner's fire may be painful, but it's preparing you for something greater than you can imagine.

When Satan can't get you off course personally, he will use other people to try to stop you. But here's the unstoppable truth—every attack, every rejection, and every setback is just confirmation that you are a threat to the enemy's kingdom. The stronger the opposition, the greater the calling.

Don't let human rejection define your divine calling. Don't let temporary setbacks derail your eternal purpose. The fire is not meant to destroy you—it's meant to purify you, strengthen you, and prepare you for the greater work God has planned.

We are the Kingdom of God; we are set apart; we are UNSTOPPABLE!

AN UNSTOPPABLE LEADER IS...
PERSISTENT

Outlasting Obstacles When Giving Up Seems Like the Only Option

By Ken A. Hobbs II

Let us not become weary in doing good, for at the proper
time we will reap a harvest if we do not give up
(Galatians 6:9 NIV).

Persistence is the heartbeat of an unstoppable leader. It's not flashy. It's not always celebrated. But it is the quiet force that keeps a leader moving forward when the path is steep, the critics are loud, and the results seem invisible. Persistence is the refusal to quit when quitting would be easier, more comfortable, and even socially acceptable.

In the Christian walk, persistence isn't just grit—it's faith in motion. It's the belief that God is working even when we can't see it. It's the conviction that the calling is worth the cost. And it's the courage to keep showing up, even when the world says, "You've done enough."

Scripture is filled with leaders who embody persistence. Think of Noah, who built an ark for decades without a single drop of rain. Or Moses, who led a grumbling people through the wilderness for 40 years. Or Jacob, who wrestled with God all night at the Jabbok River, refusing to let go until he received a blessing. His hip was dislocated, but still he declared, *"I will not let you go unless you bless me"* (Genesis 32:26 NIV).

But perhaps the most powerful example of persistence is Jesus Himself. He persevered through betrayal, abandonment, mockery, and crucifixion. He could have called down angels or walked away. But He stayed the course—for us.

Persistence, then, is not just a leadership trait. It's a Christ-like posture. It's the willingness to endure for the sake of love, truth, impact, and purpose.

Every leader faces obstacles. Some are external: lack of resources, opposition, and failure. Others are internal: fear, doubt, and fatigue. The temptation to give up often comes not when the battle is fiercest, but when it's longest; when the breakthrough is delayed, the prayers seem unanswered, and the vision looks blurry.

But obstacles are not signs to stop; they are invitations to trust.

A persistent leader doesn't deny the difficulty; they acknowledge it, wrestle with it, and then choose to keep going. They understand that obstacles are part of the refining process. God uses resistance to build resilience, and the valley is not a detour—it's part of the journey.

Persistence is not powered by human strength alone. A Christian leader draws endurance from the Holy Spirit. Romans 8:26 reminds us that the Spirit helps us in our weakness. When we don't know what to pray, He intercedes. When we feel empty, He fills us. When we feel stuck, He guides us. The Spirit empowers us to persist not only with effort, but with grace. He reminds us of the promises of God. He whispers truth when lies scream loudly and gives supernatural peace in the middle of chaos.

To persist is to lean on the Spirit daily. To say, "I can't do this alone, but I'm not alone."

Persistence isn't automatic—it's cultivated. Here are a few ways unstoppable

Christian leaders grow persistence within themselves:

- Anchor in Scripture: God's Word is a wellspring of encouragement. Memorize verses that speak to endurance, hope, and strength. Let them shape your mindset.

- Pray honestly: Don't hide your weariness from God. Pour it out. He's not offended by your struggle—He's moved by it.

- Surround yourself with encouragers: Isolation breeds discouragement; community fuels perseverance. Find people who will remind you of your calling when you forget.

- Celebrate small wins: Progress isn't always dramatic. Learn to rejoice in the little victories—they are signs that God is moving.

- Rest without quitting: Rest is not weakness—it's wisdom. Even Jesus withdrew to pray. Take breaks, but don't abandon the mission.

Galatians 6:9 promises a harvest for those who don't give up. That harvest may not come immediately. It may not look like what we expected. But it will come. Persistent leaders sow seeds in faith, water with prayer, and wait with hope. One day, they do see the fruit—not just in results, but in transformed lives, deepened character, and eternal impact.

Persistence is not just about finishing the task. It's about becoming the kind of person who reflects Christ in the process. There will be moments when quitting feels justified, the pain outweighs the progress, and the silence of heaven feels deafening.

In those moments, remember:

- You are not alone.

- You are not forgotten.

- You are not finished.

God sees your persistence. He honors it. He uses it. And He is with you in every step.

Unstoppable Christian leaders don't persist because they're superhuman. They persist because they're surrendered. They've decided that obedience is greater than comfort and faith is stronger than fear. That God is worth trusting—even when the road is long.

So keep going. Keep believing. Keep showing up.

Because persistence isn't just what you do—it's who you are. You are an unstoppable leader!

. . . .

ROB MCLAUGHLIN

Rob McLaughlin has been married to his wife, Susan, for 38 years. They have three strong-willed grown children and live on a small horse farm outside of Durango, Colorado. Rob has worked for McAlvany Precious Metals since 1986 and has thousands of wonderful clients. In addition, since 1998, he has been a Post Certified Reserve Deputy with the La Plata County Sheriff's Office.

Rob came to the Lord in June 1976 while he was working a summer job selling books door to door with The Southwestern Company, located in Nashville, Tennessee. After graduating from Furman University, Rob joined the campus ministry staff of Worldwide Discipleship Association at The University of Georgia for three challenging years, then went back to work with Southwestern, eventually becoming a field sales manager.

Rob is involved in the men's ministry at a local Four Square Church, where he also teaches the fourth and fifth graders. His primary focus is to find where the Lord is moving and get behind Him. Rob's primary motivation is, "To not be the guy looking at my shoes when I stand face to face with my Lord."

THE NARROW WAY
THAT LEADS TO LIFE

By Rob McLaughlin

One early morning years ago, as I was driving to our men's prayer breakfast at church, I was still seething about a fight my wife, Susan, and I had the night before. We were stuck in our marriage, and I could see no way forward. I'd hit a dead end.

THE BREAKING POINT

"I'm f***ing done!" I yelled to the Lord, my hands gripping the steering wheel. "Stick a fork in me—D, U, N, done! I need a word right now, and not just some happy 'Precious Moments' greeting card word. I need a cold, hard word from You right now!"

I can't explain why I was so angry, and I've never spoken to the Lord like this before or since. Writing it down for the first time brings shame. He shouldn't have answered me, but He did. In His still, small voice, this is what He said:

"Unless a grain of wheat falls to the ground and dies, it cannot live."

With tears streaming down my face, I whispered, "I don't know what that means, but I know a dead man doesn't get this angry. And sorry about the F-bomb."

A few days later, I was stopped at a red light and glanced toward the cemetery on my left. A fresh mound of dirt indicated someone had been buried recently.

"I guess that old boy's been planted," I said to the Lord.

Something almost like a vision came to me—I could see a vibrant wheat sprout next to a lifeless lump of flour. I knew which one I was. I had been ground to powder by life's circumstances and my stubborn pride. I unpacked what the Lord had shown me: flour might supply carbohydrates, but wheat sprouts are full of life and potential.

"Okay, Lord, I see what You mean, but I don't know how to die to myself. You'll have to do it."

As it turns out, I didn't have long to wait for Him to begin the process.

THE CRISIS THAT CHANGED EVERYTHING

The first part of becoming unstoppable is overcoming our inertia. It's easy to get stuck and stay self-centered. As men, we often become comfortable with routine, complacent with sin and compromise, and happy to let our wives lead while we abdicate our responsibility. A friend shared with me that when the Lord is trying to get our attention, He'll start with our wallet, maybe our health, and as a last resort, the safety of our family.

That last resort was how the Lord finally got my attention, put me on my knees, and forced me to start becoming the leader of our family.

Susan hadn't been feeling well, and our younger son, David, stayed home from school to drive her to a doctor's appointment. David called me in the middle of my workday, saying something about insurance and "Meet us at the doctor's office."

When I asked why there was a problem with insurance, he just said, "You need to come down here."

Looking back after all these years, I'm proud of how my sixteen-year-old son kept his composure, but not so proud of how annoyed I was at being interrupted. I drove to the medical complex, insurance card in hand, wondering why I "had to do everything!"

The woman at the doctor's office looked concerned as she explained that Susan was being rushed to the hospital. Following her directions, I hurried down the corridor, confusion and anxiety building.

David stood stoically behind Susan, who was hunched over in a wheelchair, clearly in excruciating pain. Sharee, the nurse checking her in, was an acquaintance of ours. She silently mouthed, "Rob, what's going on?"

We found out later that Susan was within a day of her internal organs shutting down. Her inflammation markers had skyrocketed to 175—normal is 0-3. Something had triggered a hereditary disease called Ankylosing Spondylitis that she didn't even know she had.

In that moment, watching my wife suffer while my son demonstrated more leadership and composure than I had shown in months, I realized how far I'd drifted from being the man God called me to be.

LEARNING TO LEAD THROUGH SERVING

In the days and weeks that followed, I began to pray as I never had before. I prayed for my wife's recovery from a disease with no known cure. I prayed for strength for the long road ahead. And I prayed for wisdom on how to lead and become the man I should have been all along.

> *And though the Lord gives you the bread of adversity and the water of affliction, yet your Teacher will not hide himself anymore, but your eyes shall see your Teacher. And your ears shall hear a word behind you, saying, "This is the way, walk in it"* (Isaiah 30:20-21 ESV).

It's been over ten years since that day. Susan has progressed from being bedridden and wheeled into the infusion center to becoming what I can only describe as a miracle of activity. When she's not working at the orthopedic surgery hospital as a physical therapist, she's maintaining the pasture and orchard on our little horse farm, gardening, cleaning stalls, and riding her horses. I believe her picture is in God's dictionary under the word "unstoppable."

My tough and beautiful petite wife; if I can only learn to love her the way my Lord does. This is the path I'm still on. God changed me during those years as I turned my attention from myself, humbling myself by learning to serve my wife. It's amazing how motivated I became when I realized how close I was to losing her.

As men, we all yearn for respect and admiration from our wives. That desire can become an idol. The other day, I was struck by this thought: *How great would it be if the Lord were bragging about us in heaven?* This thought led me to a profound realization about God's nature and what it means to be truly unstoppable.

Think about Satan. What arrogance gave him the idea that he could usurp the God who created him and the universe? Rather than dwell on satan, I wondered, *What is it about God that gave Satan the idea he could pull off such a coup?*

I realized God must be remarkably humble.

Satan mistook it for weakness.

I felt compelled to read the Sermon on the Mount in Matthew, chapter 5. This is one of Jesus' most well-known messages. It is a collection of Jesus' teachings given over several days on a hillside near Capernaum, and was one of the first times He addressed a large crowd. I believe that in it, Jesus was revealing the heart of God.

For days, I meditated on the first nine verses, known as the Beatitudes, pondering the thought of God's humility. When I shared my focus with a longtime friend who has a remarkable grasp of Scripture, he pointed to Jesus' words recorded in verse 5: *"Blessed are the meek, for they will inherit the earth"* (Matthew 5:5 NIV).

My friend explained that "meek" in Greek is "praus"—a term for Alexander the Great's cavalry horses. Praus meant a warhorse so well-trained it didn't need reins or a bit for control. Direction came through the rider's seat and legs alone, freeing the rider's hands to hold a shield and wield a sword.

It took years for a warhorse to become praus, and in becoming so, horse and rider became one unit. Alexander's cavalry was unstoppable—they conquered the known world.

Sermons on Matthew 5:5 often relate meekness to a powerful horse under control, but the Lord doesn't wish merely to control us. He desires us to be one with Him. Being "praus" with Him makes us truly unstoppable.

So what stands in our way? For me, the big issue was inertia. I had grown content with the way things were. Through the Lord's strength and guidance, I had overcome both alcoholism and pornography. I was well-liked at church, secure as a Senior Broker with McAlvany Precious Metals, and respected as a part-time Reserve Deputy Sheriff. I felt esteemed and successful.

The problem? To me, it was all about me. A man all wrapped up in himself makes for a pretty small package. "Satisfied-itis" is what happens when our self-worth comes to us horizontally—from people around us, instead of vertically—from the Lord.

As my wife began her recovery, her parents reached out to Ralph and Pauline Nault, true prayer warriors, asking them to pray for Susan. Ralph has since gone to be with the Lord, but while he was still on earth, he had an incredible walk with God. Ralph and Pauline, who were in their eighties, decided to drive to Colorado—all the way from Florida!—so they could lay hands on Susan.

While I had only met them once or twice, they had known Susan since she was a little girl. The Lord's peace settled around our home as they prayed and ministered to my wife. Rarely have I been in the presence of such humble, godly people. I felt grateful they had come all that way, but felt like an outsider looking in.

It was getting late as we wrapped up our prayers when Ralph walked over to me and said, "I believe the Lord wants me to pray for you." Ralph put his hands on my shoulders, bowed his head, and spoke to the Lord. Once he finished, he stepped back and said, "The Lord has something He wants me to tell you. He said He is proud of you."

Ten years later, I know now, as I did then, that I had done nothing to earn those words of encouragement from the Lord.

THE POWER OF PERSERVERANCE

While I'm not going to break my arm patting myself on the back, there's one thing I know about myself after eight seasons of playing football, seven summers of selling books door to door, 27 years as a Reserve Deputy, 39 years as a broker with McAlvany Precious Metals, and 38 years of marriage: I will not quit.

Often, it's not because I don't want to. In fact, there have been many times I've wanted to quit so badly I could taste it. But I didn't. I'm not the best, smartest, or toughest. I've fallen and been knocked down, humiliated, and hurt. I've been misguided, misunderstood, wrong, and wrongly accused.

As we all have.

Jesus can relate to being misunderstood and wrongly accused. Toward the end of His ministry, Jesus gave a difficult sermon that caused many to abandon Him:

After this many of his disciples turned back and no longer walked with him. So Jesus said to the twelve, "Do you want to go away as well?" Simon Peter answered him, "Lord, to whom shall we go? You have the words of eternal life, and we have believed, and have come to know, that you are the Holy One of God" (John 6:66-69 ESV).

I love how Peter put it—not, "where or to what should we go," but "to whom."

I knew from the moment the Lord first spoke to me almost 50 years ago. As I pondered the mystery of communion I was about to receive, I realized, for the first time, that I was taking His Spirit inside myself. And I knew how much I needed Him. I was lost. I said to myself, "I want that."

He replied, "Come, and be satisfied." Just like that. In a still, small voice from behind.

He was to be my Lord, and I was submitting my will to His. Just like a horse in Alexander the Great's cavalry, I had to learn to become "praus." It's been decades since that moment, and while I'm not there yet, He's been faithful.

We all wander. We are all tempted to walk away. And there are certainly times when we get stuck. But God never leaves us.

If we are faithless, he remains faithful, for he cannot disown himself (2 Timothy 2:13 NIV).

TAKING THOUGHTS CAPTIVE

Not too long ago, I was taking stock spiritually, thinking I was all caught up, but knowing there's always more. So I asked the Lord, "What's next?"

"Well, how about your thought life?" He asked.

Immediately, the words of the apostle Paul came to mind: *We demolish arguments and every pretension that sets itself up against the knowledge of God, and we take captive every thought to make it obedient to Christ* (2 Corinthians 10:5 NIV).

As a cop, I've arrested a few people, so I have some real-world experience with Paul's imagery. Taking thoughts captive is a little different, though. So began the next phase in my journey along the narrow way that leads to life.

As I began to monitor my thoughts, the negative thoughts multiplied. Someone would cut me off on the road, I would curse inwardly and restrain myself from giving them the one-finger international peace sign. Then I would ask Him, "Lord, am I really this angry?"

Someone would walk by, and immediately I would size them up. Upon reflection, I would ask the Lord, "Am I really that insecure or judgmental?"

Even worse, my eyes would wander, and I'd catch myself: "Wait a minute, she's not my wife!"

For weeks, the harder I tried, the worse it became. I felt discouraged, but I knew the Lord was there with me. I figured I'd struggle with this for the rest of my time on earth.

But then I read Luke 11:37-41.

Jesus was invited to lunch with a group of Pharisees, and they were surprised when He hadn't first ceremonially washed before the meal. When they brought it up, He let them have it: *"Now you Pharisees clean the outside of the cup and dish, but inside you are full of greed and wickedness. You fools! Did not He who made the outside make the inside also?"* (Luke 11:39-40 ESV).

What Jesus said next set me free: *"But give as alms those things that are within, and behold everything is clean for you"* (Luke 11:41 ESV).

I asked God, "Let me get this straight—You want me to lift up these crappy thoughts to You as a gift? Like I'm proud of them? I've only wanted to give You good things as offerings."

Then it occurred to me that this is how we started together all those years ago. When I heard His voice, I came just as I was—no turning back, no delay, not thinking I could come back later after I'd cleaned up my act. I knew I had no hope of living the Christian life or getting my house in order on my own. All I could do was surrender and trust that He wouldn't turn me into a freak or make me do something crazy.

LEARNING TO TRUST

I've lost count of the number of times the Lord has gently brought me back to the narrow way that leads to life.

Years ago, just before dawn, I walked up to the barn behind our house to let the horses out. As I reached to unlatch the barn door, I raised my left hand above my head while holding my right hand down by my waist. "Okay, Lord, the bills are up here and the income's down here. I'm going to need a little help."

It was like I could hear Him shouting from far away: "WHEN ARE YOU GOING TO TRUST ME?"

I started laughing. "How about now? Now's a good time."

Then it occurred to me that there never was a bill that didn't get paid, yet I was constantly distracted by financial pressure. It robbed me of presence with my kids as they grew up—time I'll never get back. While I hardly ever missed a dance recital, ball game, school play, or horse show, I rarely just hung out with my kids doing little things, like playing dolls, tossing a football, or having a sword fight.

Years later, I wondered if my kids grew up thinking my love hinged on their performance. I wished I had been a better dad, and I have asked them to forgive me. Thankfully, they have, and each knows how much I love them.

Urgent things are seldom important, and important things are seldom urgent.

THE NARROW WAY FORWARD

We know the Lord loves us no matter what, but we get discouraged when we fall, worried when we forget to trust Him, and distracted by the tyranny of the urgent. The narrow way that leads to life isn't about perfection or performance—it's about persistence, surrender, and becoming "praus" with our Lord.

Being unstoppable isn't about never falling down; it's about getting back up every time we do. Sometimes it's easy, sometimes it's a choice. We choose to be thankful, we choose to trust Him no matter our circumstances, and we choose to keep walking the narrow way even when we can't see around the next bend.

Like that grain of wheat Jesus spoke about, true leadership—unstoppable leadership—comes through dying to ourselves so that His life can flourish in us. When we become one with Him, when we learn to respond to His slightest guidance like a "praus" warhorse responds to its rider, we become unstoppable, not because of our strength, but because of His.

The narrow way that leads to life isn't crowded, but it's the only path worth taking. Every compromise, every detour, every shortcut leads to a dead end. But when we stay on His path, submitting to His leadership, trusting His guidance, we discover what it truly means to be unstoppable leaders.

Remember: it's not how you start the journey that matters—it's how you finish.

Finish strong!

Jeribai Tascoe

Jeribai Tascoe is an HGTV host/designer, licensed real estate agent, real estate investor, and creative entrepreneur. With a background in branding, design and development, home renovations, and real estate strategy, he helps clients navigate big decisions with clarity, creativity, and results.

Outside of work, Jeribai hones his discipline on the jiu-jitsu mats, fuels his musical creativity behind the drum kit, and brings the same passion for excellence to every area of life.

Jeribai passionately desires to see men and women move beyond fear and confusion into true identity, manifesting their unique God-given greatness within. With the heart of a coach that encourages, challenges, and motivates, he operates with a grace that combines spiritual inspiration with practical wisdom and strategy to live a powerful life.

Along with serving God and others, some of Jeribai's greatest joys are being a husband and father, and enjoying the moments of adventure and discovery with his wife and each of his children. His heart's desire is to see men truly understand the joy and fulfillment that comes from leading with love and living a life of service to others.

Keeping the Ground You've Gained

By Jeribai Tascoe

"Mr. Tascoe, we're ready for you in the operating room."

Walking down the long hallways of the birth center, I begin to remember the other times I've walked along these halls. It's a familiar place for my wife and me, as we've been here before for the birth of our other three children. What initially feels familiar, however, quickly becomes surreal, unfamiliar, and unknown. This time is different.

"How is she doing?" I ask through a muffled hospital mask.

"Your wife is doing fine," the nurse replies. "The doctors have administered the anesthesia and are ready to deliver your son."

This is it. The moment has come. We've been walking a tightrope of faith for nearly nine months, hoping and praying that God would carry our little guy all this way so we could make it to this very day. We've wanted so desperately to see his little face and hold him outside the womb.

I see the operating room doors now. We'll be there in another hundred feet. Then another nurse emerges from the doors. She sees me down the hallway, heading her way. It's our dear friend, Nurse Melissa.

"Jeribai, I'm going to get some worship music for Michelle."

I'm thinking, *Oh, that's great,* but then I remember, *I have one already.* "Oh, I have a worship playlist ready for this. Let me find it."

Even with her mask on, I can see her delight and the creases near her eyes as she smiles.

"Way to go, Dad! You're on it," she says.

I pull up the playlist and hand my phone to Melissa. She quickly moves ahead of us and disappears through the operating room doors.

We continue walking toward the doors. I can now see the movement of people and equipment through the door's windows. I have no idea what's on the other side, but my wife, my son, and our future are in there.

I'm quietly praying in the Spirit to myself, talking to God under my breath, asking for His presence to be with us, and thanking Him for bringing us this far. For keeping Michelle's health all these months, through the hardest pregnancy she's ever faced.

THE JOURNEY TO THIS MOMENT

The journey up to this very moment had been long, painful, and uncertain. It wasn't just the prior eight months. My wife and I had been trying for a fourth baby for nearly four years. Our hearts were still marked by two previous miscarriages. A potentially painful reminder was staring us in the face every time we stepped out in faith again.

I've walked with God all my life. I've been through challenging circumstances and losses. God has carried me through so many things; why would this be any different? I know He's faithful and powerful and able to do above all we could ever ask or think. While I know this, this sudden inability to have another baby was a serious challenge to what we hold onto in our faith in God.

It's so easy to quote scriptures, but it's a whole different experience to see the words of the Bible come to life in your life.

At the end of a long year of trying to get pregnant, it finally happened. After many prayers, tests, and consultations, Michelle was pregnant. Everything was going well. We got to the twelve-week mark—a moment where previous babies didn't make it—and we got the good news.

"Your baby has a strong heartbeat and sounds good," our OB doctor reported. He then went on to ask us if we wanted to do standard testing at this point in the pregnancy to screen for various potential issues.

"Sure, that's fine." We'd said yes to this test for our three prior pregnancies, and they always came back negative.

Michelle and I smiled big at each other on the way home from that appointment. She let out a sigh of relief as we held hands.

"I'm so excited and relieved," she shared with me. I could sense she'd been "holding her breath" for a couple of weeks, in a sort of quiet, nervous hope that everything would be okay.

I remember saying "Thank You, Lord" over and over as we drove home, telling Michelle we'd passed a huge milestone. We were hopeful, we were expecting, and things were going well.

"I wonder if it's a boy or girl," my wife wondered out loud.

We had names already picked out. If it were a girl, we would name her Lilly Grace Tascoe. If it were a boy, Leo Abishai Tascoe.

Thoughts of room decor and baby clothes came flooding into our minds and hearts, and we began to let the past miscarriages gently drift from our minds. *It's really happening this time... the baby is okay.*

THE PHONE CALL THAT CHANGED EVERYTHING

A couple of weeks later, Michelle received a call. It was the result of the standard screening we had chosen to do. Michelle called me and merged the call with our doctor.

"There's good news and tough news. Which would you like to hear first?"

"The good news, please," Michelle said.

"You're having a boy. Congratulations!" We held our breath as we asked for the rest of the news.

"Your baby tested positive for Trisomy 18," the doctor said. He then explained to us what the positive test meant. "Your baby potentially has a genetic disorder where three copies of chromosome 18 in the baby's DNA have formed instead of the usual two. This is just a screening, and although it's a high probability, it's not a definitive test. We'd have to schedule you for an amnio procedure."

We were fourteen weeks in. The diagnosis wasn't good. The prognosis was worse. The odds were not in our favor—ninety-some percent of babies with this diagnosis don't make it in the womb. They are miscarried or stillborn. If they beat the odds and make it to delivery, they have a very small chance of survival.

I could feel Michelle's heart sinking through the phone, and my heart was close behind hers. Thoughts were spinning up with questions and needs for clarification, but I was holding back to see what my wife was thinking. She asked additional questions, desperately trying to gain a better understanding of our options.

There were only two: keep going with the pregnancy for as long as possible, or terminate.

We decided to do the more definitive amnio procedure. Weeks later, we got the confirmation. It was Trisomy 18. It was definitive.

WRESTLING WITH REALITY, TRUSTING GOD

We were twenty weeks in. Our hearts were crushed, and we were wrestling with the reality of what was happening. Just when thoughts of past miscarriages were drifting into the past, they collided with our present reality. *Is that going to happen again? Why is this happening again?*

As a husband, it's tough to find the right words to bring any comfort to my wife in such a moment. I knew she was strong, I knew she believed, but seriously, this was a big one.

I recall saying, "Honey, I don't know why this is happening, and it's a heartbreaking situation. All I know is that I think we should give our son Leo a fighting chance, and I believe we should continue to trust the Lord, taking this one step at a time. This is hard. It's as tough as it gets—and I don't know what's up ahead, but I know this: I love you, I trust the Lord, and we'll make it through no matter how things go."

We agreed to keep going.

In those moments and for the weeks to come, the Lord reminded me not only of all He had done, but truly WHO HE IS. He IS faithful, He IS true, He IS love. He knows how we feel because He experienced all that we feel. I sensed a faith for this journey rising in my heart and even my wife's, though it was veiled with tears and sorrow. God was going to carry us. I'd seen too much evidence of His goodness, faithfulness, and miraculous works to doubt Him now.

The Lord brought me to Psalm 77:

I shall remember the deeds of the LORD;
I will certainly remember Your wonders of old.
I will meditate on all Your work,
And on Your deed with thanksgiving.
Your way, God, is holy;
What god is great like our God?

You are the God who works wonders;
You have made known Your strength among the peoples
(Psalm 77:11-15 NASB).

The Lord was speaking to us, reaching out to us from His Word. It was more than just mere words on a page—they were Words of life, breath, inspiration, health, power, and strength.

So many scriptures started coming to mind, and I wrote them in my phone's notes:

> "Do not fear, for I am with you; Do not be afraid, for I am your God. I will strengthen you, I will also help you, I will also uphold you with My righteous right hand"
> (Isaiah 41:10 NASB).

> He is not afraid of bad news; his heart is firm, trusting in the LORD. His heart is steady; he will not be afraid, until he looks in triumph on his adversaries (Psalm 112:7-8 ESV).

One of our greatest adversaries is unbelief. The enemy tries to lure us to step off the path of righteousness through doubt. Then, if we take that step off the narrow path, we end up choosing not to believe, which leads us into disobedience.

The enemy is a thief and a robber. He's desperately trying to harden the good soil of our hearts and snatch away the life-giving seeds that God's Word plants within us. Our greatest fight is to stand firm, to remain steadfast in the face of temptations and trials.

The Word of God began to illuminate for me exactly what the main challenge was in the situation with our son Leo. Yes, there were the glaring genetic and medical complications that seemed like impossible hurdles, but there was a more subtle challenge that was well within our grasp, one that we couldn't let go of.

Will we allow thoughts of doubt to fill our minds, potentially pulling us into unbelief and breaking us down to where we fold and give in to the enemy's attempts to rob us of our faith in God?

Again, the Word of God came and spoke to me:

> *He is not afraid of bad news; his heart is firm, trusting in the LORD* (Psalm 112:7 ESV).

And of course, one of my favorite scriptures since I was a boy was now resonating louder and louder in my soul than ever before:

> *Trust in the LORD with all your heart and do not lean on your own understanding. In all your ways acknowledge Him, and He will make your paths straight* (Proverbs 3:5-6 NASB).

This was the bottom line: Stand on God's Word, trust and pray without wavering, and hold fast to the confession of our hope. I sensed the challenge and asked God for the grace to endure. I committed to not doubting Him or questioning Him, no matter what the circumstances. I determined in my heart not to allow any doubt for even a moment. To not entertain any wild scenarios. To truly give no place to the enemy, but instead to release everything to the Lord in prayer.

"I believe You are good, Father! I believe You will carry us. I trust You with our lives and the life of our son. He is in Your hands, and we pray that You carry him now so we can see Leo born and held in our hands, for however long we get. We're grateful for the opportunity to be Leo's parents. Help us through in the name of Jesus. Amen."

THE FINAL WEEKS

We were thirty weeks in. Leo was still strong but growing slowly. We had bi-monthly sonograms to keep the doctors informed about Leo's development. Every doctor's visit was an up-and-down roller coaster of emotions—seeing our little guy on the sonogram screen, knowing about the diagnosis, then seeing him moving. Back and forth, up and down, every moment trying to shake our faith like a boat in a storm.

We'd get into the car to drive home, and it was often sad at first, but then the Lord strengthened us, and we just kept on going.

We finally reached about thirty-eight weeks. We attended our weekly check-in with our OB doctor, and as he checked on Leo's position in the womb, he shared some additional news.

"Your son has moved and is in a breech position. I would recommend that you do a C-section delivery."

We were ready for this, and I remember my wife with a calm smile saying, "Let's do it."

The doctor called the birth center, and they had an opening the very next morning to take us in and deliver our son.

BACK IN THE BIRTH CENTER

Back in the birth center hallways. We're at the doors now.

"Are you ready?" the nurse asks me.

"Yes, I am," I reply.

"Let's head on in then, and you can be next to your wife."

As we step into the operating room, all expectations and memories of TV show operating rooms completely vanish. There is a peace, a calmness that's so hard to explain. The delivery team, comprising doctors, specialists, and nurses, moves with poise and purpose in one of the most magnificent displays of proficiency I've ever seen. There is no clamoring of metal trays or nervous shuffling about. Everything is orchestrated, calculated, and serene. It is peaceful, but that isn't just from the people in the room.

The Lord is with us.

His presence is in the room. I can sense Him so strongly. He is ever-present to us in our time of need.

I take Michelle's hand and look in her eyes.

"You did it, Mama. You made it to delivery day, and we get to see our little boy today. You get to hold him, Sweetie!"

She gently smiles at me with tears welling up in her eyes. We listen to the worship song playing on my phone playlist. We worship, and I am still praying in tongues gently under my breath.

After a few minutes of holding onto each other in the stillness of the operating room, we hear a voice from the other side of the curtain say to us, "Your son is out, and you're looking good, Michelle."

The nurse touches my shoulder and says, "Dad, we need you over by the warming table to see your son and consult with the specialists."

I am led over to the warming table, and I see him for the first time. He is small, gray, and shivering. The nurse is suctioning his mouth and trying to perk him up. They give him some oxygen and swaddle him in a blanket. Leo is lying there looking up at me.

"Hi, my son! You made it!"

I put both my hands on him and pray for him, asking the Lord to strengthen him and keep him so that Mom can hold him. I feel a warm, powerful touch on him, and I know the Lord is sustaining him. We bring him over to Michelle.

"He's here, Honey. Your son is here," I say after carrying him over to her.

She is still being tended to by the surgeons, but she reaches for him and holds him so close. Leo looks right into her eyes. Our little miracle son has been born, beating the odds, making it to birth, and now, he is being held in the loving arms of his mama.

For the next 27 hours, we hold Leo nonstop. We have so many visitors, and my wife wants everyone to have a chance to hold our son. It is the most precious, peaceful, and anointed time in the birth center recovery room. Michelle is praying for nurses and ministering to them. Every nurse and doctor is stopping by to see our little miracle.

After those precious hours, we turn Leo over into the arms of our King Jesus. He has run his race, fulfilled his purpose, and lifted our faith to new heights. Our brave little lion only knew love. He was conceived in love, carried in love, delivered in love, and surrendered in love.

THE GROUND WE GAINED

A few months later, after the celebration of Leo's life, I was in prayer and the Lord reminded me of the story of Joshua and Caleb. They believed, they knew that with God they could take the land and possess it according to His instructions. Then it hit me: *Every place that you've gained the victory in through the faithfulness of our Lord is now the place that you fight from.*

Even though we lost our son, we gained so much because of the faithfulness of God. It was extremely painful, but it produced in us a newfound patience and purpose: To continue to trust God, no matter what the outcome may be.

We know that in all things God works for the good
of those who love Him, who have been called according
to his purpose (Romans 8:28 NIV).

The ground we gained through this trial wasn't just about enduring suffering—it was about discovering that our faith can withstand the fiercest storms. We learned that unstoppable leadership isn't about never falling down; it's about fighting from the victories God has already given.

When you've walked through the valley of the shadow of death and discovered that God's presence sustains you there, you never have to fear that valley again. When you've trusted Him with your most precious treasure and found Him faithful, you know beyond doubt that He can be trusted with anything.

The ground we gained is this: Unshakable confidence that God is faithful and good in all His ways. No matter what storm comes, no matter what diagnosis arrives, no matter what loss threatens to overwhelm us, we now fight from a place of proven victory.

We trust You, Lord. We love you, Leo. And we pray that every reader will remain unstoppable in their faith in the One who is always good.

An Unstoppable Leader Is...
OPTIMISTIC

Finding Opportunity Hidden In Every Crisis

By Ken A. Hobbs II

Optimism isn't naïve—it's prophetic. For the Christian leader, optimism is not a denial of reality but a declaration of faith. It's the ability to look at a storm and still see the sunrise. It's the courage to face a crisis and still believe in a comeback. Unstoppable leaders are optimistic—not because life is easy, but because God is faithful.

In a world that often glorifies cynicism and celebrates skepticism, optimism is a radical act of trust. It's a spiritual posture that says, "Even here, even now, God is working." The Christian leader who walks in optimism doesn't ignore pain—he interprets it through the lens of purpose.

The foundation of Christian optimism isn't personality—it's theology. It's not about being naturally cheerful; it's about being spiritually anchored.

Scripture is saturated with promises that fuel hope:

- *All things work together for good to those who love God* (Romans 8:28 NKJV).

- *"You meant evil against me; but God meant it for good"* (Genesis 50:20 NKJV).

- *Weeping may endure for a night, but joy comes in the morning* (Psalm 30:5 NKJV).

Unstoppable leaders cling to these truths when circumstances scream to do otherwise. They don't pretend the valley isn't real—they just know it's not permanent. Their optimism is a declaration that God's Word is more reliable than the world's chaos.

Every crisis carries a hidden invitation. It may be an invitation to grow, to lead, to innovate, or to trust. The optimistic leader doesn't just survive the storm—he searches it for seeds of opportunity.

Consider Joseph. Betrayed by his brothers, sold into slavery, falsely accused, and imprisoned—yet he never lost sight of God's hand. Joseph's crisis became the catalyst for his calling. He rose to power—not despite adversity, but because of it.

Christian leaders today must adopt the same lens.

- A financial setback may birth creativity.

- A broken relationship may deepen compassion.

- A business challenge may reveal a new strategy.

Optimism doesn't erase pain—it reframes it. It asks, "What is God doing in this?" rather than "Why is this happening to me?"

Unstoppable leaders don't quit when it gets hard—they dig deeper. Optimism is the fuel that keeps them moving when others stall and helps them bounce back after disappointment, rejection, or failure.

Nehemiah demonstrates this principle beautifully. When he heard that Jerusalem's walls were broken down and its gates destroyed by fire, Nehemiah could have mourned the destruction and accepted defeat. Instead, he saw an opportunity for restoration. *"Come and let us build the wall of Jerusalem, that we may no longer be a reproach,"* he declared (Nehemiah 2:17 NKJV). His optimism was contagious, and in just 52 days, they accomplished what had seemed impossible.

Resilient leaders:

- Expect setbacks, but don't let them define the future.

- Learn from failure instead of fearing it.

- Keep their eyes on the mission, not the mess.

Optimism turns a detour into a divine redirection and helps leaders keep building even when the blueprint changes.

Optimism is contagious. When a leader chooses hope, it gives others permission to do the same. In times of uncertainty, people don't just need strategy—they need strength. They need someone who believes the best is still possible.

Jesus modeled this beautifully. When the disciples panicked in the storm, He didn't just calm the waves—He calmed their hearts. When Lazarus died, Jesus didn't just weep—He declared resurrection. His optimism wasn't shallow—it was supernatural.

Christian leaders today must be thermostats, not thermometers. Don't just reflect the temperature of the room—set it. Speak life. Cast vision. Remind people of God's promises. Your optimism may be the spark that reignites someone's faith.

Optimism isn't automatic—it's cultivated. It grows when leaders spend time in God's presence, allowing Him to reshape their perspective. Prayer is where pessimism dies and hope is reborn.

When you pray, you're reminded:

- God is bigger than the problem.

- You're not alone in the battle.

- Your story is still being written.

Perspective shifts when you stop staring at the mountain and start looking at the Maker. Optimism grows when you zoom out and see the bigger picture—when you realize that even your setbacks are part of a sovereign setup.

To be an unstoppable Christian leader is to be optimistic—not because you've avoided hardship, but because you've encountered hope. Your optimism is a weapon. It's a witness. It's a way of saying, "I trust God more than I fear this moment."

So when a crisis comes, don't retreat—rise. Don't complain—create. Don't panic—pray. Look for the opportunity hidden inside the chaos. Ask God what He's building beneath the rubble. And lead with a hope that refuses to be shaken.

Because optimism isn't just a mindset—it's a ministry. And when you lead with it, you become unstoppable!

. . . .

JON MAPLES

Jon Maples is a devoted husband and father who is deeply passionate about fatherhood and cherishes every moment spent with his family. He believes that being a present and engaged parent is the most important role he can play. As the founder of a thriving investment and life insurance planning firm, Jon has built a reputation for providing expert guidance and innovative solutions to his clients. With a multifaceted career, Jon's commitment to public service is evident through his role as an elected official, where he works tirelessly to improve his community and ensure a brighter future for all.

Outside of his professional and public service commitments, Jon enjoys a range of personal interests. He is an avid reader, constantly seeking to expand his knowledge and perspectives. Additionally, Jon is an enthusiastic traveler, always eager to explore new cultures and experiences around the world that connect him to his Christian faith.

With a life dedicated to excellence in both his career and personal endeavors, Jon Maples embodies the values of an unstoppable leader.

A Journey of Faith, Marriage, and Grace

By Jon Maples

He who finds a wife finds what is good and receives favor from the LORD (Proverbs 18:22 NIV).

It was just past 3 AM. The house was quiet, and I was sitting up in bed; the only light coming from the lamp beside my journal. Journaling had become my lifeline. It was the only place I could pour out everything I was holding inside: the pain, confusion, frustration, fear, anger, and hope. Putting pen to paper gave me a way to give voice to my emotions and speak honestly with God and myself, without interruption or pretense. It was raw and sometimes painful, but it was real.

I flipped back through the pages, reading words I had written over the years. It was incredible to relive the journey through those pages, to see how far I had come. Some entries were angry scribbles, others were tear-stained pages where I had poured out my heart to God in desperation. But scattered throughout were glimpses of hope, moments where I could see God's hand at work even in the darkness.

Nineteen years of marriage have taught me that everything about marriage is simple, but the simple things are often the most difficult. Marriage to my wife, Kristi, has been filled with joy, but also with many hard seasons. Many of those hard seasons were because I lived selfishly, focusing on my business, my health, and what Jon wanted, rather than what God wanted. *All a person's ways seem pure to them, but motives are weighed by the Lord* (Proverbs 16:2 NIV). Looking back, I can see how my motives were mixed, at best, and completely self-centered, at worst.

THE BRINK OF DISASTER

My days were a blur of client meetings, market updates, and late nights at the office. I was proud of what I was building. The business was thriving, and I told myself it was all for the sake of my family. But deep down, I knew I was pouring more of myself into work than into my family waiting for me at home.

When I wasn't at the office, I was at the CrossFit gym. I pushed my body hard, twice a day, chasing a sense of control and accomplishment. Fitness became my god; the gym, my sanctuary. The endorphin rush after a brutal workout gave me a high that I craved.

The CrossFit gym was filled with people who looked like me: disciplined, confident, focused. But it was also filled with attractive, fit women who seemed to have their lives together. I began to compare Kristi to the women I saw there, and it left me feeling dissatisfied and as though I was missing something. I didn't say it out loud, but the thoughts lingered. *Why can't Kristi be more like these women?* I couldn't help it, but the comparison planted seeds of divorce.

The enemy is subtle in his attacks. He doesn't come with obvious temptation; he whispers suggestions that seem reasonable. *You deserve better. You work so hard. Look what you've accomplished. Don't you deserve a partner who matches your dedication?* These thoughts felt like my own, but

I now recognize them as lies from the pit of hell.

I started to expect more from Kristi, and when she didn't meet those expectations, anger and frustration would erupt inside me. The expectations were unrealistic and unfair—I wanted her to be a fitness enthusiast like me, to be as driven about health as I was, to match my energy and ambition in every area. But she was her own person, with her own strengths and interests.

As the unmet expectations mounted, I grew frustrated and distant, pushing Kristi away and creating a sense of isolation in our home. We started living more like roommates than husband and wife. I'd leave early for the office, come home late from the gym, and collapse into bed exhausted. Expectation of intimacy with my wife often led to more disappointment once the emotional connection between us was broken. The intimacy and connection that once defined our relationship became a distant memory.

Arguments became a cycle of me insisting I wanted more, and Kristi feeling unheard and unloved. I was like a broken record, always talking about what was missing instead of celebrating what we had. The more I tried to fix things on my own, the worse they became.

One night, during another argument, Kristi said something that made me realize I was failing her. "You never listen to me, you're never here, even when you are, it's like you want to be somewhere else."

I let out a frustrated sigh. "I'm doing this for us."

She shook her head. "You're doing it for yourself. You care more about your business and your CrossFit buddies than you do this family and our marriage."

She was right, but I didn't want to admit it. Jesus said, *"For where your treasure is, there your heart will be also"* (Matthew 6:21 NIV). My treasure was clearly in my work and my fitness, not in my family. My heart followed my treasure, just as Jesus said it would.

So, I yelled, "Because I'm working hard so we have a good life and have all the things I never had!"

She looked away and said, "I just want you. Not your money, not your muscles. Just you."

Her words echoed in my mind long after the argument ended. They haunted me during my workouts, during client meetings, during those late-night journaling sessions. *Just you.* Such simple words, yet they revealed the depth of what I had been withholding from my wife. I was giving her everything except the one thing she wanted most—my presence, my attention, my heart.

THE MOMENT OF TRUTH

I was restless, broken, and tired of fighting. I felt alone as I lay in bed with tears streaming down my face.

In the dead of night, I journaled in the darkness. God spoke to my heart: "First, become the priest of your home, then I will make you the king of your home." The words struck me with clarity. I had been waiting for Kristi to change, for her to meet my expectations, but God was calling me to lead by loving her as Christ loved the church. The change had to start with me.

> *Husbands, love your wives, just as Christ loved the church and gave himself up for her to make her holy, cleansing her by the washing with water through the word, and to present her to himself as a radiant church, without stain or wrinkle or any other blemish, but holy and blameless* (Ephesians 5:25-27 NIV).

This passage took on new meaning. I wasn't called to change Kristi; I was called to love her sacrificially, to give myself up for her just as Christ did for the church.

I knew what needed to be done, but it was a heavy lift. The call was for me to begin going through a process of change. God was calling me to return to Him, not as the man I had become, but as the man He created me to be.

I turned to journaling and the Scripture for guidance. The words of James became an anchor, a correction, and a lifeline.

My dear brothers and sisters, take note of this: Everyone should be quick to listen, slow to speak and slow to become angry (James 1:19 NIV). This verse convicted me deeply. I was quick to speak, slow to listen, and quick to become angry—the exact opposite of what God calls us to be.

Blessed is the one who perseveres under trial because, having stood the test, that person will receive the crown of life that the Lord has promised to those who love him (James 1:12 NIV). I began to see our marital struggles not as something to escape from, but as a trial that could produce perseverance and, ultimately, a blessing if I would trust God through it. I measured my approach to marriage against this standard and found myself lacking. My wisdom was earthly, not heavenly. It was self-serving, not peace-loving.

But he gives us more grace. That is why Scripture says: *"God opposes the proud but shows favor to the humble"* (James 4:6 NIV). Pride was at the root of so many of my problems. I was proud of my business success, proud of my physical fitness, and proud of my accomplishments. Pride was keeping me from the grace I desperately needed. The grace that Kristi needed from me, but I didn't have the capacity to give.

There is only one Lawgiver and Judge, the one who is able to save and destroy. But who are you to judge your neighbor? (James 4:12 NIV). I had been judging Kristi constantly, measuring her against my expectations and finding her wanting. But who was I to judge her? Only God has that authority.

These verses cut through my defenses, exposing the root of my insecurity and anger. My pride had kept me from hearing Kristi's heart.

God has a way of getting our attention. For me, it came in the form of vertigo—a relentless, dizzying sickness that left me bedridden for weeks. I couldn't stand without falling, couldn't eat without vomiting, couldn't function in any normal capacity.

I couldn't walk, drive, or even shower without help. My body, once a source of pride, became a prison. Kristi cared for me, nursing me back to health with patience and tenderness. She could have used my helplessness to get back at me for all the times I had been absent or critical. Instead, she showed me Christ-like love.

In my weakness, I saw how misplaced my priorities had been. The gym couldn't save me; only God could.

> But he [the Lord] said to me, "My grace is sufficient for you, for my power is made perfect in weakness." Therefore I will boast all the more gladly about my weaknesses, so that Christ's power may rest on me (2 Corinthians 12:9 NIV).

God was showing me that His power was perfected in my weakness, not in my strength.

I began to understand the importance of patience and empathy. Lying in that bed, completely dependent on Kristi's care, I gained a new appreciation for what it meant to serve and be served. I saw how selfless love looks in action. James asks us, *What causes fights and quarrels among you? Don't they come from your desires that battle within you?* (James 4:1 NIV). Our battle was not against each other, but against spiritual forces that sought to divide us.

For our struggle is not against flesh and blood, but against the rulers, against the authorities, against the powers of this dark world and against the spiritual forces of evil in the heavenly realms (Ephesians 6:12 NIV). This revelation changed everything. Kristi wasn't my enemy—she was my teammate in a battle against forces that were attempting to destroy our marriage and family.

Prayer and fasting were essential weapons I began to utilize, seeking to change. I wanted more from my marriage and, more importantly, I wanted more from God.

Inspired by Mark Batterson's book *The Circle Maker,* I began to pray intentionally for my marriage. Every day at 10:15 AM, my phone alarm reminded me to pray for our marriage: for reconciliation, that our hearts and minds would be pure and holy, and for protection. I realized that Satan's attacks on my wife were attacks aimed at me and our marriage, and I needed to fight for her in prayer.

Pray continually (1 Thessalonians 5:17 NIV) became my daily exercise. I circled our marriage in prayer, believing that God could do what I could not. I prayed for Kristi's heart, my heart, our daughter, and protection from the enemy's schemes. I prayed for wisdom, patience, and to love like Jesus loves.

I remembered all the times in Scripture when God made a way where there seemed to be no way: He raised the dead, parted the sea, calmed the storms, healed the sick, conquered giants, and rose from the dead. If God could do the impossible then, He could heal our marriage now.

Jesus looked at them and said, "With man this is impossible, but with God all things are possible" (Matthew 19:26 NIV). This became my anchor verse. When the situation looked hopeless, when old patterns crept back in, when I was tempted to give up, I remembered that with God, all things are possible.

Slowly, forgiveness replaced resentment. Pride gave way to humility. Anger surrendered to peace. Our marriage, once on the brink of divorce, began to heal.

For so long, I had leaned on my own understanding, trying to control every outcome. Now, I was learning to trust God with my marriage, my future, and my heart. As I surrendered my need for control, God began to exchange my fleeting happiness for lasting joy.

BIBLICAL WISDOM FOR BREAKTHROUGH

I called on God in prayer as I sought wisdom from His Word.

May the God of hope fill you with all joy and peace as you trust in him, so that you may overflow with hope by the power of the Holy Spirit (Romans 15:13 NIV). I wanted to overflow with hope, to be a source of encouragement rather than discouragement in my home.

But the fruit of the Spirit is love, joy, peace, forbearance, kindness, goodness, faithfulness, gentleness, and self-control. Against such things there is no law (Galatians 5:22-23 NIV). I studied each fruit carefully, asking God to produce these qualities in my life. Love that was sacrificial, not selfish. Joy that was deep, not dependent on circumstances. Peace that passed understanding, not the absence of problems.

"I have told you this so that my joy may be in you and that your joy may be complete. My command is this: Love each other as I have loved you. Greater love has no one than this: to lay down one's life for one's friends" (John 15:11-13 NIV). Jesus was calling me to lay down my life—my preferences, expectations, and selfish desires—for my wife.

For his anger lasts only a moment, but his favor lasts a lifetime; weeping may stay for the night, but rejoicing comes in the morning (Psalm 30:5 NIV). Even when progress seemed slow and we had setbacks, I held onto the promise that morning would come.

As I allowed my life to be shaped by God's Word, I stopped chasing happiness and started cultivating gratitude for the blessings God had already given me. I learned to see Kristi not as the source of my fulfillment, but as a gift to be cherished and served.

A friend once shared a portrait of J.W. Marriott and his son. The father was holding the master plan for their business empire. The portrait reminded me that my heavenly Father holds the blueprint for my marriage and my life. Even when joy in my marriage seemed impossible, I could trust God to guide us, one step at a time.

Trust in the Lord with all your heart and lean not on your own understanding; in all your ways submit to him, and he will make your paths straight. Do not be wise in your own eyes; fear the Lord and shun evil. This will bring health to your body and nourishment to your bones (Proverbs 3:5-8 NIV). This teaching echoed in my heart daily. I had been wise in my own eyes for too long. It was time to trust God's wisdom above my own.

People often say, "Behind every great man stands a great woman." But I've learned that my leadership is strengthened by Kristi, who stands beside me, challenges me, and trusts me to lead our family courageously in Christ. When I stopped demanding perfection and started supporting and loving her as she was, our relationship began to heal, and we experienced true joy and peace.

The journey has not been easy. Booker T. Washington said, "Nothing ever comes to one that is worth having except as a result of hard work." Marriage is hard work, but it is worth every effort. We have endured setbacks, disappointments, and moments of doubt. But through it all, God's grace has been the constant, transforming me and giving us hope in difficult seasons.

And we know that in all things God works for the good of those who love him, who have been called according to his purpose (Romans 8:28 NIV).

Even our hardest seasons, biggest failures, and deepest pain—God is already working it all together for good. Not because the circumstances were good, but because God is good, and He can redeem anything.

FROM JOURNALS TO JOY

As I read through the pages of my journals, I am amazed at God's faithfulness: How He met me in my brokenness, changed my heart, and restored joy to my marriage. The man writing at 3 AM today is not the same man who started this journey years ago. God has made me into an unstoppable leader—not because I conquered my circumstances, but because I surrendered to the God who conquers all things.

If you're reading this and your marriage feels impossible, if you're struggling to lead your family well, if you feel like you've made too many mistakes to recover from—take heart. God restored my marriage, and He can restore yours. Start with surrender. Get on your knees and admit that your way isn't working. Turn to Scripture and let His Word transform your mind. Pray without ceasing for your marriage and family. Love your spouse as Christ loved the church.

The journey of faith, marriage, and grace continues. But now I know that with God, all things are possible, even the restoration of a marriage that seemed beyond repair. That's the power of an unstoppable God working in the heart of a surrendered leader.

ANTONIO FERNANDEZ SAAVEDRA

Antonio Fernandez Saavedra is a native of Havana, Cuba, maintaining a deep love for the island's people, culture, music, and cuisine. His family experienced a dramatic transition from prosperity in Cuba to significant hardships upon arriving in the United States, challenges they met with unwavering faith and an incredible work ethic.

During a vulnerable period, Tony was drawn into what he describes as "the darkness of this world." At the age of 37, he experienced a profound spiritual transformation when he embraced his Christian faith, marking the beginning of a complete life change.

Tony built a successful career, specializing in IT and technical services. He demonstrated remarkable dedication, working full-time while serving in full-time ministry. He has retired from his position with the National Association of Boards of Pharmacy.

Tony describes himself as not truly retired, but rather "refired" by God for continued service. He ministers at the Indian River County Jail and serves on the pastoral staff at Visionary Church under the leadership of Pastor Lynne Barletta. Additionally, Tony is fully involved with the Florida Faith Alliance, an organization founded by Pastor Lynne Barletta that focuses on combating child trafficking.

Contact: agapechapelofillinois@gmail.com

From Darkness to His Marvelous Light

By Antonio Fernandez Saavedra

The stunning Atlantic Ocean embraces the beautiful white sand on the beach. The different shades of blue extend as far as the eye can see. The island is surrounded by water, and the breeze is so gentle you could say it's close to paradise. This beautiful island is Cuba, and it was my first home.

> *Here is the ocean, vast and wide, teeming with life of every kind, both large and small* (Psalm 104:25 NLT).

Our family was well-to-do. There were nannies and cooks who stayed at the house during the week. However, the beauty of the island does not always reveal what is happening within. On a night that no one expected, the southwestern coast was invaded by Fidel Castro and 1500 communist soldiers; the takeover established the awful evilness of communism on the island full of innocent people. This was the Bay of Pigs; April 17th, 1961.

After this, living conditions changed quickly for every family. Food rations limited basic goods: one box of powdered milk, one tube of toothpaste, one bar of soap, and the list went on and on. The Catholic school system completely turned to communism, which meant indoctrination. Let me explain how the younger grades were affected. The teachers would say, "Let's pray to Jesus Christ and see if He wants us to have candy." We would pray, and nothing would happen. Then the teacher would say, "Let's pray to Fidel Castro and see what happens." And of course, the candy would come out after that. Younger kids were recruited to the communist army early.

FREEDOM FLIGHT

After my mother went to the embassy almost every day of the week, it was finally time. On March 22nd, 1962, my sister, brother, and I boarded a Freedom Flight (Peter Pan) full of kids and teenagers to leave Cuba. The plane landed at an airport in Homestead, Florida, and we were taken immediately to a refugee camp. At the camp, the first two TV shows that I saw were *Sea Hunt* and *Car 54, Where Are You?* We had 24 boys in the house with one set of house parents; the bunk beds were three high. This was now home, with no family at all.

> *In everything give thanks: for this is the will of God in Christ Jesus concerning you* (1 Thessalonians 5:18 KJV).

All the family managed to leave Cuba about two years later, and we were united once again. The only one who did not make it was my grandfather—he died on the operating table due to an issue I'd rather not talk about.

Conditions in the American schools were not the same. The school system mandated segregation for those in our school. This was my first encounter with racism and being bullied.

NEW BEGINNINGS

You can't help but say, "His Grace is sufficient." After a few years, the whole family moved from Florida to inner city Chicago. My brother and I rose very early in the morning and served as altar boys at the Latin mass in the Catholic Church. I will never forget the first snowfall, which was an experience of a lifetime.

Over the next two years, we moved a bit further north. I was finally in 6th grade at a wonderful Catholic school. I continued to serve as an altar boy and was honored to serve in the first guitar mass. I also managed to make the basketball team. I will never forget one of my friends from the team teaching me English curse words.

DOWNWARD SPIRAL

As I entered 7th grade, I began to shift from focusing on God to being more involved in the world. Religion could only help you so far. Suddenly, its power began to diminish because I didn't have a personal relationship with Jesus Christ.

At the age of 15, I started smoking marijuana in high school, drinking, and doing acid. I know the Holy Spirit was trying to get my attention, but I was focused elsewhere, walking on the dark side. I managed to graduate, but college was nothing but a continuous party. I somehow made it through a year and a half of college, walking away with credits in data processing.

In my early 20s and 30s, my life was a total wreck. I lost a wonderful marriage to a very beautiful Swedish woman because of drugs. The divorce returned me to a life as a bachelor, which took me to a period of freebasing cocaine, during which I had a lot of crazy relationships that amounted to nothing.

To make ends meet, I asked a roommate to move into a 2-bedroom apartment, and a new level of life began. After a while, he started dealing with cocaine, and I fell back into the darkness. We went to a bar and there was a beautiful blonde. My roommate said, "I'll bet you $100 you can't pick her up."

I said, "I'm coming back to collect." She and I started dancing and conversing, and we had a couple of cocktails. We started dating, and I came to find out she was the ex-girlfriend of a very big drug dealer.

I had worked my way up to become a computer room supervisor. This was before personal computers were available, so I was earning a good salary. Unfortunately, my income was not enough for her. Next thing you know, after a period of time, I gave in and became part of a cartel and was dealing drugs. In no time at all, with five people under me, we were moving $175,000 worth of drugs every week. This, however, did come with a price. I developed a $50,000 a year cocaine habit along with drinking and smoking pot and, of course, cigarettes. I was on a highway to hell with no exit.

> *There is a way which seemeth right unto a man,*
> *but the end thereof are the ways of death*
> (Proverbs 14-12 KJV).

THE CRASH

The roller coaster ride continued, and then right around the 3 1/2-year mark, things suddenly changed. One night, I smoked a couple of joints and went to bed. All of a sudden, a 50-pound sledgehammer came through the front door. It was the local police, the FBI, the DEA, and a SWAT team. They immediately grabbed me, pulled the sweatshirt over my head, and began to inflict physical damage to gain information. In a cartel, you do not divulge information. Sure enough, they found a lot of drugs in the house, and I was handcuffed and taken to the Cook County Jail.

The police informed the news stations that I had $3,000,000 worth of drugs in the house. Because of that, my bond was set at $1,500,000, putting me right up there with the murderers. In that jail, I was shaking and sweating, having major drug withdrawals with no medical assistance. After a few court appearances, I knew I was looking at 88 years in jail.

Be sober, be vigilant; because your adversary the devil,
as a roaring lion, walketh about, seeking whom
he may devour (1 Peter 5:8 KJV).

DIVINE INTERVENTION WITH ROCK BOTTOM PRAYER

After coming back from court, my new reality set in. The devil cannot wait to take out your legs from under you. I sat in jail during the quiet of nighttime, and suddenly felt the urge to get down on my knees. It was just me in that cold, clammy jail. I knelt, and all I said was, "Jesus, if You're real, show me."

For whosoever shall call upon the name of the Lord
shall be saved (Romans 10:13 KJV).

I truly believe the Lord heard my sincerity and desperation; He knew the cry of my heart was filled with true repentance. One of my youngest sisters was part of a ladies' Bible study that my future wife attended, and they began praying for me. Things started to happen. Somehow, in the evidence room, the amount of drugs I was busted with was drastically reduced. Also, the drugs in my body were leaving, giving me a much clearer mind and a better appearance. I knew this was not my doing; the Lord had intervened in my situation completely.

To them God has chosen to make known among the Gentiles
the glorious riches of this mystery, which is Christ in you,
the hope of glory (Colossians 1:27 NIV).

More things continued to happen. The two lawyers representing me got me released from jail. I only needed to show up for the remaining court hearings. The verdict had not yet been reached, but my goodness, I could feel the Lord moving.

While on the outside, the Lord sent an Angel that I surely did not deserve. Between Jesus, the Angel, and one of my sisters, Jesus came into my heart. I experienced the most incredible transformation of salvation—from darkness to His marvelous light. I could feel the Spirit filling my heart, and suddenly, the darkness began to dispel. I was filled with joy and felt like my vision had been enhanced; I knew why I was born. And all of me was alive like never before.

Salvation is a life-changing experience like no other. You become full of God.

I could not wait for the church doors to open. I was His and He was mine.

In no time, my love affair with Jesus began with intimacy, deep love, and a friendship evolving into a relationship. It was marked by the newness of life. I felt distant from the past with the knowledge that the price for my sins had been paid. I crossed the veil into His heart, was made new, and experienced the physicality of the Holy Spirit. I could go on and on because I'm still living it. Oh hallelujah! He is alive! And so are you, in Christ Jesus.

For I am persuaded, that neither death, nor life,
nor angels, nor principalities, nor powers, nor things
present, nor things to come, nor height, nor depths,
nor any other creature, shall be able to separate us
from the love of God, which is in Christ Jesus our Lord
(Romans 8:38-39 KJV).

MIRACLE VERDICT

The day came when the lawyers called me and told me to brace myself because the final verdict was being handed down; my life was in the balance. I have always believed that there is power and trust in God. There is power in praying in tongues. Exercising faith opens up new possibilities for expectations. The acronym for FAITH is For All I'm To Have.

These things I have spoken unto you, that in me ye might have peace. In the world you shall have tribulations: but be of good cheer; I have overcome the world (John 16:33 KJV).

I had been praying all morning. In getting ready, I put on a suit and combed my hair after getting a haircut. I kept looking up to heaven, knowing that the $65,000 I paid the lawyers meant nothing if my Jesus was not involved in the equation.

As my case was called, I realized the moment had arrived, and I knew Jesus had arrived, too. The lawyer and the judge went back and forth. They were going over everything—discovery, evidence, background, and many other things. All of a sudden, there was a hesitation; nobody was speaking. Then the gavel went down, and the judge began to speak, revealing the verdict. I was fined $5000 and given a five-year probation.

Jesus looked at them and said, "With man this is impossible, but with God all things are possible" (Matthew 19:26 NIV).

An 88-year sentence had just been wiped clean. And my heart finally slowed down from pounding through my chest. I still have the picture in my mind of what the judge looked like, what he spoke, and how, in the blink of an eye, I was given a fresh start to live my life again. Thank You, Jesus.

> Now thanks be unto God, which always causeth us to
> triumph in Christ, and maketh manifest the savour of his
> knowledge by us in every place (2 Corinthians 2:14 KJV).

A TEST OF FAITH

Readjusting to life was not easy. Finding permanent employment with a Double Class X Felony was challenging. I decided to study for and take the insurance exam, which I passed. I started mainstreaming back in society; although the adjustment to the small checks humbled me, I was very thankful.

About a year went by; life was good. Then, all of a sudden. I found out that the FBI had conducted a sting operation, arresting over 120 members of the cartel across the United States, and my name came up. I was extradited to the West Coast to stand court with the cartel members who were busted. By the grace of God, I found a lawyer who was a former judge. I was looking at 80 years in jail because I had been mixed up with the cartel that was also dealing with kilos of cocaine.

People of God, know that your faith will be tested every single day, if not every single minute. The key is always to remain as prayerful as you can.

When my case came up and my lawyer was talking to the judge, I was praying in tongues under my breath. At the beginning, the judge said, "I see no other way but to give you time." As the case progressed and it came down to the final decision, I was able to speak for just a few minutes to the judge directly about what I had done with my life. Again, he got quiet, hesitated, and spoke, saying, "Five-thousand-dollar fine and a five-year probation."

I couldn't believe what happened, because the truth was that a 168-year sentence in two states had just been wiped clean. Can man do that? No, only God Almighty, Almighty God. Other members had to do time. Thank You, Jesus.

For whosoever is born of God overcometh the world: and this is the victory that overcometh the world, even our faith (1 John 5:4 KJV).

FULL SPEED AHEAD

After that, I was so empowered by what happened that I felt like I heard, "Full speed ahead for Jesus."

Soon, with just a pastor and a witness in a simple room, I got married to my Angel. Six months later, we had saved up enough money to host a reception, as neither of our parents could afford it. The exact cost of the reception was the same amount of money that was given back to us by those who attended. Jesus!

My wife had been saved five years before I was. She was the rock of faith that helped ground me so I could grow in Christ. We're in the world but not of it. I had become an usher and also led the men's group at Good News Christian Center under the strong-faithed Pastor Tim Roames. For five years, my wife and I led one of the two groups that went to the Cook County Jail, where I had been locked up. In our spare time, we would minister to the hurting.

As our journey continued, I was ordained a deacon, preached regularly, and organized evangelistic outreaches. Through time, the Lord has also ordained me as an elder, evangelist, and assistant pastor. Know that promotion comes from the Lord.

The Lord even helped us in deciding to open a church for Him. We opened that church, which is still alive and led by a pastor we installed.

I want you to know that God does not call leaders; he creates the leaders for the call.

There is hope for all of us. When we lean into Him for everything, the doors will begin to open.

> *Then he answered and spake unto me, saying,*
> *This is the word of the Lord unto Zerubbabel, saying,*
> *Not by might, nor by power but by My spirit, saith the*
> *Lord of hosts* (Zechariah 4:6 KJV).

Yes, I was ordained as a pastor in November of 2013; what an honor it was. I still live by what Jesus calls me: His servant.

There is more, but my story is also written in heaven. Currently, my beautiful wife of 33 years and I are preaching at the Indian River County Jail. We are on the pastoral staff at Visionary Church under the great Pastor Lynn Barletta. This is an awesome Holy Spirit-filled church. Our other involvement is with Florida Faith Alliance, founded by Pastor Lynne, which is an incredible organization that fights against child trafficking.

People of God, He is looking for the earthen vessels that will rise. He can't wait to equip you. What Jesus has done for me, He can do for you. What the devil meant for bad, God turns around for the good.

> *And we know that all things work together for good*
> *to them that love God, to them who are called according*
> *to his purpose* (Romans 8:28 KJV).

YOUR CALL

My heart has heard You say, "Come and talk with Me." And my heart responds, "Lord I am coming" (Psalm 27:8 NLT).

Now I would not be a good pastor if I did not say this: God is calling you. Are you coming?

From losing paradise in Cuba to finding true paradise in Christ, my journey proves that no matter how far you fall into darkness, His light will always dispel the darkness. God does not call leaders; He creates leaders for the call.

The same God who turned my 168-year sentence into probation and transformed a drug dealer into a pastor is calling you today. True unstoppable leadership comes when you realize you're completely stopped without Him, and completely unstoppable with Him.

The question isn't whether you're qualified. The question is: are you willing to let Him qualify you?

An Unstoppable Leader Is...
EMPOWERING

Build Leaders, Not Just Followers

By Brett Dabe

> *Iron sharpens iron; so a man sharpens his friend's countenance* (Proverbs 27:17 WEB).

Leadership isn't measured by how many followers a person has, but by the leaders they have helped develop. Unstoppable leaders understand that their ultimate legacy isn't *what* they accomplish, but who they empower to accomplish great things long after they're gone.

Moses gives us the perfect example of empowering leadership. When God called him to lead Israel out of Egypt, Moses could have tried to do everything himself. Instead, he listened to his father-in-law Jethro's advice and appointed capable men to handle smaller disputes while he focused on the bigger issues.

Moses' most significant act of empowerment was training Joshua. Moses didn't wait until his time of leadership was over to start developing his replacement. Instead, he brought Joshua along on the mountain when he received the Ten Commandments and allowed him to lead military campaigns, preparing him for the responsibility of leading God's people into the Promised Land. When the time came for Moses to pass the torch, Joshua was ready—not because he was naturally gifted, but because Moses had invested years developing him. That's empowering leadership.

Jesus took the same approach with His disciples. He could have accomplished His mission alone, but He chose to invest three years training twelve ordinary men to carry on His work. Jesus didn't just preach to crowds, leading the masses; He also developed leaders who would plant churches, write Scripture, and lead the world to Christianity after He no longer walked the earth in the flesh.

Jesus didn't choose the most qualified candidates. He chose fishermen, tax collectors, and other regular guys. Then He poured Himself into them, teaching them through words and example. He sent them out to minister while He was still with them, letting them make mistakes and learn from experience. When Jesus returned to heaven, His disciples were ready to lead the early church. Not because they were perfect, but because Jesus had empowered them with knowledge, experience, and the Holy Spirit.

Barnabas followed the same pattern. When he saw potential in John Mark after the young man had quit Paul's first missionary journey, Barnabas took Mark under his wing. Paul had written Mark off as unreliable, but Barnabas saw what he could become with the right mentoring. Years later, Paul would write to Timothy: *Get Mark and bring him with you, because he is useful to me for ministry* (2 Timothy 4:11 NKJV). Barnabas' investment in Mark's development paid off. Mark went on to write one of the four Gospels and became a valuable ministry partner.

Empowering leaders see potential in people that others miss. When Samuel was looking for Israel's next king, he almost overlooked David because he was the youngest son doing the humble job of watching sheep. But God saw David's heart, and Samuel anointed him for future leadership.

Elijah did the same thing with Elisha. When God told Elijah to anoint his successor, Elijah found Elisha plowing with oxen. Elisha wasn't in ministry school or serving as a prophet's assistant; he was a farmer. But Elijah saw his potential and invested in his development. When Elijah was taken up to heaven, Elisha received a double portion of his spirit and performed twice as many recorded miracles. Elijah's empowerment of Elisha multiplied his impact far beyond what he could have accomplished alone.

An empowering leader doesn't offer all the answers. Instead, he asks questions of those he is leading, helping them learn to make decisions themselves. When King Solomon asked God for wisdom, God didn't download everything Solomon needed to know. Instead, He gave Solomon the ability to discern right from wrong and make wise decisions. The same principle applies to developing other leaders. Instead of solving every problem for your team, ask them questions that help them think through solutions. "What options do you see?" "What would success look like?" "What resources do you need?" This approach takes longer initially but builds capability that lasts.

Empowering leaders also create stretch opportunities for the people they're developing. When Mordecai mentored Esther, he didn't protect her from challenging situations, but he did prepare her for them. When the crisis came and the Jewish people faced genocide, Mordecai reminded Esther: *"Who knows but that you have come to your royal position for such a time as this?"* (Esther 4:14 NIV). Esther's courage to approach the king and expose Haman's plot saved her people. Mordecai's empowerment helped her rise to the occasion when it mattered most.

Empowerment requires trust, and trust requires risk. When Elijah passed his mantle to Elisha, he risked his successor taking the ministry in a different direction. When Jesus sent His disciples out two by two, He risked them making mistakes that could hurt His reputation. Empowering leaders are willing to take these risks because they understand that people learn by doing, not just by watching. They'd rather have someone try and fail than never try at all. They know that failure is often the best teacher.

An empowering leader holds themselves and those under them accountable.

Moses set clear expectations for the judges he appointed. Jesus gave His disciples specific instructions for their ministry trips. Empowering leaders maintain high standards while providing high support.

Most importantly, empowering leaders are secure enough to celebrate others' success without feeling threatened. When Jonathan saw that David was God's chosen king instead of him, Jonathan didn't become jealous. He helped David succeed and celebrated his victories.

Building an empowering leadership style requires intentional effort. Start by identifying the people in your sphere of influence who have leadership potential. Look for character, not just competence. Find people who are faithful in small things and give them bigger opportunities. Then, create development plans for each person you're mentoring. What skills do they need to develop? What experiences would stretch them? What resources could help them grow? Be intentional about their development, not just their current contribution.

The kingdom needs leaders at every level who can think strategically, solve problems creatively, and develop others effectively. This kind of distributed leadership can only be developed through intentional empowerment.

Your legacy as a leader won't be determined by what you accomplish, but by who you develop. Are you building people who will carry on your mission long after you're gone? That helps ensure leadership that is truly unstoppable.

. . . .

ERIC BUCHER

Eric Bucher has always had a passion for entrepreneurship. At just 13, he launched his first business mowing lawns in his parents' neighborhood. By summer's end, he had saved $3,000—enough to open his first stock portfolio.

By age 22, Eric owned 13 rental units across three counties while also pursuing Microsoft certifications through evening classes.

In 2006, at age 26, Eric relocated to South Florida, where he now lives with his wife, Yolanda, and their 11-year-old son, Xander.

In 2009, Eric founded Quantified IT, growing the company from a single employee to a 45-person team with offices in West Palm Beach, Florida, and Atlanta, Georgia. In 2021, he successfully merged Quantified IT with Applied Innovations to form QIT Solutions, a managed IT services company delivering end-to-end technology solutions—from AI development to helpdesk support.

In 2015, Eric also founded CallSprout, a hosted VoIP telecommunications company serving clients nationwide.

Today, Eric ministers to a growing number of men, speaks on repentance, surrender, and obedience to the Father, sharing the love of Christ with all whom he encounters.

FROM DEATH TO LIFE

By Eric Bucher

Success had always been my measuring stick. As a CEO who had just completed a marathon, I embodied what I thought was the American Dream: wealth, achievement, and the relentless pursuit of more. But on April 14th, 2023, lying in a hospital bed with my legs shaking uncontrollably, I heard words that would shatter my entire worldview: "You're having a major heart attack."

I was in shock. *You don't know me, I thought. I'm an athlete. I JUST ran a marathon. I JUST ran three miles this morning!* But the dozen medical professionals surrounding me, inserting needles into both arms, were telling me a different story. My legs, seemingly having a mind of their own, were also telling me a different story.

The doctor whispered in my ear, "You need to calm down, take deep breaths. We're trying to stabilize your heart." Then I saw my wife in the hallway, with a look of disbelief and shock that any spouse would express having just heard those words. The fear, pain, and nausea on my face reflected in her eyes. It was a moment I'll never forget.

I didn't realize in that terrifying moment that God was about to take me on a journey from physical death to spiritual rebirth, transforming me from a successful businessman into an unstoppable leader for His kingdom.

THE VALLEY OF PHYSICAL DEATH

Almost immediately, I was loaded into an ambulance for transport to another hospital. That was the only point during the whole ordeal when I thought I was going to die—and for a few minutes during that ride, I wanted to.

The doctors had already pushed three doses of morphine into my veins, with two more administered during transport. But chest pain from a heart attack is incredibly severe. Add nausea, and you have a recipe for wishing death would come quickly. The rush-hour ride on I-95 in South Florida's emergency lane made every bump and jolt of the rumble strips feel like torture. Imagine being suspended in midair with a vice grip on your chest and back, then being jostled five times per second.

Upon arrival at the second hospital, nurses began preparing me for surgery. Within seconds, a surgeon was inserting a catheter with a tiny camera into a vein in my groin to examine my arteries and blockages. "STEMI," I heard him say. "Placing the stent now."

Then, like magic, the pain vanished immediately. As I'm writing this, I still can't believe how quickly the pain and nausea disappeared. A nurse approached and said, "I'm going to give you some fentanyl now." Little did anyone know I was a former addict, but I figured I got a free pass on the morphine and fentanyl. Before that thought fully registered, I drifted off as they wheeled me into recovery.

I was told I'd be hospitalized for days, but being a man of incredible will, I left exactly 24 hours later. Besides receiving the largest stent they manufactured, I left with nagging questions and a new fear that would consume me.

THE SEARCH FOR PURPOSE

Until that point in my life, my purpose had been simple: generate wealth, provide for my family, be a good person, and embody the American Dream.

I was succeeding by all measures, but leaving the hospital, I felt there was much more to life than material success.

What is the purpose of life? Why are we here? I couldn't shake these questions. I'd lie awake at night, sometimes all night, pondering them. That led to a new fear I'd never experienced before—dying. I became so afraid of dying in my sleep that I couldn't sleep. My nine-year-old son needed his father, my wife relied on me financially, and I hadn't prepared adequately to leave them at 43 years old.

During my recovery, I took a month off work, and I discovered just how deep YouTube rabbit holes can go—starting with creation theories, studying the Big Bang, and ending on the ten dimensions of reality. I realized after several days that both paths led to the same conclusion: God. Until that point, my belief in God had been nothing more than a hedge against hell—a childhood insurance policy. I had no understanding of faith until I began reading the Bible and discovered Hebrews 11:1: *Now faith is confidence in what we hope for and assurance about what we do not see* (NIV).

The Lord was drawing me to Himself, just as Jesus promised in John 6:44: *"No one can come to me unless the Father who sent me draws them, and I will raise them up at the last day"* (NIV). Looking back, I can see how God was orchestrating every detail of my journey, confirming what Jeremiah 29:11 declares: *"For I know the plans I have for you," declares the Lord, "plans to prosper you and not to harm you, to give you hope and a future"* (NIV).

As summer passed and I returned to work, I stepped away from operational responsibilities to reduce stress. When I announced to my team that I'd be stepping back from operations, instead of panic, I saw relief. Apparently, I'd been a "shiny object chaser" who could rally the team in any direction— sometimes the wrong direction. This change empowered my team and allowed much-needed foundations to be built.

Just as I was settling into this less stressful routine, I received a call that would change everything.

October 8th, 2023: "Your dad is in the hospital. His colon ruptured in the middle of the night. He's septic. Get here now."

Living 1,000 miles away, I had to fly to reach him. I canceled my calendar and bought a ticket to Lexington, Kentucky. On the way to the airport, my wife asked, "What can I do? What do you need?" I've never been one to ask for help, but without sleep and fearing the worst for my father, I began to weep.

Only during active drug addiction 17 years prior had I felt so out of control. It was surreal—seeing myself in a dark pit with a hundred chains wrapped around my neck, unable to escape. I was a mess while driving—weeping and talking to my wife. I couldn't lose my dad. Despite our differences and past mistakes, he was my measuring stick for success in life.

Arriving in Lexington, my mom picked me up from the airport and drove me to the hospital. At the ICU and seeing him—a crumpled mess with dozens of tubes coming from his body—I broke in half. I spent four days in deep thought, sometimes pulling out my laptop and deconstructing my life one keystroke at a time.

I learned two crucial things about myself that week. First, I was a "chrome polisher"—I had an innate ability to shrug off anything, act as if nothing was wrong, and properly present myself while pressing forward. But inside, I was rotting out. There wasn't enough chrome polish left to protect my shiny exterior. Rust was showing through, and holes were forming.

> *"Woe to you, teachers of the law and Pharisees, you hypocrites! You are like whitewashed tombs, which look beautiful on the outside but on the inside are full of the bones of the dead and everything unclean"* (Matthew 23:27 NIV).

Second, I realized I didn't believe in Jesus. He wasn't real to me. I couldn't wrap my head around Him being the only way to heaven. *So many good people exist in the world—are they destined for hell?* As it turns out, yes, if they don't believe in the life, death, and resurrection of Jesus Christ. Romans 3:23 makes it clear: *For all have sinned and fall short of the glory of God* (NIV), and Romans 6:23 explains the consequence: *For the wages of sin is death, but the gift of God is eternal life in Christ Jesus our Lord* (NIV).

On my flight home, I sat next to a retired Baptist preacher who was busy preparing papers for a keynote speech. Realizing he might have answers to my questions, I asked if he had five minutes. I quickly explained about the heart attack and asked, "What's the purpose of life? Why are we here?"

He smiled and said, "That's the easiest question I've been asked all day. To glorify God."

I thanked him and spent the rest of the flight trying to understand what it meant to glorify God. I assumed it meant being good to others since we're created in God's image. As it turns out, that wasn't the complete picture.

I shared these revelations with my wife—a lifelong believer. I nearly gave *her* a heart attack when I told her I didn't believe Jesus could be the only way to heaven. Before we could finish our conversation, we had to take our son to hockey practice.

Driving past a small, old church, I noticed their sign: "Jesus? - John 14:6." My interest piqued, so I asked my wife to find the verse. Before she could locate it, my son in the backseat began reciting: *"I am the way and the truth and the life. No one comes to the Father except through me"* (NIV). We later discovered our son had memorized this verse for school just weeks before.

When the Bible speaks of signs and wonders, don't discount literal signs—they can have wonders associated with them too.

That evening, we went to some friends' house for a playdate. My wife knew special guests would be there but didn't tell me, fearing I'd back out. During our visit, an older couple arrived—they were friends of our friends without children. For the next 45 minutes, I sat fascinated as the couple shared stories from China, Indonesia, Thailand, Europe, South Africa, and Brazil.

Without my uttering a single word, they'd answered almost every question I had about Jesus Christ. I abruptly interrupted and asked, "Who are you people?"

"We are missionaries," they replied. When I asked what that meant, they explained they were disciples of Jesus Christ, referencing Luke 9, where Jesus sent out the twelve disciples to spread the good news. They told me I'd never know Jesus until He revealed Himself to me—something that confused me completely. *How can you know a dead person?*

As we said goodbye, they told me to read the book of Hebrews, saying it would explain everything. My wife disagreed, suggesting I read John instead. Being a good student, I went home and read Hebrews first, which left me with more questions than answers.

THE MOMENT OF SURRENDER

October 17th, 2023, I followed my wife's advice and read the entire book of John in one sitting—something I recommend to everyone. For the first time in my life, the Bible came alive. I felt connected to the people and was transported into their world. I became excited, seeing the Bible's relevance and truth for today, just as it was 2,000 years ago.

After our usual family routine that evening, once my wife went to lie with our son, I felt called to pray. I got on my knees and asked Jesus to reveal Himself to me, just as the missionaries had instructed.

"Jesus," I prayed, "if You are real, please reveal Yourself to me. I can't live my life in fear of dying anymore. If You want to take my life in the night, go ahead and take it. Otherwise, use me, clean me out, and make me Your own.

I don't want to drive anymore—take the keys. Amen."

Afterward, I went peacefully to sleep and woke at 1:45 AM, giggling uncontrollably like a little boy. Waking my wife, she asked what was happening. I told her, "We're going to be in heaven together!"

If you've ever had the veil between heaven and earth split open and received a baptism of the Holy Spirit in the middle of the night, you understand there's NO WAY to go back to sleep. Jesus had revealed Himself to me, and for nine days, we walked side by side as He tattooed the Bible to my heart. Every single word jumped off the page and made immediate sense. This supernatural experience fulfilled what Jesus promised in John 16:13: *"But when he, the Spirit of truth, comes, he will guide you into all the truth"* (NIV).

For a week and a half, I repented of my sin in written prayers, silent prayers, vocal prayers—to my wife, my son, his teachers, and anyone who would listen. I understood for the first time what 1 John 1:9 meant: *"If we confess our sins, he is faithful and just and will forgive us our sins and purify us from all unrighteousness"* (NIV).

The only way I can characterize those nine days is "chaotic joy," which culminated on November 2nd—my wife's birthday. Each year, I take this day off to spend with her, and this particular day included a hair appointment, lunch, a manicure, a pedicure, and a foot massage.

When you have a foot massage, they wash your feet first. Within seconds of the masseuse washing my feet, heat welled up inside my chest that was unlike anything I'd ever felt. When it left minutes later, I was overcome with peace. I walked out of that place a new human being—reborn and renewed.

> *Do not conform to the pattern of this world, but be transformed by the renewing of your mind. Then you will be able to test and approve what God's will is—his good, pleasing and perfect will* (Romans 12:2 NIV).

LIVING AS AN UNSTOPPABLE LEADER

As of this writing, it's been two years since my heart attack and 18 months since I came to know Jesus. Nothing in my life remains as it was. Every bit of willful sin left me almost immediately, by God's grace. Things I could never stop on my own—like nicotine addiction—were simply removed. I went from smoking two cigars daily and using nicotine pouches every waking hour to quitting cold turkey without withdrawal, anxiety, or any desire to return.

Lust and desires of the flesh were also taken from me nearly overnight. The mere thought of pornography turns my stomach, and I pray for those women, their absent fathers, and the men who gave them false hopes of stardom. May they, too, come to know Jesus, repent, and find freedom, salvation, and forgiveness.

Jesus came for sinners. He broke bread with tax collectors, prostitutes, Samaritans, Gentiles, the demon-possessed, thieves, and criminals. The only difference between followers of Christ and non-followers is that followers have found strength in their weakness. Through vulnerability and humility, they've admitted they're powerless over sin and need a Savior.

In the Sermon on the Mount, Jesus taught that sin starts in the mind. *"But I tell you that anyone who looks at a woman lustfully has already committed adultery with her in his heart"* (Matthew 5:28 NIV). We're all born with a sin nature—there's no escaping it.

So what is the good news? Jesus is! Throughout history, animal sacrifices were made for sin's atonement, but sin continued. However, John 3:16 declares: *For God so loved the world that he gave his one and only Son, that whoever believes in him shall not perish but have eternal life* (NIV).

Because of God's faithfulness and love, He sent His only Son as a living sacrifice for what we couldn't do ourselves. As Jesus died on the cross, He said, *"It is finished"* (John 19:30 NIV), and gave up His spirit. They buried

Him in a tomb, and three days later He rose again. He ministered for 40 days and appeared to over 500 people before ascending to heaven, telling His disciples to wait for the Father's gift. Ten days later, on Pentecost, the Holy Spirit fell upon His disciples.

THE PURPOSE REVEALED

What is the purpose of life? Why are we here? We are here to live in the truth that is Jesus Christ, understanding that nothing comes from our will—it's God's will that leads to life. The Way of Jesus Christ is the only way to freedom, both here and for eternity.

It is tempting to get caught up in yesterday's regrets or tomorrow's anxieties, forgetting what's happening now. There's only one thing happening in real time, each and every second: Life.

We're called to live abundantly through Jesus Christ, projecting His character and nature by loving God and loving others. We're saved by faith through grace, and grace is a gift we don't deserve (Ephesians 2:8). We are to share grace with all those we encounter, spreading the good news, making disciples, and planting seeds of faith.

Our old way of living must pass away so we can receive the boundless joy that a relationship with Jesus Christ provides. He died for you—don't let His death be in vain. Seek Him and ask Him to reveal Himself to you. I promise, when you're ready, He will.

The heart attack that nearly killed me became the catalyst for my eternal life. The fear of death that paralyzed me became my doorway to fearless living. The business success that once defined me pales in comparison to the purpose I now carry as an unstoppable leader in God's kingdom.

True leadership isn't about driving your own agenda or achieving the American Dream. It's about surrendering the keys to the One who knows the destination, trusting His will over your own, and allowing Him to transform you from the inside out. When you stop trying to polish your exterior and let God clean out your interior, you become unstoppable—not because of your strength, but because of His power working through your surrendered life.

I have been crucified with Christ and I no longer live, but Christ lives in me. The life I now live in the body, I live by faith in the Son of God, who loved me and gave himself for me (Galatians 2:20 NIV).

Joshua P. Clark

Joshua P. Clark is a Senior National Sales Director with Primerica and a successful business owner, leading a high-performing team with an annual payroll of $2.5 million. Over his career, he has promoted 12 Regional Vice Presidents, helping them achieve both professional and personal success. Prior to his work in financial services, Joshua worked in the healthcare and oil field industries.

While earning a Bachelor's and Master's Degree, Joshua played football and wrestled—serving as captain of both teams. This experience instilled in him a deep sense of discipline and teamwork, along with a competitive drive that continues to shape his leadership style.

Based in the Akron, Ohio, area, Joshua is a devoted husband to his wife, Emily, and a proud father to their two children, Cameron and Colette. After what he describes as a "tug of war with God," Joshua became a committed Christian in 2016, a turning point that shapes his values and vision today. Outside of his business, he enjoys golf, studying apologetics, reading, and hosting family and friends. Joshua's life reflects his dedication to faith, family, and empowering others to achieve their fullest potential.

Led by THE Unstoppable Leader

By Joshua P. Clark

It began on a quiet winter night in 2023. The kind of night where silence presses down around you and questions grow louder than the wind outside. I sat at my desk, eyes fixed on the glowing search bar. *Should I even ask?*

<Does God really exist?>

It felt almost like a betrayal, as if I was crossing some unseen line. I was supposed to be a Christian! Raised in the Catholic Church, I'd always believed in God—at least on the surface. *Yes, God exists. Yes, Jesus is who He said He was.* But those affirmations had never taken root beyond tradition or surface-level sentiment. Figuring out why I believed was also like an unwritten and undeclared item on my to-do list: it was not urgent, although I knew it was important. Like so many things we push to the back burner, it took me years to finally get around to it. *WHY do I believe? No clue.*

Sometimes I wondered if my prayers were just me talking to myself. I wasn't sure if the answer I sought was even available or knowable. *Is the answer to my question a treasure that doesn't exist? Or is it just buried, waiting for me to care enough to find it?* I wanted to know the truth—objectively, historically, philosophically. I needed to know why I believed what I believed. And if I had been wrong all along, I wanted to know that too. I was ready to follow the evidence wherever it led, even if it cost me everything I wanted to believe.

Years earlier, at age 29, I had hit a low point both personally and professionally. Life wasn't working. My business was struggling, my purpose was foggy, and I felt untethered from anything meaningful. Success had always been my identity, but when that crumbled, I discovered I had nothing solid underneath.

Twice, I had been invited to a men's bootcamp called Band of Brothers; I said NO both times. I was skeptical, and honestly, I thought it might be some kind of Jesus freak cult. "Nah, I'm good", I'd say dismissively. Finally saying yes took having an engagement ring thrown in my face, being kicked out of my fiancé's home, and sleeping on a twin bed at my younger sister's. And, oh yeah—one more ask. Then I caved.

And we know that in all things God works for the good of those who love him, who have been called according to his purpose (Romans 8:28 NIV).

While I was at this bootcamp, something unexpected happened. On Saturday morning, November 5th, 2016, I encountered Jesus in a way that shattered my assumptions. It wasn't logical or scientific. Instead, my experience was deeply emotional and spiritual, like a blindfold had been ripped off, allowing light to flood in. I knew God was real, and I knew He loved me. I knew I needed to be forgiven, and I knew I needed a savior. I accepted Jesus Christ not because of evidence, but because I knew He was real. I felt it. I finally, for the first time, heard the offer of Christianity, and I wanted it to be true.

Therefore, if anyone is in Christ, the new creation has come: The old has gone, the new is here! (2 Corinthians 5:17 NIV).

Many things started to change. I changed. My spiritual, personal, and business life became an upward spiral. Right after I swore off women to focus on my spiritual life, I met and married my wife, Emily. I love Yahweh's sense of humor. Men, please hear this: She is the first woman from whom I did not seek my validation as a man. I had learned how to receive it from our Father in heaven. I was also able to forgive and connect with my earthly father, my dad. He and I, for the first time, talked through the past wounds I had been carrying. Hearing, "Son, I love you and I'm proud of you," was like food for the soul of a man and helped me answer *yes* to the question, *Do I have what it takes?* Emily and I had our first son, Cameron. But after a few years, the honeymoon phase of being a new Christian, on fire for God, started to wear off. And though my heart believed, my mind still wrestled with disbelief and questions.

Had it all been in my head? Was Christianity just a comforting story?

I found myself in a strange place—emotionally connected to Jesus but intellectually uncertain about Christianity. I became a poser about my faith. All while I evangelized others and brought dozens of men to the same Band of Brothers bootcamp I had gone to, I secretly doubted and questioned. I played the part of the humble, Christian husband and businessman. My prayer life became inconsistent. Reading the Bible felt forced. I was living a divided life, and it was exhausting. The joy I'd experienced as a new believer was fading, replaced by uncertainty and shame.

I knew I couldn't live divided like that. Either Christianity was true, or it wasn't. I had to know. So I returned to that question I'd typed into the search bar. The question I feared would make me an atheist.

<Does God really exist?>

> *Ask and it will be given to you; seek and you will find; knock and the door will be opened to you* (Matthew 7:7 NIV).

THE INVESTIGATION

I read, watched, listened, and learned—and to my surprise, this journey didn't weaken my faith—it transformed my faith. My belief went from emotional to rational, from fragile to firm. Here's what I found.

Philosophy is the study of fundamental questions about existence, knowledge, values, reason, mind, and language. The Greek means "love of wisdom". That seemed like a good place to start. Our world says, "You do you" and "Live your truth." But that's nonsense. Truth isn't subjective. If two beliefs contradict, they can't both be true. That's the Law of Non-Contradiction. If Christianity is true, then other worldviews can't also be true in the same way.

Objective truth exists. That was the first bit of relief I felt in a while.

Next, I considered: *What about the existence of God?* Seeking an answer, I explored science, logic, and history.

I found the cosmological argument. The universe is either eternal or it had a beginning. If it had a beginning, it needed a cause. The Big Bang is a confirmation that the universe had a beginning—time, space, and matter all began in an instant. Everything coming from nothing defies natural explanation. That fact points to a supernatural cause. Something—no, someone—outside of time, space, and matter, chose to create. Since the universe includes all of space, time, and matter, the cause must be spaceless, timeless, and immaterial. That sounds a lot like God.

Then there was the question of life: Can life come from non-life? I learned this has never been observed. Despite decades of trying, scientists have never been able to create life from non-living matter. The complexity of even the simplest cell is staggering. DNA operates like a computer code, but contains more information than any computer program we've ever written. Just like written software, information requires an intelligent mind to produce it.

If the materialist worldview is true, why are some things immaterial yet undeniably real? Examples would be mathematics, logic, inherent moral standards, and free will.

Every arrow pointed toward a creator, lawgiver, and designer.

The heavens declare the glory of God; the skies proclaim the work of his hands (Psalm 19:1 NIV).

I also considered, *Are miracles real?* I asked, *What's the greatest, craziest miracle in the Bible? The resurrection? Jonah and the whale?* The answer, amazingly, is in the first verse. I recognized that creation itself is the greatest miracle, and if God created everything out of nothing, then parting the Red Sea or raising the dead would be a walk in the park for Him, since He created the park! The greatest miracle is creation itself from nothing.

Accepting that God could intervene in our world, I no longer dismissed biblical miracles as improbable.

Is the Bible historically accurate? I studied the methods historians use to evaluate ancient events, texts, and claims. I learned that by their standards, the New Testament events and documents are the most reliably known in recorded ancient history. We have more early manuscripts of the New Testament than any other ancient work by a mile. We can trace the chain of custody back to the original apostles and Paul. We know what they wrote. We know Jesus was an actual person more confidently than any other ancient figure, such as Julius Caesar or Alexander the Great.

Then came what I now believe is the crown jewel of my investigation. I asked: *If God were to become a man, what would that have looked like?*

If God entered the human story as one of us, He might fulfill specific prophecies from the past about Himself. He did. Jesus fulfilled over 300

Old Testament prophecies. The mathematical probability of one person fulfilling just 48 prophecies by chance is 1 in 10^157. That's a number so large it defies comprehension.

He might perform miracles, displaying His supernatural power over the world He created and over the natural laws he created to govern it. He did. Jesus walked on water, controlled the wind and waves, created food out of nothing, healed the human body, knew the unspoken hearts and minds of people, and raised the dead back to life. Even His enemies and critics did not deny the miracles Jesus performed. Interestingly, Christ referred to His miracles as evidence and testimony.

God, if He were to become human, would teach the greatest spiritual truths ever uttered. He did. He would surely be the most impactful human being who ever lived. He was. He would speak as no man ever spoke. He did. Jesus claimed to be God in the flesh, yet distinct from the Father and Spirit, which would also make the Trinity doctrine of God true. That claim would make him either a liar or a lunatic. Jesus said, *"[I am] also Lord of the Sabbath"* (Mark 2:28 NKJV), which is a divine institution of Yahweh in the Old Testament. He claimed He had existed eternally before the world was made, and identified Himself by the divine name of Yahweh God, *"Before Abraham was born, I am!"* (John 8:58 NIV). The New Testament writers backed up His claim both directly and indirectly—for example, by taking over 50 Old Testament passages about Yahweh and crediting them to Jesus.

But would God save His creation from eternal death? Well, that's exactly what Jesus claimed. The love of God and the justice of God came together at the cross of Jesus Christ. *So, is that true?*

RESURRECTION EVIDENCE

The evidence for the death AND resurrection of Jesus is staggering.

First, Jesus' death by crucifixion is affirmed by multiple historical sources—

both Christian and secular. Even skeptical historians acknowledge that Jesus was crucified under Pontius Pilate. It is the best attested fact in ancient history. And the earliest Christian creeds date to within months of Jesus' death, which is essential to note because that means there was no time for these events to turn into myth or legend.

Second, regarding His resurrection, even Jesus' enemies acknowledged the tomb was empty. And no one could produce the body.

Third, many saw Jesus in the flesh after He rose from the dead— Paul tells us there were over 500 people who saw Him at the same time that, at the time of his writing, *most of whom are still living* (1 Corinthians 15:6 NIV). The apostles not only saw Jesus, but they were radically changed after His resurrection. These were men who had fled in terror when Jesus was arrested and had hidden themselves in a room after His death. Suddenly, they were boldly proclaiming Jesus' resurrection in the very city where He'd been crucified. They suffered, bled, and even were put to death—but not one ever recanted their testimony. Twelve powerful men in the Watergate scandal couldn't keep a lie for three weeks; you're telling me twelve apostles held onto a lie for forty years under scorn, imprisonment, and torture? That's absurd.

The resurrection wasn't just possible; given the evidence, it is the most probable, best explanation of the events surrounding the death of Christ.

SURRENDERING

I came to the conclusion that belief in the Christian story is not blind faith. It is based on evidence, grounded in truth, and sealed by experience.

Christianity explains why we're here (created for a relationship with God). It explains what went wrong (sin separated us from God, and sin must be punished because God is just). It explains the solution (Jesus' death and resurrection). It explains what's coming (resurrection, restoration, and eternal life for those who live their lives in Christ).

Other worldviews left me with more questions than answers. Atheism can't explain the beginning of the universe, the fine-tuning of physical constants, or the existence of objective moral values. Eastern religions are unable to explain the reality of evil or the value of individual persons, and have very little to no historical evidence for their claims. Islam gave me many reasons to doubt. One is that Islam violates the Law of Non-Contradiction because its "holy writings" claim the Bible is true. Yet if the Bible is true, then Islam is false. There are some religions that claim to be Christian but deny the true deity of Christ, leading to a works-based salvation system. And Judaism started in truth, but is incomplete.

Every other religion that is about a relationship with the divine presents a "hope" for acceptance at the end based on what has been done in life, but they present no assurance. True Christianity stands apart and is unique, stating that God's acceptance of His children comes at the beginning of the relationship because of His mighty works, not ours. My heart leaps as I type that.

> *If you confess with your mouth that Jesus is Lord and*
> *believe in your heart that God raised him from the dead,*
> *you will be saved* (Romans 10:9 ESV).

Only Christianity provides a complete, coherent explanation for reality. It answers the big questions: *Where did we come from? Why are we here? What's wrong with the world? How can it be fixed?*

Finally, I made the decision to surrender—not just emotionally, but intellectually. I chose to follow Jesus with my heart, my soul, and, after a drawn-out tug of war, my mind.

But in your hearts revere Christ as Lord. Always be prepared to give an answer to everyone who asks you to give the reason for the hope that you have. But do this with gentleness and respect (1 Peter 3:15 NIV).

FOLLOWING THE UNSTOPPABLE LEADER

Please don't take my word for all I have presented. Ask the hard questions; the truth of Christianity can handle your doubt. And don't settle for "I don't care" or "I'll figure it out later." I beg you not to procrastinate. Eternity is too long to be wrong or apathetic about.

Here's how to begin:

- Repent: Turn from sin, toward God. Admit your need for help and forgiveness.

- Believe: Trust that Jesus lived, died, and rose again—for you personally.

- Receive: Accept the gift of eternal life that is offered freely by God.

- Study: Read the Bible systematically (I recommend starting with the Gospel of John).

- Connect: Find a Bible-believing church and a mentor who lives out their faith authentically.

- Disciple: Share what you've found with others who desire truth.

I still experience doubt sometimes, especially before my first cup of coffee in the morning. There are still questions I can't answer. But now, my foundation is solid. I've tested it. I've pushed against it. I've tried to break it. And it stood firm.

That's why I'm a Christian. Not because it makes me feel good. Not because

I was raised in it. But because I know it is true.

Here's a quick life update since I began my investigation. My wife and I had another child, our daughter Colette. I still get my validation as a man from the uncreated Creator of the universe, which helps me in every situation and relationship. I have shed being a poser, although I consistently work on being the real deal that God wants. It is very freeing to no longer need the approval of others, which used to be an addiction, as it is to most people. *Knowing is better than feeling* has become a mantra for me, which has freed me from slavery to my feelings and the ups and downs of life. I know now we deserve nothing. We are entitled to nothing, yet God showers us with love, blessings, and grace. My joy is rooted in my salvation through trust in Jesus Christ. After all, compared to our eternal life, what else in this earthly life matters as much? I don't just believe in God, I trust God. My business continues to grow and produce leaders now all over America. I lead with integrity and authenticity.

I cannot claim to be an unstoppable leader—I proved that when my life fell apart. But I serve the One who is. Jesus Christ is THE Unstoppable Leader, who conquered sin, death, and hell. He's the Leader who takes broken men and makes them whole. He's the Leader who transforms doubt into faith, fear into courage, and failure into victory.

Under His leadership, I've learned what it means to lead others: Not through manipulation or intimidation, but through service and sacrifice. Not by demanding respect, but by earning it through integrity and authenticity. Not by hiding my weaknesses, but by being transparent about my struggles and God's faithfulness.

All of the blessings in my life are fruit from allowing God to be the Unstoppable Leader I need.

> *And He said to me, "My grace is sufficient for you, for power is perfected in weakness." Most gladly, therefore, I will rather boast in my weakness, so that the power of Christ may dwell in me* (2 Corinthians 12:9 LSB).

So today, I follow Him—not blindly, but boldly. I hope you will, too.

All glory and praise and honor and worship to my Savior, my eternal Captain, and my Unstoppable Leader, who is our Lord Jesus Christ.

An Unstoppable Leader Is... DECISIVE

Making Bold Moves Without Analysis Paralysis

By Brett Dabe

*If any of you lacks wisdom, let him ask of God, who gives to
all liberally and without reproach; and it will be given to him*
(James 1:5 WEB).

While the fear of making a wrong decision paralyzes many people,
unstoppable leaders understand that the greater risk is not deciding at all.
They also recognize that success is often the by-product of prompt action,
so they've learned to move forward with faith when they have enough facts
to make a wise choice.

Joshua demonstrated decisive leadership at its finest. When God told him
to have the Israelites cross the Jordan River while it was at flood stage,
Joshua didn't call for a committee meeting or request more time to study
the situation. He told the priests to step into the water, trusting that God
would stop the flow as He had promised. And God honored Joshua, parting
the river the moment the priests' feet touched the water.

That's decisive leadership: Moving forward based on God's promise before
seeing the complete solution.

When the Israelites faced the fortified city of Jericho, Joshua could have spent months developing siege strategies or leading his people to build better weapons. Instead, he followed God's unusual battle plan: March around the city for seven days, then shout and blow trumpets. It made no military sense, but Joshua decisively obeyed God, and the walls came down.

Elijah showed us the same principle at Mount Carmel. When the people of Israel couldn't decide between serving God or Baal, Elijah forced the issue. *"How long will you falter between two opinions?"* he challenged them. *"If the Lord is God, follow Him; but if Baal, follow him"* (1 Kings 18:21 NKJV). Elijah didn't complain about the people's indecision; he set up a decisive test that would settle the question once and for all. When God answered with fire from heaven, the people finally chose to serve the Lord. Sometimes leaders have to create moments of decision for others.

Decisive leaders understand that waiting for perfect conditions usually means waiting forever. Gideon learned this lesson when God kept reducing his army size. Gideon started with 32,000 men, which seemed reasonable for fighting the Midianites. But then God reduced his force to 300 men with trumpets and torches. From a human perspective, it was military suicide for this small group of 300 to go into battle against the enemy's army of 135,000 men. But God wanted it to be clear that their victory came from Him, not from human strength or strategy. Gideon had to decide: Trust his military training or trust God's unusual plan? He chose to trust God and led his tiny army to overwhelming victory.

The key to godly decision-making is seeking God's wisdom first, then acting with faith.

Solomon asked God to grant him the wisdom he needed to lead Israel, and God gave him discernment beyond any other king. Yet Solomon still had to make tough choices based on that wisdom. Nobody said that being a godly leader is easy. When two women came to Solomon claiming the same baby, he had to determine decisively which woman was the child's mother. His threat to cut the baby in half revealed the truth immediately. Wise decisions often require bold actions.

Jesus also modeled decisive leadership throughout His ministry. When He called His disciples, He didn't give them weeks to think it over. "Follow me," He said, and they left their nets immediately. When He cleansed the temple, He didn't form a committee to study the problem. He made a whip and drove out the money changers.

It is important to note that Jesus made these decisive actions only after spending time in prayer with His Father. He didn't act impulsively. He acted with divine guidance and perfect timing. That's the model for Christian leaders: Pray for wisdom, then act with confidence.

King Hezekiah faced a life-or-death decision when the Assyrian army surrounded Jerusalem. His advisors were divided about whether to surrender or fight. Hezekiah could have spent weeks debating options while the enemy grew stronger. Instead, Hezekiah took his problem directly to God in prayer, then acted decisively based on the prophet Isaiah's counsel. When he refused to surrender, God destroyed the Assyrian army in one night. Hezekiah's decisive faith saved his nation.

Esther faced a crucial decision when Mordecai asked her to approach the king uninvited to save the Jewish people. This could have cost her life. Esther could have spent days weighing the risks, but she made her choice quickly: *"If I perish, I perish!"* (Esther 4:16 NKJV). Esther's decisive courage saved her people from genocide. Sometimes the right decision requires risking everything you have for something greater than yourself.

Building decisive leadership skills starts with developing a decision-making framework based on biblical principles. When facing choices, ask yourself: *Does this align with Scripture? Will this advance God's kingdom? Have I prayed about this decision? Do I have enough information to move forward wisely?*

Practice making smaller decisions quickly to build your decision-making muscles. Don't spend an hour choosing what to eat for lunch or which route to take to work. Make the choice and move on; this trains your brain to process options efficiently.

Study how biblical leaders made tough decisions under pressure. Notice how they combined prayer, wisdom, available information, and faith to move forward. Learn from their examples of trusting God's guidance even when the path wasn't completely clear.

Set deadlines for your decisions. Don't let choices drag on indefinitely. Gather the information you can within a reasonable timeframe, seek wise counsel, pray for guidance, then decide. Indecision is also a decision—usually the wrong one.

Remember that most decisions are reversible if new information emerges. Don't let the fear of making a mistake paralyze you. Make the best decision you can with the information you have, then adjust course if needed.

God's kingdom needs leaders who can cut through complexity and move forward with faith-based decisions. While others may get stuck in analysis paralysis, decisive leaders progress toward God's purposes.

In a world full of indecision and endless debate, decisive leadership becomes a powerful testimony to trusting God's guidance. People are drawn to leaders who can make tough choices and move forward with confidence.

The question every Christian leader must answer is: Do you make decisions based on your faith in God, or does the fear of making mistakes paralyze you?

Decisive leaders choose faith and trust God with the outcome.

· ·

JOSHUA AJINI

Joshua Ajini is a husband, leader, and purpose-driven entrepreneur committed to transforming lives through faith and financial empowerment. Raised in the Maronite Catholic tradition, his life took a radical turn at age 22 when he became a born-again Christian—an encounter that reshaped his values, vision, and mission.

In 2015, Josh launched his financial services business with a clear goal: to equip families with the tools, strategies, and confidence to protect what matters most and build lasting wealth. Through integrity, education, and personalized guidance, he has helped countless clients move from uncertainty to financial clarity.

Josh's leadership extends beyond business. Since 2021, he has served on the Band of Brothers leadership team, where his influence has inspired nearly 100 men to step into deeper faith, authentic brotherhood, and personal growth.

Anchored in biblical principles—purity before marriage, loving his wife as Christ loved the Church, and surrounding himself with wise mentors—Josh leads with conviction, authenticity, and vision. His mission is simple yet profound: to help people live with purpose, lead with faith, and leave a legacy that outlives them.

FROM SELF TO SERVANT

By Joshua Ajini

I was born and raised in Michigan. Like many children in culturally religious families, we attended a Maronite Catholic Church—full of heritage and tradition. The only problem was that I couldn't understand it. The services weren't in English, and as a kid, I didn't have the maturity or the spiritual hunger to press through the confusion. I didn't encounter Jesus there, at least not in a way that made sense to me. So, by the time I was around nine or ten, we had stopped attending. Church faded into the background. Religion became a memory.

Looking back, I can see the truth of Proverbs 22:6—God was still working in my life, even when I couldn't see it. Those early seeds would eventually find soil in my heart—but not for many years.

Train up a child in the way he should go; even when he is old,
he will not depart from it (Proverbs 22:6 ESV).

THE WANDERING YEARS

Without a spiritual foundation to stand on, I started learning about life the way most young men do: from culture, music, movies, and my peers. Nobody sat me down to explain biblical purity or God's design for relationships. I didn't even know sex before marriage was wrong. Everything around me encouraged the opposite. Sleeping around, drinking, and living for yourself were normal, even admirable. And that's precisely what I did. My teenage and early adult years were marked by addiction to porn, multiple sexual relationships, and alcohol.

Underneath it all, I was chasing something deeper—validation. I wanted to feel like I mattered, like I was enough. But no matter what I chased, nothing ever satisfied me. *All the ways of a person are clean in his own sight, But the Lord examines the motives* (Proverbs 16:2 NASB). I thought I was living freely, but I was actually enslaved to my appetites and insecurities, and the emptiness grew.

I was walking the wrong path, believing the lies that the world was teaching me about what it meant to be a man. The enemy was stealing my purity, killing my potential, and destroying my future, but I couldn't see it yet.

> Jesus said... "The thief comes only to steal and kill and destroy; I came that they may have life and have it abundantly" (John 10:7, 10 ESV).

DREAMS, DOUBTS, AND A DIVINE CALLING

In January 2015, I started a business. It was exciting, and honestly, it was a way for me to prove myself. I thought if I could be successful, make money, and become "somebody," then maybe I'd feel whole. But success without purpose is empty, and I was beginning to feel that ache. Business was hard. I had moments when I wasn't sure if I was going to make it. I doubted my ability to lead. I doubted whether I'd ever find a wife. I even started saying, half-jokingly, that I'd just be "married to the money."

*Hope deferred makes the heart sick, but a desire fulfilled
is a tree of life* (Proverbs 13:12 ESV).

For what will it profit a man if he gains the whole world, and loses his own soul?
(Mark 8:36 NKJV). I was gaining some worldly success but losing my soul
in the process. The business world taught me about goals and achievement,
but it couldn't address the spiritual emptiness inside.

But God had a plan and a calling for my life.

In 2016, I met Kayla through my business. We connected quickly and got
married just five months later. For some people, that timeline seems rushed.
For me, it was divine. Our relationship and commitment marked the
beginning of the most transformational season of my life.

Proverbs 18:22 teaches, *He who finds a wife finds a good thing and obtains
favor from the Lord* (ESV), and I had definitely found favor. *Two are better
than one, because they have a good return for their labor: If either of them falls
down, one can help the other up* (Ecclesiastes 4:9-10 NIV). God was preparing
to use my marriage as a tool for my spiritual growth.

Around the same time, I became a born-again Christian. At 22 years old,
it was the first time I truly encountered Jesus, not as a distant religious
figure, but as a personal Savior. I began reading Scripture and realizing just
how different God's ways were from everything I'd believed. One verse in
particular impacted me: *Husbands, love your wives, just as Christ loved the
church and gave himself up for her* (Ephesians 5:25 ESV).

That verse became my mission. It redefined for me what it meant to be
a man, a husband, and a leader. I realized that love wasn't about control,
performance, or even passion—it was about sacrifice. Christ loved the
church by laying down His life for her. That meant my role as a husband

was to do the same: to lead through serving, to die to myself daily, and to prioritize my wife's needs above my own.

> In the same way, husbands ought to love their wives
> as their own bodies. He who loves his wife loves himself
> (Ephesians 5:28 NIV).

Being a good husband wasn't just about being nice; it was about fundamentally changing how I saw myself and my role. I was to serve my wife. *For even the Son of Man did not come to be served, but to serve, and to give his life as a ransom for many* (Mark 10:45 NIV).

Marriage brought both joy and refinement. My wife had her own history of pain—especially with people who claimed to be Christians but had hurt her deeply. That reality shaped the way I approached our relationship. I was determined to be different. I wanted to be the kind of man who didn't just talk about Jesus but lived like Him, especially behind closed doors. My desire to be a godly husband became one of the most significant catalysts for my spiritual growth.

Likewise, husbands, live with your wives in an understanding way, showing honor to the woman as the weaker vessel, since they are heirs with you of the grace of life, so that your prayers may not be hindered (1 Peter 3:7 ESV). I was learning that how I treated my wife directly affected my relationship with God.

Thankfully, when God calls us to grow, He doesn't expect us to navigate the path alone. One of the greatest blessings He has given us is brotherhood and mentorship. I made a decision early on that I didn't want to figure things out on my own or rely on my own wisdom. So I surrounded myself with Christian men who were walking the path ahead of me—in marriage, in business, in leadership, and in faith. These mentors didn't just give advice;

they walked with me, corrected me, challenged me, and encouraged me. I learned that leadership isn't about having all the answers. It's about being teachable, humble, and accountable.

> *Without counsel plans fail, but with many advisers they succeed* (Proverbs 15:22 ESV).

> *Iron sharpens iron, and one man sharpens another* (Proverbs 27:17 ESV).

These godly relationships became the forge where God shaped my character. *The way of a fool is right in his own eyes, but a wise man listens to advice* (Proverbs 12:15 ESV).

I was discovering that my authentic leadership would begin with submitting to God and continue with respecting the wisdom of the godly men He sent to guide my growth.

A CALL TO LEADERSHIP

Over time, God began to grow something deeper in me: a passion for helping others. This desire did not stem from a place of superiority, but from recognizing that because of our shared struggle, I now had something to offer others. I knew what it was like to be lost. I knew what it was like to search for identity in all the wrong places. I knew what it was like to doubt your worth, future, and ability to lead. And now, by God's grace, I also knew what it was like to be restored.

Blessed be the God and Father of our Lord Jesus Christ, the Father of mercies and God of all comfort, who comforts us in all our tribulation, that we may be able to comfort those who are in any trouble, with the comfort with which we ourselves are comforted by God (2 Corinthians 1:3-4 NKJV).

God didn't waste my pain; He repurposed it, using it to further His kingdom. *And we know that in all things God works for the good of those who love him, who have been called according to his purpose* (Romans 8:28 NIV). The struggles I'd been through, the mistakes I'd made, the lessons I'd learned, they were all being transformed into tools for helping other men. I discovered the power of vulnerability and transparency. Men are hungry for authentic leadership, not perfect presentations.

In 2021, I stepped into a new level of responsibility and calling by joining the Band of Brothers leadership team—a ministry focused on calling men to a deeper purpose, deeper faith, and deeper brotherhood. Since joining, I've had the privilege of helping lead two major events each year. Nearly 100 men have attended these events due to my involvement, whether they received a personal invitation, heard my testimony, or were impacted by my consistent role in leadership.

Band of Brothers Bootcamps aren't retreats. They're encounters. Men come broken, worn down, and spiritually dry; they leave refreshed, realigned, and on fire for Christ. I've watched men cry for the first time in decades. I've seen chains of addiction break. I've heard stories of restored marriages and renewed faith. And every time, I'm humbled to think that God used me to help make this happen—not because I'm great, but because I said yes.

> *But he said to me, "My grace is sufficient for you, for my power is made perfect in weakness." Therefore I will boast all the more gladly of my weaknesses, so that the power of Christ may rest upon me* (2 Corinthians 12:9 ESV).

God used my brokenness and healing as a bridge to reach other broken men and show them how God can make us new. *Therefore, if anyone is in Christ, he is a new creation. The old has passed away; behold, the new has come* (2 Corinthians 5:17 ESV).

If there's one thing I've learned about leadership, it's this: Leadership starts with surrender. The world says leadership is about control, dominance, and image. God says leadership is about service, humility, and obedience. Jesus didn't lead from a throne; He led from a cross.

> But Jesus called them to him and said, "You know that the rulers of the Gentiles lord it over them, and their great ones exercise authority over them. It shall not be so among you. But whoever would be great among you must be your servant, and whoever would be first among you must be your slave, even as the Son of Man came not to be served but to serve, and to give his life as a ransom for many"
> (Matthew 20:25-28 ESV).

That truth now shapes every area of my life.

In business, I lead with integrity, not ambition. I care more about people than profit. I see my team not just as coworkers, but as souls. *Whatever you do, work heartily, as for the Lord and not for men* (Colossians 3:23 ESV).

In marriage, I lead with gentleness, not pride. I ask for forgiveness. I pray with my wife. I pursue her heart, not just her time. *Love is patient and kind; love does not envy or boast; it is not arrogant or rude. It does not insist on its own way; it is not irritable or resentful* (1 Corinthians 13:4-5 ESV).

In ministry, I lead with urgency and authenticity. I'm not interested in performing. I want to be a vessel for God's truth, God's grace, and God's love.

YOUR CALL TO LEAD

Just as God called me—first to walk with Him, then to grow, and now to lead others—He is also calling you. If you doubt what I am saying, read back through this chapter and apply each Bible verse to your own life. Ask God what His divine plan is for your life. I guarantee you, He has someone waiting for your leadership.

To any man reading this who feels unqualified to lead, know that I understand. I was addicted, insecure, prideful, and broken. But God doesn't call the qualified. He qualifies the called. All He needs is your yes.

Say yes to His will and His way wherever you are today.

If you are unmarried, say yes to purity. Don't believe the lie that you need experience to be valuable. You don't need to test the world to appreciate God's design. Purity before marriage isn't old-fashioned; it's holy. It's powerful. Purity will protect your future marriage more than you realize. Flee from sexual immorality. *Every other sin a person commits is outside the body, but the sexually immoral person sins against his own body* (1 Corinthians 6:18 ESV).

Say yes to your wife, whether you've met her yet or not. Choose now to be the kind of man who will love her like Christ loved the church. That kind of love takes guts. It takes prayer. It takes dying to yourself daily. But it's worth it. *An excellent wife is the crown of her husband* (Proverbs 12:4 ESV).

Say yes to mentorship. Don't try to figure your path out on your own. You were never meant to. God uses people to grow people. Find men who walk with Jesus, and ask them to walk with you. *Listen to advice and accept instruction, that you may gain wisdom in the future* (Proverbs 19:20 ESV).

And when God calls you, say yes to leadership—not for the spotlight, but to serve His kingdom. The world is desperate for real godly leaders, not just loud voices or flashy influencers, but men who serve, sacrifice, and stand for truth. *"Have I not commanded you? Be strong and courageous. Do not be frightened, and do not be dismayed, for the Lord your God is with you wherever you go"* (Joshua 1:9 ESV).

I'm still becoming the man God created me to be. Every day, I ask Him to help me lead better, love deeper, and serve stronger. I'm not there yet, but I'm on the journey. And the journey is worth it.

Being confident of this very thing, that He who has begun a good work in you will complete it until the day of Jesus Christ (Philippians 1:6 NKJV). God isn't finished with me yet, and He's not finished with you either.

The question isn't whether you're qualified to lead. The question is whether you're willing to let God qualify you through the process. Will you say yes to His call on your life? *Then I heard the voice of the Lord saying, "Whom shall I send? And who will go for us?" And I said, "Here am I. Send me!"* (Isaiah 6:8 NIV).

The world needs unstoppable leaders—men who can't be stopped because they're powered by something greater than themselves. Men who lead from the cross, not from the crowd. Men who understand that *"God opposes the proud but gives grace to the humble"* (James 4:6 ESV).

That's the kind of leader God is calling you to be. That's the kind of leader the world desperately needs. And that's the kind of leader you can become—not because you're perfect, but because you serve a perfect God who specializes in using imperfect people for His perfect purposes.

Will you answer the call?

DAVID S. STROUP

David S. Stroup is a difference maker! He has been making a difference in the lives of students since 1992 in both the Christian school and public school settings. He is currently teaching social skills and teacher development in a public school south of Atlanta.

David also gets to make a difference in a local church by leading worship every Sunday. He works hard planning services, rehearsing, and communicating with the worship team so that they are all prepared to lead in the worship of Jesus Christ!

Since 1997, David has also been making a difference in the lives of his clients as they purchase and sell houses. He is currently a real estate agent and is licensed to work with sellers and buyers throughout Georgia. (StroupGroup@gmail.com)

David prays that this book will make a difference in the lives of everyone who reads it. The reason he breathes is to make a difference. He is so focused on making a difference that he wrote a song about it, which you can find by searching YouTube for "David Stroup Make A Difference."

OUR GOD CAN

By David S. Stroup

Unstoppable leader! In the story you are about to read, I lived out a true miracle as the leader of a children's musical in Germany. I guess some may have looked at me as their unstoppable leader; however, it was only because I serve an unstoppable God!

I can do all things through Christ who strengthens me (Philippians 4:13 NKJV) sends a clear message that we can accomplish anything when we rely on God's power. Many of us may have a small idea of what the word "all" means in this verse. Sure, God can heal the sick if He chooses. He can certainly provide my needs as He does for the sparrows of the air. He can still perform many miracles. But can the God who stopped the sun and moon in their tracks in Joshua 10:13 still alter the patterns of the earth and the weather if He chooses?

In 2001, God proved to me He can indeed do *all* things! I experienced a week of ministry that will always remind me that God is in control, He listens, and He loves.

THE CALL TO ADVENTURE

I had been asked to put together a children's musical drama show at a church on the south side of Atlanta. We called this theater group Shirah, which is Hebrew for the phrase "my song." The Shirah team, along with many of the children and parents, decided to take this musical on the road... to Germany! Yes, Germany!

We packed up our props, musical instruments, suitcases, and everything we needed for this massive undertaking. It took many weeks to schedule and iron out all the details. As we prepared, I kept thinking about Jeremiah 29:11—*"For I know the plans I have for you," declares the Lord, "plans to prosper you and not to harm you, to give you hope and a future"* (NIV). I had no idea how prophetic this verse would become.

Traveling from Hartsfield-Jackson Atlanta International Airport, we arrived in Germany safely, surprised that all of our items also arrived intact. At the airport, an English-speaking pastor and his wife from a nearby church welcomed us. Their church was established for and served primarily English-speaking military personnel and their families, but was welcoming to the surrounding German community.

On Monday, we began to prepare on-site for our Saturday show. First, we were introduced to a few other people who would be part of the ministry that week. They walked us around the church property and discussed the location for the musical, explaining that people from the German community would not enter the church building. To minister to them, we would have to perform the musical outside. Additionally, we realized that to make the greatest impact, the script would have to be translated into German.

This news could have been discouraging, but I remembered the words of Joshua: *"Have I not commanded you? Be strong and courageous. Do not be afraid; do not be discouraged, for the Lord your God will be with you wherever you go"* (Joshua 1:9 NIV). We all got busy working on the set and painting the remaining props that were needed. The small orchestra rehearsed, the children reviewed their lines, and the script was being translated. All went well on Monday. It was encouraging to finally be there and see all the hard work paying off.

On Tuesday, the shining sun and gentle breeze made for a perfect day, and we continued our work outside. Everything was falling into place.

On Wednesday, we decided to rehearse inside the church building. The children were seated in the front section on the left side of the church auditorium as I led them in songs and rehearsal. Suddenly, a huge thunderstorm unexpectedly took over the entire city. It was massive and had snuck up on us in no time.

The lady missionary who lived there came into the auditorium and told me to walk with her to the front door of the church. As we looked out, she explained that the sudden downpour was typical. In the ten years she had lived there, she had learned that every single time a thundercloud appeared over the mountain, they had less than ten minutes to take cover before the skies opened up, soaking everything.

We continued rehearsing as it poured outside. The rain continued through the night, but by the next morning, it had finally stopped.

On Thursday, while we were rehearsing, the same missionary lady came into the auditorium and asked to speak with me again. I gave the musicians a brief break and went to her. She said that she felt like I needed to have a Plan B for Saturday's outdoor musical in case of rain. She explained that the day before, when we had experienced the sudden deluge, the chance of rain had been 65%. Saturday's chance of rain was 84%.

I remembered that the musical had to be outside in order to reach the local Germans who refused to ever set foot into the church building. I also knew that God didn't have us travel across the globe to get rained out. It was a defining moment for my leadership. *Should I trust human wisdom and make backup plans, or should I trust the God who called us to this mission?*

I called the musicians, the children, and the other adults into the auditorium and shared the news with them. We decided to pray that God would hold back the rain and allow His ministry to continue. As we prayed together, I was reminded that the Bible instructs us to *Trust in the Lord with all your heart and lean not on your own understanding; in all your ways submit to Him, and He will make your paths straight* (Proverbs 3:5-6 NIV).

As soon as we stopped praying, God gave me another idea. Up to this point, I haven't told you that the musical was the story of Joshua. That was definitely orchestrated by God many months before this day because He had a plan. I knew that God was unstoppable, but I didn't know what He was about to tell us to do.

That's right, just like Joshua in Joshua chapter 6, we lined up the musicians and the children and silently walked outside. We walked around the area of the stage as well as the places where the Germans would be sitting to watch the musical. We walked around in a single file, with our lead character, Joshua, leading the way—you guessed it—a total of seven times. We walked in silence just as Joshua had commanded his army in Joshua 6:10: *"Do not give a war cry, do not raise your voices, do not say a word until the day I tell you"* (Joshua 6:10 NIV).

As we walked those seven circles, I felt the weight of leadership and the power of obedience. *"Be strong and courageous, because you will lead these people to inherit the land I swore to their ancestors to give them"* (Joshua 1:6 NIV). We then walked back inside the church building, prayed together, and continued to rehearse. I didn't know what God's answer would be, but I did know that I was being obedient to what He had placed on my heart!

Friday was our dress rehearsal, and it went on without any major hiccups. This was also the day we finished translating and copying the script. After the dress rehearsal, we rehearsed a couple of scenes and a few songs, then ensured that all the props and staging were in place. It was all coming together nicely. The small orchestra then polished up a couple more songs while the children were placing their costumes in their designated places.

Everything that happened on Friday just proved to me that all of the hard work was paying off. However, the chance of rain for Saturday had now gone up, from 84% to 88%. It wasn't looking good from a human perspective, but I held onto Romans 8:28.

> *And we know that in all things God works for the good of those who love Him, who have been called according to His purpose* (Romans 8:28 NIV).

A DAY OF MIRACLES

Saturday, we woke up and had our usual breakfast and devotions. We were all a little nervous because it was the day we had been looking forward to for so many months. We had completed the necessary tasks and were as prepared as possible.

That afternoon, still with the 88% chance of rain, a few Germans trickled in to see what was going on. The younger crowd was excited to see the translated scripts, which had already been placed on the seats. The orchestra continued to warm up as the children put their costumes on for the last time.

At 3:00, it was showtime.

Many more Germans had come out to the musical, and there were several children in the crowd as well. It encouraged me to see so many local Germans in attendance.

There was an excitement in the air. The welcome and the opening prayer went great. And after a big, deep breath, I started the four count to bring in the orchestra to start the first song of the musical. The orchestra began playing without a hitch, and the children were right on cue, smiling and singing as they entered the stage. The weather was looking great with no signs of rain in the sky.

Scenes one and two, along with the first three songs, went beautifully. During scene three, I could feel the weather getting cooler and the wind picking up, but nothing else had changed. Then it happened...

Song four was well underway, and I could hear the thunder coming in from behind me. I could smell the rain in the air. I remembered that history had proven that every single time the thunder clouds came, there was less than ten minutes before a deluge drenched the whole area. *What to do?* As the leader, I could do nothing but trust in God, who can do all things. All I could do was trust in the God of the Impossible, the Creator of the universe, the One who controls the weather and the world. That is what I did.

THE GOD OF THE IMPOSSIBLE

As song four continued and the wind continued to pick up, I was still conducting the musical when a huge drop of rain landed directly in the middle of my director's book. I looked down and noticed that it had soaked the middle of my music. Then, on the back of my neck, I felt it. *Would the rain keep coming and force us all to run inside? No, absolutely not!*

What I felt was *not* huge raindrops. On the back of my neck, I felt the brightest sunshine I could ever remember feeling in my entire life. The air dried up, the wind completely stopped, and the angelic voices of those children soared. As song four was coming to an end, I continued to direct the musical as I stood up from the front row and made a complete circle, staring into the sky.

I could not believe what I was witnessing with my own eyes! But God! To my surprise, the thunderclouds were still rolling, and the rain was still dumping—in a 360-degree circle all around us. This was incredible to see. The God of the universe showed up that day! The God of the Impossible showed up that day!

*"Ah, Sovereign Lord, You have made the heavens
and the earth by your great power and outstretched arm.
Nothing is too hard for you"* (Jeremiah 32:17 NIV).

We were experiencing a modern-day miracle. I was leading in the center of God's supernatural intervention.

The show was unstoppable, not because of me, but because God had a plan, and He orchestrated His plan. The rest of the musical went on without any concerns. The Germans in attendance that afternoon loved the musical. The musicians were so excited that the musical went so well. The leaders and the older children could not wait to share their thoughts on the absolute miracle they saw that day.

THE GOD WHO STILL MOVES

On the plane as we flew back to the USA, for the next several months, and occasionally still to this day, we talk about the miracle in Germany in 2001. Several Germans that day asked us about our faith and wanted to know more about the God who could control the weather. Seeds were planted; only eternity will reveal the full harvest.

The God of the universe showed up and showed off that day in front of all of us. He made us realize that He is a personal God who cares for His people. He showed us that His plans are perfect. He demonstrated His awesome power, which can even move storms so that His ministry can continue without any delays or interruptions.

This really should not have surprised us. He is the same God who, as recorded in Joshua 3, performed a miracle many of us have learned about.

So when the people broke camp to cross the Jordan River,
the priests carrying the ark of the covenant went ahead
of them. Now the Jordan is at flood stage all during harvest.
Yet as soon as the priests who carried the ark reached the
Jordan and their feet touched the water's edge, the water
from upstream stopped flowing. It piled up in a heap a
great distance away, at a town called Adam in the vicinity
of Zarethan, while the water flowing down to the
Sea of the Arabah (that is, the Dead Sea) was
completely cut off (Joshua 3:14-16 NIV).

Now, you might think that God holding back the water for the Israelites would be enough, but there was more. The ground that had been under the Jordan River became completely dry, allowing for their safe passage. And God wanted His people to share this with future generations, so we, too, would know God's glory.

"In the future when your descendants ask their parents...
tell them, 'Israel crossed the Jordan on dry ground.'
For the Lord your God dried up the Jordan before you
until you had crossed over. The Lord your God did to the
Jordan what He had done to the Red Sea when He dried it
up before us until we had crossed over. He did this so that
all the peoples of the earth might know that the hand of the
Lord is powerful and so that you might always fear the Lord
your God" (Joshua 4:12-24 NIV).

This same God is the one and only true God who cares for you!

This same God cares so much that He sent His Son, Jesus, to die on a cross. By His death, Jesus paid the final price for our sins, and through the death and resurrection of Jesus, we can all know that we will be with Him in heaven for all of eternity.

> *For God so loved the world that He gave His one and only Son, that whoever believes in Him shall not perish but have eternal life* (John 3:16 NIV).

You may feel that you are in a storm. Perhaps you have even lived in a pattern of getting caught up in life's storms for years. As a leader that day in Germany, I was reminded of the Lord's words: *"When you pass through the waters, I will be with you; and when you pass through the rivers, they will not sweep over you. When you walk through the fire, you will not be burned; the flames will not set you ablaze"* (Isaiah 43:2 NIV).

God doesn't always remove the storms. Sometimes, He puts us right in the center of His supernatural protection.

THE LEADERSHIP LESSON

I want you to know two very important truths I learned from my trip:

First, the God of the Bible and the God of the Germany 2001 event is the same God—the One and Only God—who still exists today and will exist forever!

Second, when we trust God, He will still do miracles if He chooses.

As leaders, we will face impossible situations. The weather forecast might be against us. The odds could be stacked high. People might suggest we need a Plan B. But unstoppable leaders serve an unstoppable God. Our job isn't to figure out how God will work—our job is to obey what He tells us to do, even when it looks as unusual as walking in circles seven times.

My God is the Creator! My God is the miracle worker! My God is the forgiver of all! My God is the God who can reach down and save even you and me because He has already proven His love for us in the death of His only Son, Jesus!

As a reminder of this miraculous German event in 2001, I still have the wooden stick that our Joshua carried as he led us all around the outdoor area, praying and silently walking around seven times. Yes, the same wooden stick that he used throughout the rehearsal and the musical. After the musical, all of the cast members and musicians signed it and gave it to me as a gift. I keep it in my bedroom.

I will never forget what God did that day in Germany in 2001. That same God still loves, still forgives, still cares, and still has a plan that we must follow. No matter how difficult your life becomes, no matter how stressed you are about a situation, remember that God is the God of miracles, and He can even change the weather to make His plans come to pass.

When you face your impossible situation, remember: Our God can do all things. He's still in the miracle business. And He's looking for unstoppable leaders who will trust Him completely, even when life's forecast says otherwise.

An Unstoppable Leader Is...
VISIONARY

Seeing Tomorrow's Possibilities, Not Just Today's Problems

By Brett Dabe

Where there is no revelation, the people cast off restraint; but one who keeps the law is blessed (Proverbs 29:18 WEB).

The best Christian leaders I know aren't fortune tellers—they can't predict the future any better than you can. But they've got something more valuable: They can see God's possibilities in the middle of impossible circumstances.

Abraham is the perfect example. God told him to leave everything familiar and go to a land he'd never seen, promising to make him the father of many nations. Two problems: Abraham was 75 years old, and his wife was barren. From a human perspective, what God said made no sense, but Abraham saw past the present limitations and envisioned God's future promises.

Abraham didn't have a GPS or a detailed business plan; he just had God's Word and a vision showing him descendants as numerous as the stars. That vision kept him moving forward for 25 years before Isaac was even born. I bet most men would have given up after the first year.

That's visionary leadership. Not seeing what is, but believing what God says can be.

Ezekiel demonstrated this same principle during Israel's darkest hour. The people were in exile, the temple was destroyed, and hope seemed dead. Instead of wallowing in despair, Ezekiel saw visions of dry bones coming back to life, a new temple being built, and God's glory returning to His people. Ezekiel's visions didn't make sense to people living in the Babylonian captivity. But he painted such vivid pictures of restoration that the people began to hope again. He saw God's future when others only saw their present problems.

Visionary leaders don't get paralyzed by present problems; they allow future possibilities to energize them. They understand that God often calls us to things that look impossible from where we're standing.

Caleb is one of my favorite examples of a visionary with persistence. When twelve spies checked out the Promised Land, ten of them focused on the giants. Only Caleb and Joshua concentrated on God's promise. While the others essentially said, "We can't do it," Caleb said, *"Let us go up at once and take possession, for we are well able to overcome it"* (Numbers 13:30 NIV).

Here's the amazing part: Caleb held onto that vision as the Israelites wandered in the wilderness for the next 40 years. When they finally did enter the land, Caleb was 85 years old and still claiming his mountain. *"Give me this mountain,"* he told Joshua (Joshua 14:12 NKJV). That's vision with staying power.

Vision without action is just wishful thinking. Let's look at Noah. Noah didn't just envision an ark; he built one. This guy spent decades building a massive boat in a place where it had never rained. His neighbors thought he was crazy. But Noah held onto God's vision of the coming judgment and stayed faithful to the building project. When the floods came, Noah's vision became the world's salvation. Sometimes your vision seems foolish to others because they can't see what God has shown you. Keep building anyway.

Zerubbabel faced the enormous task of rebuilding the temple after the exile. The foundation looked tiny compared to Solomon's original temple. The older men who remembered the first temple wept when they saw how small this new beginning looked. But Zerubbabel didn't let present limitations kill his vision, as he heard God say, *"For who has despised the day of small things?"* (Zechariah 4:10 NKJV). Zerubbabel understood that God's great works often start with small beginnings. He kept building, and the temple was completed.

King Josiah caught a vision for spiritual revival when he was just eight years old. By age sixteen, he was tearing down pagan altars and restoring worship to the true God. Most people would have said he was too young to lead such massive changes. But God doesn't call the qualified; He qualifies the called. Josiah's vision of a nation returned to God drove him to make difficult decisions and unpopular changes. He didn't wait until he was older or more experienced; he acted on his God-given vision and led Judah back to righteousness.

The church needs men who can look past current limitations to see God's unlimited possibilities. Men who can look at broken marriages and see restoration. Men who can look at struggling businesses and see a breakthrough. Men who can look at discouraged communities and see revival.

What vision has God put in your heart? What future possibility makes you come alive when you think about it? You aren't just daydreaming; God is showing you what He wants to do through you.

Don't wait for perfect conditions or complete clarity. Noah built the ark before the first raindrop fell. Abraham began walking before he knew the destination. Ezekiel prophesied restoration while still in exile.

God gives vision to men who will act on it. The question isn't whether you're qualified or ready; the question is whether you're willing to trust God's vision more than your limitations.

. . . .

SANUL CORRIELUS

Dr. Sanul Corrielus is a board-certified cardiologist, visionary entrepreneur, and Amazon best-selling author whose life's work blends medical expertise with a passion for holistic wellness. As the founder and CEO of Corrielus Cardiology in Philadelphia, Dr. Corrielus has pioneered a heart health model that integrates advanced cardiovascular care with lifestyle medicine, prevention, and community engagement. His bestselling books, *Healing the Spartan: A Roadmap to Heart Health* and *Longevity and Hypertension: Killing the Silent Killer,* reflect his mission to empower individuals to reclaim their health by addressing not only physical symptoms but also emotional, mental, and spiritual well-being.

A sought-after keynote speaker, mentor, and faith-driven leader, Dr. Corrielus inspires audiences with his unique ability to connect science, compassion, and purpose. His leadership extends beyond the clinic—advocating for underserved populations, combating the epidemic of heart disease, and equipping leaders to live and lead with integrity, resilience, and balance. Whether speaking from the stage, consulting with patients, or mentoring the next generation, Dr. Corrielus embodies a message of hope, healing, and transformation.

Learn more about his work, upcoming events, and heart health resources at corrieluscardiology.com.

STRENGTH IN SURRENDER

By Sanul Corrielus

Leadership has a way of placing us on a pedestal—whether we ask for it or not. And if we aren't careful, the view from the top can blur our vision of the very ground we are standing on. God has taught me, through my ups and downs, that the strength I need to be an unstoppable leader comes when I surrender to Him.

THE ARMOR I WORE

I am the youngest of nine children, raised in the rural heart of Haiti. My mother was the true Spartan in my life; her strength and commitment were evident in the many hats she wore—provider, protector, teacher, and spiritual guide. My father left when I was only three years old, traveling to the United States in search of a better life for our family. With no documentation, he was unable to return home. Our only connection for much of my childhood came in the form of handwritten letters and a single, cherished annual phone call.

Our family's livelihood came from the land. We farmed crops and cared for livestock. As a boy, I watched my older siblings labor in the fields; while observing them, I learned early lessons in discipline, patience, and resilience. The success of the crops meant the survival of our family. There was no backup plan; if the harvest failed, we didn't eat. My mother's tireless dedication to ensuring we had food, education, and faith was my first lesson in leadership.

From her, I learned that resilience is not just enduring hardship—it's finding ways to thrive in the midst of it. When school fees were due and money was short, she sought help from neighbors, her word as good as any written contract. She built a community of support and modeled faith that never wavered. Her actions echoed the truth of Philippians 4:19: *And my God will meet all your needs according to the riches of his glory in Christ Jesus* (NIV).

Faith and education became my cornerstones. Enrolled in a Catholic all-boys school, I excelled academically, fueled by my mother's insistence that knowledge and faith were our keys to a better life. I started small businesses—tutoring children in math, raising chickens to sell—which helped me learn not just about money, but about responsibility and service. And in those early days, even as I prayed before exams and proudly sang in the church choir, I felt God preparing me for a mission I could not yet see.

THE WARRIOR'S BREAKDOWN

After years of longing, I reunited with my father in America when I was 17. The joy of our reunion was short-lived. Within a year, he was gone—claimed by heart disease. Watching him struggle with shortness of breath and swollen legs, relying on misguided home remedies like leeches, I felt both helpless and angry. His cardiologist had handed him prescriptions without truly educating him or equipping him to fight for his health. My father, who had sacrificed everything for us, had not known how to protect his own heart.

His death became my call to arms. I realized then what my years of "training" had been preparing me for. My enemy was not a rival army—it was cardiovascular disease. From that point on, my path was clear. I would become a cardiologist. I would fight the battle my father never had a chance to win.

I worked relentlessly, studying chemistry at Brooklyn College, doing bench research, and later earning a scholarship to the University of Rochester School of Medicine. From there, I pursued a residency at Temple University and a fellowship specializing in cardiology at Howard University. Outwardly, I was thriving. I was the picture of success: a physician, husband, and father.

But inwardly, I was unraveling.

I carried myself like a Spartan warrior, armored in achievement and resilience. I equated strength with silence and considered vulnerability to be weakness. I compartmentalized my pain, pushed through exhaustion, and became the one everyone relied on, the one with answers. Yet beneath the armor, my heart was heavy.

The signs of fatigue, anxiety, and disconnection became apparent. I noticed an increasing distance in my marriage, where conversations had grown functional rather than intimate. Even when I was present with my children, I realized I was not truly engaged. And the quiet between patients had become heavier than the often difficult diagnoses I delivered.

Then came the breaking point. Alone in my office one evening, staring at the degrees on my wall, I felt an emptiness I couldn't name. I had spent my life helping others find healing, yet I was carrying wounds I had never addressed. For the first time in years, I wept. And in the quiet of those tears, I heard God's whisper: "Take off the armor. Let Me heal your heart."

Matthew 11:28 came alive in that moment: *"Come to me, all you who are weary and burdened, and I will give you rest"* (NIV).

THE HEART OF THE MATTER

The real battle was never just against the demands of my profession, the crushing weight of responsibility, or the unresolved trauma of my past. Those were real and heavy burdens, yes—but they were only the surface currents. Beneath it all, the true war was waged in the quietest of places: my own heart.

For years, I had guarded one thing more fiercely than any medical credential, title, or accomplishment—my image of strength. It was the armor I wore into every operating room, every board meeting, and every family dinner. I thought it kept me safe. I thought it made me worthy of respect. I thought it was the only way to lead. But what I didn't see was that my armor had also become my prison.

When I began writing my book, *Healing the Spartan,* I imagined it would be a helpful health resource, a bridge between medical science and practical lifestyle wisdom. But as the words poured out, I realized I wasn't just writing for my patients. I was writing for myself. The manuscript became less of a professional project and more of a spiritual reckoning—a peeling back of layers I had long kept sealed.

Page after page, I confronted the truth: I had been living on fumes. My body could endure the long hours and mental strain, but my soul was gasping for air. I was pushing myself toward an undefined finish line, believing the lies that leaders must be unshakable, that showing weakness would diminish my authority, and that my value was directly tied to my output.

And then, God disrupted my narrative.

I began to notice how many leaders—especially men—were living exactly as I had been: being praised publicly for their strength, yet privately withering under the weight of unspoken burdens. We called our long hours "perseverance," when in reality, they were avoidance. We called our relentless pace "ambition," when much of it was just grief disguised as productivity.

Psalm 34:18 pierced through the noise: *The Lord is close to the brokenhearted and saves those who are crushed in spirit* (NIV). I had preached that verse to others. I nodded in agreement when patients told me how it comforted them in their suffering. But now it was no longer a verse to quote—it was a lifeline to cling to.

And that meant doing something I had resisted for years: admitting I was brokenhearted.

I sought counseling—not as a formality or as a box to check, but as an act of surrender. I sat across from a counselor and, for the first time in decades, allowed my words to come out unfiltered. I spoke of the constant pressure, the fear of letting anyone down, and the moments I felt invisible despite being "important." I confessed that sometimes the man in the white coat felt like a stranger to the man in the mirror.

I reclaimed the Sabbath—not as a passive day off, but as a sacred appointment with God. I turned off my phone, stepped away from the noise, and learned that rest is not laziness—it is obedience. Each Sabbath became a reminder that my worth is not in my work, but in my belonging to Him.

I invited my wife and children into the emotional corners of my life that I had kept locked. It was uncomfortable at first. I had spent years mastering the art of compartmentalizing, believing I was protecting them. But as I began to share my struggles—the fatigue, the doubts, the loneliness—I saw something shift. My vulnerability became a bridge for deeper connection. My children didn't need a perfect father; they needed a present one. My wife didn't need an untouchable hero; she needed an honest partner.

As I grew by facing the truth, the Holy Spirit met me—not as Dr. Corrielus, the cardiologist with all the answers, but as Sanul, the man in need of grace.

From there, the way I interacted with others began to change. In my medical practice, I started asking more soul-searching questions, listening beyond the symptoms to the stories behind them. A patient's chest pain wasn't just a matter of blood flow—it was often tangled up in loss, fear, or years of silent stress. My consultations became less about transactions and more about transformations.

With my family, I began to prioritize presence over performance. I didn't just attend my son's game—I strived to leave the work behind in my mind so I could truly cheer from the stands. Having dinner with my wife became more than an appointment to eat together as I put down the phone and leaned into the conversation.

In leadership, I moved away from the myth of the invincible figure at the helm. Instead, I began leading my team with transparency, admitting when I didn't have all the answers, inviting them to collaborate, and trusting them with both the challenges and the victories.

This shedding of armor was not an overnight transformation. Some days, I felt exposed and unsure. But I began to realize that true strength is not the absence of vulnerability—it is the courage to embrace it.

I also started paying attention to my physical temple in ways I had neglected. Not only did I go to gym sessions and tweak my diet, but I also focused on the holistic care of my body as a sacred vessel. Exercise became less about aesthetics and more about honoring the gift of health. Eating well became less about discipline and more about stewardship.

And perhaps most importantly, I learned to pray differently. My prayers became less about asking God to help me "do more" and more about asking Him to help me "be more"—more present, more surrendered, and more attuned to His Spirit. I began to sit in silence with Him, not rushing to fill the space with words.

As the months passed, I noticed something remarkable: I was finding an altogether different kind of strength, which no longer came from titles, accolades, or accomplishments. Instead, I exhibited strength built on the unshakable foundation of God's love. And my ability to hold it all together no longer defined my identity.

And in that truth, I discovered the paradox of leadership: When you stop trying to be unbreakable, you become unstoppable.

THE HEART OF AN UNSTOPPABLE LEADER

Here's what I've learned, and I can say this with absolute conviction: God is not impressed by our résumés, titles, or long list of accomplishments. He is not moved by the letters after our names or the accolades we display on our walls. What moves the heart of God is our surrender.

It took me years—decades, really—to understand that distinction. I used to think leadership was about projecting competence, proving capability, and pushing through at all costs. I believed that the respect of others was earned by how much I could handle without breaking. I had perfected the art of "managing" both my image and my responsibilities, believing that showing weakness would mean forfeiting my credibility.

But God had other plans.

True leadership does not begin on a stage, in a boardroom, or behind a title. It starts at the altar—when we place our ambitions, fears, wounds, and need for control into God's hands. To be authentic leaders, we must decide that who we are becoming matters more than what we are achieving.

When God transforms our hearts, we stop leading from insecurity and start leading from identity. We no longer need to pretend we have it all together, because we trust the One who holds it all together. We become conduits of His grace, not just managers of our own resources.

I have found that when we stop hiding behind the armor of perfection and choose instead to embrace our authentic selves, something shifts. The pace of life may not slow, and the demands may not disappear, but the way we meet them changes. We are no longer dragging our burdens alone—we are walking with the One who promised, *"My yoke is easy, and My burden is light"* (Matthew 11:30 NIV).

That is what makes a leader unstoppable—not the absence of obstacles, but the presence of God's power in the midst of them.

Jesus' words recorded by Paul in 2 Corinthians 12:9 have become a personal anthem for me: *"My grace is sufficient for you, for my power is made perfect in weakness"* (NIV). Those words used to feel like a contradiction. How could weakness be the place where power is perfected? But now I see it: my weakness is not a liability—it's an entry point for divine strength.

Today, I still wear a white coat. I still step into exam rooms and operating theaters. I still make decisions that carry weight. But I no longer hide behind the coat. I no longer use busyness as a badge of honor or excellence as an excuse to neglect my soul. I still pursue excellence, but never at the expense of my peace.

I lead differently now. I lead from overflow, not emptiness. My work is no longer about proving myself—it's about serving from the abundance that comes when I stay rooted in God's presence. That shift has changed not only how I lead *others* but also how I lead myself.

To the leader reading this who feels worn thin, I want to offer you an invitation—not as a motivational speaker or as someone who has mastered every aspect of balance, but as a fellow traveler who has tasted both burnout and breakthrough:

Take off the armor.

You don't have to be perfect to be powerful. You don't have to be fearless to be faithful. You don't have to have all the answers to walk in authority. You only have to be available—available to God's leading, available to those who need your presence more than your performance, and available to be reshaped into the leader God created you to be.

We live in a world that celebrates the Spartan—the one who fights, endures, and wins at all costs. But God does not call us to be Spartans in spirit. He calls us to be servants. Servants who lead with humility, listen before they speak, and kneel before they command. He calls us to be His sons and daughters first. He longs for us to experience His healing, knowing we can then lead others to Him for healing. When we place our identity in God and strive to serve Him and those we walk with on this planet, we will fulfill the unique leadership role He created for us.

That's the kind of strength that endures—the kind that can withstand storms—because it is anchored in something more firm, secure, and everlasting than circumstances.

When we live under God's authority and by His grace, our legacy will not be defined by how much we achieved, but by how deeply we loved and how faithfully we served. Our children will remember less about the positions we held and more about the presence we gave them. Our teams will remember less about the targets we hit and more about the trust we built. Our communities will remember less about the events we organized and more about the hope we inspired.

If there is one thing I want you to carry away from my story, it is this: Being unstoppable is not about being unbreakable. An unstoppable leader is unyielding in their dependence on God. The world will try to convince you that strength means standing tall on your own. Heaven knows that true strength is found when you are on your knees.

So, as you step back into your own sphere of influence—whether that's in a hospital, a classroom, a kitchen, a courtroom, a pulpit, or a business— remember this: Your title may open doors, but your surrender will change lives.

Don't be afraid to lead with your scars visible. They are not signs of failure—they are proof of survival and, more importantly, evidence of God's faithfulness.

In the end, the most unstoppable leaders are not the ones who have never fallen. They are the ones who have learned to rise—not in their own power, but in the power of the One who called them and claims them as His own.

That is the strength worth cultivating. That is the legacy worth leaving.

DWIGHT W. BELL

Dwight W. Bell is the president and founder of Wings of Grace Ministries, Inc., based in Melbourne, Florida. The mission of the ministry is to guide teenagers, helping them discover their potential, build confidence, nurture hope, and live life with purpose. Wings has developed several innovative programs to mentor teens, the premier of which is an aviation program where a student can earn a private pilot's license by performing community service.

In addition to the teen ministries, Wings of Grace is also a provider of affordable housing with 30 rental units in Brevard County. The homes serve as stepping stones to home ownership for individuals and families who have difficulty finding housing due to credit or criminal histories. Wings of Grace has begun developing apartments for children aging out of the foster care system. The ministry has 24 units under construction, soon to be followed by three additional projects with about 110 units. The vision is to scale this nationwide.

Dwight is a licensed pilot with both helicopter and airplane ratings. He is also a licensed real estate broker.

The Thrill of Being a Godly Leader

By Dwight W. Bell

I could write a whole chapter on my life before Christ—the negative things I did to myself and other people. While my story is unique and might be somewhat interesting, it is really the same story that affects all of us.

We are all born in a lost and sinful world. We are all enemies of God, destined for eternal punishment because of our sin, with no way to save ourselves. In fact, Christianity tells us that we are so lost we can't even find God on our own. Sounds hopeless, doesn't it? It would be, except for the gospel of Jesus Christ—the good news. Because He loves us so much, God sent His son, Jesus, to come and dwell with us. Jesus seeks us out and leads us to Him. See, Jesus willingly gave His life, dying on the cross to pay the penalty of our sin, so that when we put our faith and trust in His finished work, He offers us forgiveness and His own righteousness so that we will no longer be lost. That is good news!

However, following Christ doesn't just benefit our future. Following Christ will take you on an adventure that is full of thrills better than you can imagine!

CALLED TO JESUS

As I entered adulthood, I didn't know anything about faith in God. And looking back, I recognize I was far from submissive. I had problems with authority and thought that rules didn't apply to me. My goal was to be super rich; I believed that would bring me happiness. But wanting to be rich and thinking the rules don't apply to you is a recipe for a lot of pain. Although I didn't know it at the time, Jesus was right there, using that pain to draw me to Himself.

After many years of struggling to achieve wealth, I slowly began to respond to Jesus, shifting my thinking from worldly ways to the ways of God's kingdom. God had a plan in allowing me to attain what I wanted, even though I partially desired it due to a purely selfish motive. He provided for my success, positioning me to do what He had planned all along. I can see a series of stepping stones He used to mold me more and more into His likeness. Over time, He also eliminated my own selfish stepping stones, allowing my life to become more fulfilling and fruitful.

As I surrendered more and more of my decisions to God, things began to get better; life became more purposeful and joyful. One of the first blessings I received was my beautiful wife, Angelia. She is a wonderful, godly wife who has brought me great joy, including two sons and a step-mother to my oldest son.

As I submitted to Him further, God gave me a measure of financial wealth that had previously eluded me. I was operating a small title search company in Port St Lucie, Florida, out of a spare bedroom. In the late 90s, banks were making a lot of home equity loans, and they needed a simple title search showing who owned the property and if there were any open liens or mortgages. I didn't make a whole lot on these individually, but with the volume of business, I was able to pay the bills. I offered my friend John, a real estate broker, a job soliciting business. He was so successful that I was able to rent an office and hire some staff.

John was on the board of Habitat for Humanity. When the market for vacant lots in town crashed, there were hundreds of for-sale signs and very few buyers. People began donating their lots to Habitat to get rid of them, but Habitat didn't want them either. So they assigned John to sell them, and he was successful in doing so. One day, John told me he was stepping out of the office to put a for-sale sign on a donated lot. Before he even returned, someone called and bought the lot over the phone. John attributed his sales success to displaying the lot's price on the sign. He figured that if people could see that they could purchase a lot for $1,200 or $1,500, they would jump at it. That gave us an idea.

We got the names of ten people who owed back taxes on their lot and sent each of them a letter with a $1,000 offer. We knew we wouldn't have to pay the back taxes on a lot until we sold it, so we would have very little capital outlay. From the first ten letters, we received one response. We quickly sold it and netted about $400. Realizing this was an easier way to make money than doing title searches, we mailed out 100 letters. From 2000 to 2007, we flipped over 4,000 lots. We had multiple years of over $25 million in sales.

With our success came all the bling: custom suits, a condo on the beach, a Jaguar, and a Mercedes convertible. I learned to fly, bought a brand-new helicopter, and flew it back from California. I had finally arrived, or so I thought. But God continued His work in me. From these stepping stones, He began to draw me into ministry.

CALLED TO MINISTRY

During my wealth-building years, I began to acknowledge more and more that God's ways are the best. I realized that if I had known this when I was younger, especially in my earlier teens, I could have saved myself—and other people—a lot of grief. The Lord began calling me to minister to youth—to teach and show them the ways of the Lord instead of the dead-end ways of the world.

One day, while flying the chopper down the beach, it hit me that aviation would be a great connecting point. Successfully flying an airplane or helicopter is a microcosm of living a successful kingdom life. Flying involves several key steps: Training. Following instructions, rules, and regulations. Self-discipline. Planning. And setting goals. All these are also needed to live life successfully. So I began developing a teen program, using aviation as the "hook" to teach about Jesus.

I equated aviation principles with biblical principles—for example, the preflight procedure. Before firing up an airplane or helicopter, the pilot must conduct a thorough preflight, which includes checking the flight controls for proper movement, the oil in the engine, the air pressure in the tires, and ensuring there is no water or contaminants in the fuel. This procedure provides the pilot the opportunity to find any problems on the ground rather than in the air. What is the spiritual correlation? Apostle Paul writes, *Put on the full armor of God, so that you can take your stand against the devil's schemes* (Ephesians 6:11 NIV). Do you think your day would go better if you would "preflight" yourself with the armor of God as a pilot preflights the aircraft?

Another principle is the "accident chain." An aircraft doesn't just all of a sudden fall out of the sky and crash. There is a chain of events that leads up to the accident, sometimes years in the making. A part of pilot training is to recognize the accident chain and break it before the chain of events overwhelms the pilot. In the same way, you don't wake up one morning and decide to go to divorce court or file for bankruptcy. A chain of events leads you to that day (usually successive bad decisions). The kingdom training is to recognize the "accident chain" you have created and nip it before devastation occurs.

With this basic vision, my wife and I founded Wings of Grace Ministries, Inc. in 2010, based in Brevard County, Florida. I placed some yard signs out around our church with a simple three-line message: "Teenagers, free flight lessons," and my cell number. Our first class started with 19 students. We like it when our students join us in their early teens because it gives us many years to share the gospel and model Jesus before they graduate and go off into adulthood. This arm of our ministry has grown tremendously, with 11 chapters in the Southeast US and one in The Bahamas. The impact we have seen has been tremendous. We have developed strong relationships with our students, with many coming to know Jesus and earning a pilot's license. Several students have later returned as flight instructors to teach the younger students—that is a true joy.

Another set of God's stepping stones was the development of our affordable housing ministry. While aviation is a great (and fun) way to do ministry, it is very expensive. Our cost to give flight instruction to our teen students is nearly $200 an hour. God had financially blessed my wife and me; however, I could see that offering free flight lessons to hundreds of teenagers would quickly drain all our savings.

In 2010, with house prices low, I had the idea of having the ministry purchase some foreclosed homes to create a rental income stream. The students could earn flight time, improve their work ethic, and learn home improvement skills by working on the homes. We purchased three bargain homes to get this project started. Besides learning to fly, many teens have learned how to make an ugly home look nice with cleaning, painting, and landscaping.

As we continued to purchase homes, Wings of Grace became known as a housing provider. The calls from struggling people looking for housing became more and more frequent. Many days, I received multiple phone calls from people needing housing. After much prayer, we decided that all of our properties would be affordable housing units, which began another avenue to share the good news of Jesus.

If our prospective tenants have poor credit, a criminal history, or evictions on their records, we tell them that we might have a home for them. We share that it's not where they have been that's important, but where they want to go. We inform them that they can actually buy their own home, because this is America. And if you can't do it here, where can you? We also share that they may need to change the way they think, especially about money and relationships, saying, "Let us tell you about a radical way of life that brings peace and joy and abundance! This radical way of life is called the kingdom of God, and the King is Jesus! And if you embrace it, you will find that your life will be much better, and in a short time, you can own your own home."

CALLED TO THE FAITH ZONE

My desire for wealth and bling had diminished, and our ministry was growing rapidly as we added new students, airplanes, and houses. I wanted my resources to be used in God's kingdom. With our success, I had a question for the Lord: "Are we achieving success because we are making it happen out of our strength and ability, or is it You bringing this success? How can I know?" I devised a test.

I began praying for projects I knew I could not possibly do. I figured if I was praying to do something I knew I couldn't do, and it happened, then it must be God doing it. I called it putting myself in the faith zone. By entering the faith zone, we have seen God answer huge prayer needs in ways we never would have expected. While unsettling at first, living in the faith zone is the only way to go! Every day is an adventure!

By 2020, we had expanded our portfolio to 30 rentals, and we had seven tenants go on to purchase their own homes. Everyone I shared this statistic with thought it was great, but to me, it seemed awful. After ten years and thirty properties, we had only seven tenants successfully purchase a home. I asked the Lord another question: "Lord, am I empowering people or enabling people?" The answer was both. Although we had some success, most of our tenants simply used our inexpensive rentals to muddle through life, not taking advantage of the opportunity offered. As I prayed on how to increase our success, I kept hearing "widows and orphans." This didn't make any sense to me, but we were approaching the next stepping stone quickly.

A week later, I received a call from a lady named Pam who started a ministry to provide services for youth aging out of foster care. Children in foster care are the orphans of today; I realized that this was a God-ordained call. I invited Pam over to our ministry headquarters, where she shared stories of young people who are hurt over and over again by those who are supposed to love them. She also shared that when a foster child turns eighteen, the funding to the foster parents stops; therefore, 25% of children who age out of foster care end up homeless within a year. This leads to a higher percentage of incarceration, substance abuse, unwanted pregnancies, and decreased high school graduation rates.

As Pam shared the stories of the abuse, betrayal, abandonment, and pain these young people suffer, my heart began to break. How can this happen in our country with great freedom and wealth? *How can Christians allow this to happen when there is so much scripture commanding us to care for them?* Perhaps it's because most of us are oblivious to the plight these young people face when entering adulthood. That is where I was—ignorant of their pain. But as I was made aware of this scourge on our society, I felt called to do something about the problem.

We immediately began a major shift in our affordable housing ministry. I was given a vision to build apartments so young adults who age out of foster care could have a safe, stable home to move into instead of being cast out onto the streets. The housing would include intense discipleship, so they could discover who they are in Christ, find their God-given purpose, and enter the life of abundance that Jesus came to give. As they prosper, they would move into a new home, preferably one they own, which would free up the apartment for the next one entering adulthood. As I discussed the enormity of the problem with Pam, we figured we would need to build or acquire 150 apartments in our community and 10,000 nationwide to solve the problem.

A quick calculation gave me a rough bottom-line figure of 20 to 30 million dollars to solve the issue in our local area. My pocket calculator gave me an error when I tried to calculate a nationwide figure—billions at least. I was thrilled at being presented with a project that I knew our ministry could not possibly do! I was ready to step into the faith zone. I told Pam that our ministry had a parcel of land across the street where we could build 20 or so apartments to begin. I knew even building 20 units would be a challenge for us, but I wanted to see God move in a mighty way. He began almost immediately.

About two weeks later, a team seemed to appear around our ministry conference table miraculously. I could feel the spirit of the Lord at work. Besides Pam, there was an engineering consultant and an architect. The local housing authority director attended and said he could get special HUD housing vouchers for our new residents. The finance guy guaranteed us the financing. Getting a loan commitment before even applying for the loan was proof enough that God was making this happen!

From that meeting, we began the development of Capernaum Place Apartments. Capernaum was Jesus' hometown, and Matthew records Jesus beginning his public ministry in this region after being tested in the wilderness. Jesus went to this region to fulfill the scripture, *The people walking in darkness have seen a great light* (Isaiah 9:2 NIV). The young adults we will be housing and discipling have been living in a type of darkness, and we want to bring them the light of Jesus, so Capernaum is a fitting name. As it turns out, we received approval to build 24 one-bedroom, one-bath apartments. Each resident will have their own brand new, beautiful apartment with cathedral ceilings and stainless-steel appliances. More importantly, they will be unconditionally loved and come to know that they are valuable, have a God-given purpose, and have an incredible future ahead of them. We expect to have our new residents moving into their new homes around September 2025.

God is continuing to bless the vision He gave us. A young lady who will be moving into Capernaum Place made a decision for Jesus and began attending weekly Bible studies with my wife. She is the first of many! We have acquired land for an additional 110 units in Brevard County, Florida, and land for nearly 50 units in Tennessee. Will Wings of Grace actually build 10,000 apartments nationwide? Maybe. But as our work becomes known, I am receiving calls from other churches and ministries inquiring about being a part of the solution. I have no doubt that Christians working together, with ideas and resources, can solve this issue. I believe this would be the better way. However God does it, I'm good with it.

EXPERIENCING THE THRILL

I have had a lot of thrills and successes in my life. I love wheeling and dealing in real estate, building businesses, flying helicopters, and loving my wife, kids, and grandkids. The greatest thrills, however, are seeing God move in the life of one of our students or residents and witnessing how He answers prayer when I step out in faith.

When you submit and give your life to Jesus, He secures your salvation in heaven, which is the greatest thrill of all. But He also has a plan and a purpose for every day of your life here on earth. Commit to serving and following His call; as you do, the thrills and adventures He will provide are greater than you could ever imagine.

Step into the faith zone. And remember, with God, all things are possible!

An Unstoppable Leader Is...
INFLUENTIAL

Inspiring Action Through Connection, Not Just Commands

By Ken A. Hobbs II

Leadership in the kingdom of God isn't about domination—it's about demonstration. The Christian leader who is truly unstoppable leads not by issuing commands, but by cultivating connection. Influence isn't measured by how many people obey you—it's measured by how many hearts you've touched, how many lives you've lifted, and how many souls you've stirred toward Christ.

Jesus Himself modeled this perfectly. He didn't come with a crown or a sword—He came with sandals and scars. He didn't bark orders from a throne—He walked dusty roads, sat at dinner tables, and wept beside grieving friends. His influence was magnetic because it was relational. Jesus inspired action not through fear, but through love.

Unstoppable leaders understand that before you can move someone, you must first meet them. Influence begins with proximity—with being present, available, and attentive. Jesus didn't just preach to crowds; He pulled people close. He knew their names, their stories, and their wounds.

Jesus led through connection:

- He called Zacchaeus down from a tree and dined with him.

- He touched the leper before healing him.

- He wept with Mary and Martha before raising Lazarus.

Each act of our Savior's was a connection before it was a command. That's the blueprint for Christian influence: Relationship first; transformation second.

Modern Christian leaders are called to follow this model. Whether you're leading a ministry, a family, or a business, your influence will grow when people feel seen, heard, and valued. You don't need a pulpit to be influential—you need compassion.

Connection opens the door, but integrity keeps it open. People may be drawn to charisma, but they stay for character. A Christian leader's influence is only as strong as their consistency. Do your words match your walk? Do your convictions show up in your conduct?

Jesus didn't just teach truth—He embodied it. He didn't just tell us to love our enemies—He forgave those who nailed Him to a cross. His influence was unstoppable because His life was unshakable.

For today's leader, integrity means:

- Apologizing when you're wrong.

- Leading with humility, not ego.

- Making decisions that reflect Christ, not culture.

When people see that your faith isn't just a Sunday performance but a daily posture, your influence deepens. You become a lighthouse—not because you shout, but because you shine.

Commands may change behavior temporarily, but influence transforms hearts permanently. Unstoppable leaders don't just tell people what to do—they help them see who they are in Christ. They speak life, cast vision, and awaken purpose.

Jesus did this with Peter. He saw a fisherman and called him a rock. He saw a denier and called him a shepherd. His words didn't just instruct—they ignited.

As a Christian leader, your influence grows when you:

- Call out the gold in others.

- Speak prophetically into others' potential.

- Encourage those who are weary.

- Challenge those who become complacent.

Your voice becomes a vessel of God's truth. Your words become seeds of destiny. And your influence becomes a catalyst for spiritual growth.

Unstoppable leaders don't build empires—they build people. They don't hoard power—they release it. Influence multiplies when you empower others to lead, serve, and grow.

Jesus didn't keep His ministry to Himself. He sent out the twelve. Then the seventy. Then He said, *"[You] will do even greater things"* (John 14:12 NIV). His influence exploded because He equipped others to carry it forward.

Christian leaders today can empower others by committing to:

- Mentor the next generation.

- Delegate with trust, not fear.

- Celebrate others' success.

- Create space for others to shine.

Your influence isn't diminished when others rise—it's amplified. The mark of mature leaders is not how many people follow them, but how many people they've raised up to lead.

To be an unstoppable Christian leader is to be influential—not through control, but through connection. Not through commands, but through compassion. Not through dominance, but through discipleship.

You don't need a title to be influential; you need a testimony. You don't need a platform; you need presence. You don't need to be perfect; you need to be real.

So lead like Jesus. Connect deeply. Walk in integrity. Speak to hearts. Empower others. And let your influence ripple through eternity.

Because when your leadership reflects Christ, your influence becomes unstoppable.

. . . .

TIM MAY

Timothy May, a native of Girard, Ohio, is a devoted husband to his wife, Alisson, and a proud father to their three children—Zachary, Benjamin, and Grace. An entrepreneur and ordained minister, Tim's life journey reflects a powerful story of transformation and faith. Although he grew up in the church and was familiar with God and religion, his relationship with Christ deepened in a life-changing way through the influence of Band of Brothers, United Men of Honor, and the encouragement of faithful brothers in the Lord.

Before the transformation he shares about in his chapter, Tim faced significant challenges—financial struggles, poor health, and spiritual emptiness. Yet, through the work of the Holy Spirit, he experienced a complete turnaround, becoming physically fit, spiritually grounded, and financially prosperous as a leader and business owner in the financial services industry.

Tim's mission is to inspire others with the message that real change is possible when we fully surrender to God's divine purpose. His story stands as living proof that no situation is beyond God's power to redeem and restore.

From 467
to Freedom

By Tim May

As we drove down the highway, I looked at my wife with the kids sleeping in the back seat, and I said to her, "Well, maybe I should just f***ing kill myself."

There's a lot in my story that led me to say that, and I hope I can provide the context for you. This is my testimony of how God can take a man at his absolute lowest point—spiritually broken, physically destroyed, and emotionally bankrupt—and transform him into the leader He always intended him to be.

AN UNHEALTHY BEGINNING

I was brought up in a Christian household. We attended church every Sunday, my parents facilitated Bible studies, and my mom was the head of the women's ministry. From the outside looking in, I appeared to be living a respectable Christian life, and everything seemed great.

I had a lot of women in my life: my mom, her mom (my grandmother, who lived with us), and three much older sisters who were 15, 17, and 19 years older than me. I was the apple of everyone's eye—the baby boy.

There was plenty of love in our family. I wanted for nothing and was coddled constantly. My mom stayed at home while my dad built his business, so I really wasn't around my dad a lot. No one ever went hungry in my mom's presence; she was always cooking, making something delicious with all her heart. The main ingredient in everything she made was love.

When I was in second grade, I tripled in weight. I weighed around 50 pounds in first grade, and within a year, I was wearing adult sizes and had gained almost 100 pounds. This slippery slide toward obesity continued throughout my life. I was a rather sedentary youth and young adult. Sports and outdoor activities were not my strong suits, so I did not gravitate toward them.

By high school, I weighed almost 300 pounds. Completely addicted to sugar and, more importantly, completely addicted to the approval of other people. I was always trying to make people laugh, deflecting my hatred for myself with humor.

What I lacked in physical capabilities, I made up for with intellectual prowess. I consistently excelled academically in school, finishing at the top of my class in every grade level and ultimately serving as the salutatorian for my graduating class. I was accepted to a prestigious college and thought I wanted to be a doctor, so I declared a pre-med major.

SEEKING COMFORT

College was a continuation of my slippery slope. My constant longing for home, need for others' approval, and desire to feel accepted always led me to what brought me comfort: food.

I continued to gain weight as I navigated a family trial—my mom was dying from renal failure. She was the spiritual light in my life, and I was her baby boy. I was her masterpiece. Right in the middle of my sophomore year, I received a call that I needed to meet my sisters and dad at the Cleveland Clinic. My mom was unconscious, and they were signing a DNR. This was goodbye. Goodbye to everything that I knew as normal. Goodbye to the love that my mom had for me.

He heals the brokenhearted and binds up their wounds
(Psalm 147:3 NIV).

I couldn't see that truth then, but God was already working even in my deepest pain.

Everything changed. I left college and came home, transferring to a school that was more affordable and more accessible to ease our strained financial situation. My dad's business was devastated as he and my mom actually ran it together; when she died, the business failed horribly. My childhood home ended up getting repossessed by the bank. I'll never forget the four months that I was homeless.

On top of losing my mom, I lost my dad, too. He became an emotional wreck, and his old coping mechanisms and habits resurfaced as he tried to deal with my mom's loss: Lust. Drugs. Partying. I didn't have a dad anymore—I had a best friend who liked to party. I did things with my dad that most men wouldn't even do on their bachelor party night.

That was when my wife, Ali, entered the picture. Ali and I had known each other for basically our entire lives. Our families knew each other; we grew up in the church together, and we attended youth group and high school together. We had even dated for a couple of years. After I went away to college, we grew apart. But when I returned after my mom passed, it was like gravity. She and I found each other again.

She had also just lost her mom, but in a different way. Her parents went through a very messy divorce. Ali was deeply wounded and was looking for a source of comfort and acceptance. Together, Ali and I began relying on unhealthy coping mechanisms: Food. Sex. Alcohol. Marijuana. A lot of toxic habits.

In 2015, I fell into a deep, dark depression. Alcoholism and drug use were taking over my life. I was also pushing 450 pounds. Ali gained weight, too, so I didn't think it was that big of a deal. We were on our second child at that point.

There were moments when I thought things were getting better. I did find sobriety for a period of time, but I did not change mentally or spiritually. I finished my degree and was working a job I completely hated, but I did have a side business. By 2017, we were on our third child, and that summer, I'd saved enough money to quit my job and develop my business into a full-time venture.

Things were going well. At least I thought they were.

But there was something dark inside of me. An attachment to food, an addiction to the comfort and love I was yearning for. Nothing would fill the hole that the passing of my mom had left. Nothing even helped.

THE BREAKING POINT

This brings me back to the beginning of my story. In February 2021, we won a free trip to Universal Studios. My wife, being a huge Harry Potter fan, was elated. She'd been asking me to take her for years, and go figure—I won a free trip. What a dream, right?

We arrived in Florida and checked into our hotel with our eldest son, Zachary, who was 10, and my wife's little sister, who was 18. At that point, I had reached my highest recorded weight of 467 pounds.

I didn't realize how much walking I would be doing on the trip. Before we even reached any of the parks, my feet were already hurting, my knees were swollen, and my back was tight and sensitive. I was very, very irritable. Unfortunately, I made that clear at every point.

This amazing dream of a free trip, a trip that my wife had been waiting years for, was completely ruined. I was miserable, and I made everyone around me miserable. I kept having to sit down everywhere I went. I was ashamed and humiliated that I couldn't get on certain rides. I took jabs at my wife and the kids, biting their heads off whenever I could about stupid things, just because I was so unhappy with myself. I turned our dream trip into a nightmare.

After spending our day in the park going from seat to seat because I didn't want to walk or stand, I made the rest of the trip pointless for everyone else. Everything was about me. I grumbled about the blisters on my feet and how we weren't properly prepared. I griped about problems with the room. I complained about everything I could complain about. Looking back, I'm surprised my wife didn't leave me at the hotel in Florida and come back to Ohio without me.

As we were driving home, both kids were asleep in the backseat, and my wife and I were bickering about something. To this day, I don't remember what it was, but at some point, there was a straw that broke the camel's back. In the middle of our back-and-forth, I exclaimed to Ali, "Well, maybe I should just f***ing kill myself."

She continued driving, just staring at the dashboard and not saying a word. She stayed calm, cool, and collected. I was boiling over, teeming with tears that I was trying my best to hold back. I was so angry at myself, with her, and with the current state of my life. I hated myself, and I hated what I had become.

GRACE AND GUIDANCE

Our life looked okay from the outside. We were making more money in our business than I had been making at my day job. I had more freedom and flexibility than most of my friends. Ali and I had three beautiful children. We owned a home and even a few rental properties.

Spiritually, though, I was a mess. I was broken. And in my lowest moment, after ruining a trip for my family, my wife showed me grace and mercy. She could've yelled at me, could've demeaned me, or even could've left me (I'm sure the thought crossed her mind more than once). But what she did next surprised me.

As Ali continued to drive, she remained silent for about 10 to 15 minutes. Then, she put on her blinker and took an exit ramp, pulling into a gas station to top off the tank. Before she got out of the car, she looked at me with tears in her eyes and said, "I can't help you—only God can. I recommend you get out of the car and make a phone call. I don't know who you're supposed to call. But you're not getting back in this car until you talk to someone."

The Lord is close to the brokenhearted and saves those who are crushed in spirit (Psalm 34:18 NIV).

In that gas station parking lot, God was closer than I had ever imagined.

I listened to my wife, with tears in my eyes too, and then exited the car. I called a friend of mine who is a pastor. I pleaded with him to counsel me, saying I needed a mentor and a friend. He prayed with me, calmed me down, and gave me some sound advice. But most importantly, that friend introduced me to another pastor.

We got home, and within 48 hours, I was in Pastor Bill's office at my first counseling session. I had attended Christian men's conferences before, such as Band of Brothers. I realized I had a huge wound from my father and another from the loss of my mom, and that I was filling those wounds with food, pornography, lust, and other things.

I started to meet with Pastor Bill twice a week for an hour. God, working through him, showed me a set of steps to help me break soul ties and generational curses in my life. Having another man to open up to and talk to consistently helped me find strength. But more importantly, it helped provide me with a set of guidelines and steps to take, ensuring that I was progressing in my spiritual life, shedding the old me, and finding God's purpose in my life.

TRANSFORMATION TO FREEDOM

Through counseling, I realized I could change. Just getting some of the spiritual and emotional baggage off my back took a huge weight off my shoulders. Over the next three months, without making significant changes to my diet or lifestyle, I lost approximately 40 pounds, solely from being more spiritually and mentally fit. My emotions had always been linked to food—it's how I felt love. When I began to shed my need for love and focus my gaze solely on the validation of my heavenly Father, things started to change dramatically.

> *Therefore, if anyone is in Christ, the new creation*
> *has come: The old has gone, the new is here*
> *(2 Corinthians 5:17 NIV)!*

That verse became my reality as God began transforming me from the inside out.

I began to explore additional ways to enhance my physical well-being, and I gained a sense of clarity regarding many of the decisions I had to make. After much prayer, in December 2021, I decided to pursue gastric bypass weight loss surgery. Choosing this certainly wasn't the easy way out. It required extensive research and planning, along with making a commitment to change how I lived. I had to be intent on doing the right things for my body.

Over the next three months, I continued my counseling with Bill and added psychological counseling for weight loss surgery. I lost another 30 pounds.

Then, in March 2022, I went under the knife and had surgery. Right around my three-week post-op mark, I started walking and hitting the gym. I found a fantastic routine and a community. I found uplifting, heavy Christian music. I continued to attend counseling sessions with Pastor Bill. I prayed constantly. I fostered relationships differently. I changed as a leader for my family and in my business. I discovered that incorporating daily discipline into my life edified my heavenly Father, helped me treat my body like a temple, and made these steps and processes sustainable.

Over the next two years, I lost 200 pounds, going from 467 pounds at my highest down to just over 200. I became more mentally and spiritually sharp, to the point where I even started quoting scripture when faced with trouble or when people asked me for advice. My business started to thrive even more, and our income doubled. I began to see God's masterpiece—loose skin and all. I got ordained and began to follow God's calling on my life, serving in a para-ministry role, counseling others through mental and physical struggles, and providing marriage counseling, as well as performing weddings.

I can do all this through him who gives me strength
(Philippians 4:13 NIV).

Philippians 4:13 wasn't just a verse on a wall anymore—it became the foundation of my new life.

I went from thinking that taking myself out was the best option for my family, to becoming the most physically, spiritually, and mentally fit version of myself I've ever been in my life. I'm healthier at 35 than I was at 25. I had early-onset type 2 diabetes, high blood pressure, and sleep apnea. I was mentally distressed most days, allowing depression and anxiety to rule over my life. I used to let all of my emotions control me and all the decisions I made. Not only were all these physical ailments cured, but I no longer needed medication for any of the symptoms.

If the old me were to walk past the man I had become on the street, he wouldn't even recognize me.

I am now able to be a more present father, actively engaging my three very high-energy children, Zachary, Benjamin, and Grace. I coach them in sports without having to catch my breath or rest because my knees and back hurt.

I am also a more present leader for my team. Additionally, I'm more mentally sharp and don't get tired as easily, having more energy than I've ever had.

I am a more present husband. I no longer make excuses (or at least as much, ha-ha).

The Lord expands our territories if we yield to Him. My transformation and spiritual growth came after I sank to one of the lowest points in my life and received my wife's graciousness and mercy. She saw my heart, instead of the emotions I was wearing on my sleeve.

There are many things I attribute to my success, including long hours in the gym, dedicated meal planning, visits to doctors and professionals for blood work, therapy, and counseling. But what really saved me?

What really saved me was knowing that the Creator of the universe, God, our heavenly Father, has so much reckless love for me that He sent His only Son to die for my sins.

Every mistake I made. Every wrong decision. Every time I cursed Him. Every time I ate something that shouldn't have been in my body. Every time I looked at another woman. Every time I made up an excuse so I didn't have to play with my kids. Every time I made somebody feel less than..

For every single one of those things, I have a Savior who died on a cross to wipe my slate clean... leaving me innocent.

I have an advocate. A friend. A confidant. A Father.

It was only when I shed the disguise of who I thought I wanted to be and assumed my role as the son of a King that I finally started to change and become the man God created me to be.

> *But God demonstrates His own love for us in this: While we were still sinners, Christ died for us* (Romans 5:8 NIV).

God's reckless love changed everything.

Losing over 200 pounds can be really shocking. It's easy to see that I've changed physically—that I've let God change me. But my internal change is double, maybe even triple, that of my outward change.

Transforming my body took discipline, but no discipline is more important than going to our knees and remaining plugged into God, our ultimate power source.

When we plug into God and surrender our broken selves to Him, He will transform us into all He created us to be, giving us the opportunity to impact the lives of all those He has placed around us; the opportunity to be unstoppable leaders.

RYAN OTTO

Ryan Otto is a husband, father, and pastor with 12 years of experience in ministry. He has served as a pastor, as a missionary to more than 20 countries, and as a chaplain in the United States Air Force. He is also the business owner of Light of Life Coaching & Consulting and Light of Life Wedding Services, offering services as a wedding DJ and officiant. Ryan also coaches high school football and serves as the director of distribution for "The Heaven Guy" non-profit ministry.

Ryan deeply loves his family, loves football, and is passionate about being from the great state of O-H-I-O. Above all, he identifies as a son of God, born for such a time as this, with a passion to inspire and remind others of their identity and destiny in Christ. His calling is to help people know and experience the true hope of God and to be awakened to who they are and whose they are, walking confidently in their God-given purpose, identity, and destiny. He can be reached at ryanotto11@gmail.com or on social media @ryan.otto11.

ON THE TEAM, IN THE GAME

By Ryan Otto

Have you ever wondered why you're alive or what your true purpose is in this life? Have you ever wondered if you were an accident or a mistake in this world, if you were truly born for a purpose, or where you are supposed to be going in this life? If you've answered yes to any of these questions, then you're not alone. Throughout my life, these questions have burned deep within me, causing me to wonder, doubt, and search for who I truly am and why I'm alive on this earth. I want to share with you some wisdom I have learned in this journey called life: To know where you're going, you have to know where you are, and to know where you are, you have to be willing to dig deep into your past to understand the path you've been on and how you got to where you're at within your life.

BROKEN FOUNDATIONS

Growing up, I didn't always feel accepted, wanted, or chosen by others, especially by my dad. Please don't get me wrong—I had an amazing village around me who loved me deeply and took care of me, including my mom, grandparents, aunts, and uncles. But deep within me, I always sensed that something was "off" or "different" about me compared to my friends. Something didn't fit, and as much as I tried to fit in and push the feelings, doubts, and fears away, they were always there in some way.

I grew up with no memory of my parents ever being together. My mom recently sent me a couple of pictures of her and my dad together holding me, with a message on a post-it note saying she sent them in case I wanted to remember us as a family all together. When I read that, it felt like I was trying to read a foreign language that I had no understanding of. In all honesty, I was shocked she sent them because, in my view, we were never a family; I have no memories or recollection of us all being together.

My parents were high school sweethearts who went to college together. During their first semester at college, my mom became pregnant. She dropped out of school, giving up her hopes and dreams to move back home with her parents to prepare to be a mom. My dad stayed at college, continuing to live the college life until circumstances brought him back home. After I was born, my dad focused on his job and growing his career. My mom focused on me, trying to become the best parent she could be. They stayed together off and on until I was two years old, but both lived separately at their parents' houses.

Shortly after my parents went their separate ways, my dad found the woman who would become my step-mom; they got married a couple of years later. He had a successful job that moved him around the country.

I lived with my mom most of my life. She found her life partner and husband when I was in eighth grade, and they married the summer before my freshman year.

I know this is common for some readers, but growing up, I felt different, angry, and lost. Although many amazing people loved me (grandparents, aunts, uncles, and more), I never had the family I longed for. And deep down, I never felt like I fit. My dad started a family with his new wife, and they had four kids together. My stepdad already had two daughters from a previous marriage, and then he and my mom had a son together. So, I grew up mostly as an only child, but I somehow have seven brothers and sisters, two of whom are much younger than I am. One is nineteen years younger, born during my freshman year of college, and the other is 20 years younger, born when I was a sophomore. When he was born, I was the same age my mom was when she had me.

I share this to say, I grew up questioning who I was and why I was alive. I was filled with anger, fear, and pain, always wondering if my dad really loved me, truly wanted me, or was ever genuinely proud to have me as his son. Deep inside, I always knew my mom loved me, but it was challenging to always believe that when different boyfriends came into her life or when she got married and started to focus more on her future family.

Things in my childhood started to go downhill when my mom and I moved away from my grandparents' house to another city. I got arrested in fourth grade for trying to steal cigarettes from a grocery store, and then got put into a hospital in fifth grade for suicidal thoughts, depression, and obsessive-compulsive disorder. My mom was trying her best, but she was trying to be both my mom and dad, and, in all honesty, just couldn't handle me by herself. My grandpa stepped in and supported us both tremendously, but because he didn't live with us, there was only so much he could do.

After my two weeks in the treatment center, my parents decided that I should go live with my dad and step-mom for a year. Following a year of ups and downs, I ended up moving back home with my mom when my dad got a new job out of state. My dad and I didn't live in the same state again until I moved to Florida about a year and a half ago, which was almost 30 years later.

I ended up getting arrested again in high school for underage drinking and should have gotten arrested for much more, including drugs, drinking and driving, theft, and vandalism. But then my focus shifted to sports, popularity, girls, and doing whatever I could to fit in as I tried to fill the big hole in my heart from not feeling accepted, wanted, and believed in.

My senior year in high school, my world came crashing down when I was deemed ineligible to play football. My grades were good enough, but one of the classes I took didn't count as a full credit course, and my counselor and I had both missed it. Football was my life. My high school had a powerhouse football team that consistently played the best opponents and went to the playoffs every year. Being part of that team felt like being in the movies. It was my dream to run out onto that field as a varsity starter, playing for my school, my team, and my friends and family. A week or two before our first game, that was stripped away from me, and there was nothing I could do to get it back.

So once again, I was on the team, but couldn't play in the game. Even though I was at every game, I couldn't put on the pads and actually play. I couldn't run out on that field with my brothers to fight and make a difference; all I could do was watch from the sidelines. I was on the team, but I wasn't in the game.

This is how I had felt most of my life. I had a family that loved me, yet sometimes I just didn't feel like I fit and wasn't really accepted, loved, or wanted. I had friends growing up, but I was always on the outskirts of the friend group and felt like I was looking in. I was on the team, but never got to be in the game. From the outside in high school, it looked like I had it all together, but on the inside, I was a fake—a scared boy who didn't know who I was or whose I was. I was mad at God, my parents, and this life for the hand I had been dealt.

> "For I know the plans I have for you," declares the Lord,
> "plans to prosper you and not to harm you, plans to give
> you hope and a future" (Jeremiah 29:11 NIV).

This verse would later become my anchor, but at the time, I couldn't see past my pain.

After high school, I managed to gain admission to college despite being on academic probation. I remember one of my family members telling my grandma that I would flunk out after the first semester. Hearing that was all the motivation I needed to empower the underdog I had always felt like and prove everyone wrong.

DIVINE APPOINTMENT

I often felt doubted, counted out, and not truly believed in for most of my life. I felt like a misfit who just hurt the people around me, and I was told some pretty hurtful things from people I loved and trusted—people who should have been protecting me instead of hurting me. So I started to believe it. To this day, I struggle with what people think of me and say about me, but I had to learn a valuable lesson that changed and turned my life around. I had to learn to lose my life. Let me explain:

> *"For whoever wants to save their life will lose it, but whoever loses their life for me will save it"* (Luke 9:24 NIV).

As the verse says, I was trying to save my life, but in reality, I was losing it. I was attempting to fill the void and replace the emptiness, sadness, anger, rejection, and feeling lost with whatever would give me temporary happiness and fulfillment. I put my hope in drugs, drinking, girls, popularity, sports, working out, a new car, money, image, and most of all, what people thought of me. My goal was to make everyone believe everything was great on the outside so that no one could see the cracks on the inside.

But God wanted me to lose my life and allow Him to save it. Growing up, I was a believer, but I didn't grow up a belonger. Let me explain: I grew up believing in God, saying the sinner's prayer, and going to church because I was forced to. I had always believed *in* God and believed that Jesus Christ was our Lord and Savior. But most of the time I prayed as a kid, I felt like He was angry at me and wanted to punish me (similar to how I felt toward my dad). I knew of God, but I didn't personally know Him as a Father, Savior, and Friend. I believed in Him, but didn't belong to Him, at least not yet.

When I was in college, a girl I really liked invited me to attend a young adult service at a cool new church in town. Ironically, two other people I knew had previously invited me, which I had declined. But when the girl I liked asked me, I said yes, of course (God knows how to get us!). I attended the church service with her and was impressed by the young people who were there not because they had to be, but because they genuinely wanted to be. I was amazed at how cool and real most of them were, yet they had this light about them and loved God.

I continued attending the service that summer. Even after the girl I liked and I went our separate ways, I knew I needed to continue attending that young adult service on Sunday nights. I was getting tired of the drinking, the partying, and living for things that I knew would give temporary fulfillment, but in reality were just taking me deeper into the hole of my past and pain.

One night during the summer before my junior year of college, I was struggling with so much depression and feeling so lost inside. I went to the service for the first time by myself; while there, I felt and experienced something completely new. The senior pastor of the church was a guest speaker at the young adult service, and even though he didn't know me at all, it felt like he had been following me around my whole week and was talking directly to me. At the end of the service, they did something special they didn't always do: They invited people up to surrender their lives to Christ and ask Jesus into their hearts to be their Lord and Savior.

I wanted to jet for the doors; I didn't want anyone to see me getting emotional. But something, or better yet, Someone, picked me up from my chair, and I walked up front. I think I was the only one. Instead of being scared of what others thought, I felt a love, a freedom, and a presence like never before. Even though my eyes were closed, I could feel and see a bright light shining down on me. Although I didn't know who they were, hands from all around started touching me as they prayed for me. It literally felt like angels were putting their hands on me to pray for me and welcome me home to God's kingdom.

I was crying like a baby, and I kept saying, "God, I give it all to You. I give you the drinking, I give you the girls, I give you everything that is holding me back from being the man that You created me to be. I believe in You, Jesus. I believe in You, Jesus. I believe in You, Jesus. Please come into my heart, make me new, and make me the man that You created me to be."

Even though I felt extreme tiredness, as if I had just played a football game, I felt so free, so light, and so full of peace and love. As I walked out, I stopped and looked back at the cross, and for the first time in my life, I felt accepted, loved, and not alone.

I had spent so many years trying to "save my life," when in fact I was slowly losing it. But as the Good Book says, when I had the courage and faith to "lose my life" in Christ, He found it and saved it.

WALKING IN PURPOSE

I was 21 years old when I got saved and surrendered my life to Christ. Ever since then, it has been a wild and amazing adventure full of ups and downs, learning, discovering, and growing in who I am and Whose I am in Christ. God has shown me that I can't know my destiny in this life until I truly know my identity. We can't know what we're meant to do until we know who we are, and we can't know who we are until we truly know and experience Whose we are.

> But you are a chosen people, a royal priesthood, a holy nation, God's special possession, that you may declare the praises of him who called you out of darkness into his wonderful light (1 Peter 2:9 NIV).

Since then, I've graduated from college, earned my master's degree, traveled to over twenty countries sharing the message of Jesus, and served as a pastor for nine years. I am now a chaplain in the United States Air Force, a football coach, a life coach, and living out this adventure of faith in God everywhere I go, reflecting His living hope that is alive within me to this world.

I'm not perfect—trust me. Or ask my wife. I'm not the strongest, the bravest, the smartest, or even the most godly, but one thing God has taught me is not to quit. I might not finish the race first, and I might even be the last one to finish, but I will finish, one step of faith at a time, remembering the One who is with me and has been with me since I was born.

Despite all I've been through, I struggled when I was asked to write in this book, thinking, *I'm not an unstoppable leader.* But then, I was reminded of a principle God has taught me: Never give up, and never stop remembering and believing in who you are and Whose you are. I must lose my life in Christ and let Him continually find me, lead me, and show me who and Whose I am.

So, are there unstoppable leaders out there? Are there people who are "fearless"? Personally, I don't think so. But I do believe there are people out there who look fear straight in the eyes with faith and choose not to give up. They live out this life through the ups and downs, the thick and thin, one step of faith at a time, choosing to persevere and never give up, remembering the One who lives within us who will never give up on us.

I can do all this through him who gives me strength
(Philippians 4:13 NIV).

Even though in the world's eyes I wasn't planned, I was certainly planned in God's eyes, and so are you.

For we are God's handiwork, created in Christ Jesus to do
good works, which God prepared in advance for us to do
(Ephesians 2:10 NIV).

So my question to you is this: What will you do with this one and only life you have been given and chosen to live? I encourage you to lay it all down. Surrender your life, lose it in Christ, and trust that He will find it, and He will show you the person and unstoppable leader He created you to be. You are not an accident or mistake—you have been created for such a time as this, for a special, anointed, and appointed reason.

The question isn't whether you're strong enough, smart enough, or good enough. The question is: Will you trust the One who is all of those things and lives within you? Will you choose to be unstoppable not because of who you are, but because of Whose you are?

It's time to stop watching from the sidelines, and it's time to step out in faith, face your fears, and get back into the game.

An Unstoppable Leader Is... ADAPTABLE

Thriving in Chaos, Not Getting Paralyzed by Change

By Brett Dabe

A man's heart plans his course, but Yahweh directs his steps
(Proverbs 16:9 WEB).

Instead of spending their energy trying to control every detail of their future, unstoppable leaders have learned to dance with uncertainty. They understand that in a world where God is the only constant, adaptability isn't just practical, it's essential for following His leading.

Jesus demonstrated perfect adaptability throughout His ministry. He taught in synagogues and on mountainsides, in homes and by lakeshores. He healed with touch, with words, with mud, and from a distance. He reached out to religious leaders and tax collectors, fishermen and prostitutes. His methods constantly changed, but His message never wavered.

When the religious leaders tried to trap Jesus with questions about taxes and marriage, He adapted His responses to each situation while staying true to His principles. He was like water—flexible enough to fit any container but powerful enough to carve through rock over time.

Paul demonstrated the same principle in his missionary journeys. This guy had a plan to preach in Asia, but the Holy Spirit redirected him to Macedonia. He could have insisted on his original strategy, but instead, he adapted to God's leading and ended up planting churches that changed the world.

When Paul got thrown in prison, he didn't spend his time complaining about his disrupted ministry plans. Instead, he adapted and began writing letters, which became half of the New Testament. Prison became his seminary, and the chains that bound him became his credentials as he encouraged other believers facing persecution.

Adaptable leaders understand the difference between principles and practices. Their core values and relationship with God remain constant, but their methods stay flexible. These leaders are like skilled sailors, adjusting their sails to the changing winds while keeping their eyes on the destination.

Elisha had to learn to be adaptable when Elijah was taken up to heaven. Elisha had been following Elijah's ministry model for years, but when he inherited the mantle, Elisha couldn't just copy his mentor's approach. So he adapted, finding the right approach for *his* calling and the needs of his generation. Elisha performed twice as many miracles as Elijah, but his style was completely different. Whereas Elijah was dramatic and confrontational, Elisha was practical and relational—purifying poisoned stew, making iron float, and helping a poor widow pay her debts. The source of his power was the same, but he used a different approach.

The key to godly adaptability is always staying close to God, so when change comes, you are already positioned to follow Him. When circumstances shift, adaptable leaders don't panic; they pray. They don't immediately react; they seek God's wisdom. And they understand that what looks like a setback just might be God's setup for something better.

Jonah learned this lesson the hard way. When God told him to preach to Nineveh, Jonah ran in the opposite direction. He had his own ideas about how God should handle Israel's enemies. But God used a storm and a great fish to change Jonah's course. Even after Jonah obeyed and preached in Nineveh, he struggled to adapt to God's mercy toward his enemies. But God patiently taught Jonah that His plans are bigger than our prejudices and preferences.

Ezra faced constant challenges that caused him to adapt while rebuilding Jerusalem's spiritual foundation. When he discovered that the people had intermarried with pagans, he could have despaired or become angry. Instead, he wept, prayed, and worked with the people to find solutions that honored God's law while showing compassion to families.

Adaptable leaders are like Ezra—they hold their plans with open hands, ready to adjust when God shows them a better path. They understand that the path to God's promises rarely looks as we expect it to, but it always leads where He intends.

Being adaptable doesn't mean being wishy-washy or having no convictions. Daniel adapted to Babylonian culture without ever compromising his faith. He learned the language, studied their literature, and served in their government, but he didn't eat the food God had forbidden, and he certainly didn't worship other gods. On the contrary, Daniel found ways to honor the one, true God while thriving in a pagan culture. When the king's decree conflicted with his prayer life, Daniel adapted by praying in his room with his windows open, which faced Jerusalem. He knew this might cost him his life, but he was determined. Sometimes adaptability requires creative courage.

Becoming adaptable begins with holding your plans loosely. Make plans— good stewardship requires it. But hold your plans with open hands, prepared to adjust when you encounter an obstacle or God shows you a different path. Pray over your plans and stay sensitive to His leading.

Study how biblical leaders handled unexpected changes. Notice how they maintained their faith and character while adjusting their strategies. Learn from their examples of trusting God's sovereignty even when circumstances didn't seem to make sense.

You can build your flexibility muscles with practice; seek God's wisdom to make minor adaptations. When traffic forces you to take a different route, practice going with the flow and intentionally enjoy the extra time alone with God. When meetings get cancelled, recognize it as an opportunity to tackle something else on your list.

The business world changes rapidly, but God's character always remains the same. Adaptable leaders anchor themselves in His unchanging nature while staying flexible about everything else. Seasons change, markets shift, and opportunities come and go, but God remains faithful through it all.

Don't spend your energy fighting adjustments you can't control. Instead, use that energy to invest in adapting wisely to the new reality God has allowed. Sometimes, He closes doors to open better ones. Sometimes, He allows detours to teach us lessons we couldn't learn on a more direct path.

As you lead, the question isn't whether change will come. It will. The question is whether you'll fight it or flow with it while trusting God's good purposes. Adaptable leaders choose to flow, and God uses their flexibility to accomplish things they never could have imagined.

. . . .

GREG COURY

Since 1979, Greg Coury has been a devoted follower of Jesus Christ, a faith that has shaped his life both personally and professionally. He believes in the power of faith and integrity, using these principles to lead with honesty and compassion.

Greg is an accomplished mortgage consultant with over four decades of experience in the financial industry. His deep industry knowledge has made him a trusted advisor in the mortgage lending field. With a career built on trust, a life grounded in faith, and a love for family and personal growth, Greg continues to inspire those around him. His dedication to excellence, service, and living a purposeful life has made him a respected figure in both his professional and personal circles.

One of Greg's most cherished roles has been that of a single father. He embraced the responsibilities of parenthood with unwavering commitment. His fatherhood is a testament to his deep devotion to family, including his new wife, Debi.

In his spare time, Greg's passions are studying God's Word, watching sports, exercising, playing golf, enjoying fine cigars, cooking, and playing the guitar.

From Broken to Blessed

By Greg Coury

I put a pen to my life experience to encourage anyone who is battling with Satan as he tries to kill, steal, or destroy you or someone you love. Jesus came to give me an abundant life, and He offers that to you as well. Trust Him.

> *"The thief comes only to steal and kill and destroy;*
> *I have come that they may have life, and have it to the full"*
> (John 10:10 NIV).

WHEN LIFE FELL APART

At age 8, my happy family life changed very quickly. My parents got divorced after my father got involved in illegal activities, smuggling marijuana into Texas over the Mexican border, and was sent to prison for 10 years. I was devastated. I didn't get to see or talk to my dad for many years afterwards.

At age 10, I fell in love with Jesus. He became my superhero after watching *King of Kings*, with Jeffrey Hunter playing the role of Jesus. At that time, all my friends' superheroes were Batman, Superman, and Spider-Man. I was so intrigued by Jesus that I even went to a missionary camp for two years during summer school breaks to become a Catholic missionary.

Approximately three years later, my mother married a second time. Her new husband was much younger than she was. He was also strong and athletic, which helped make my brother and me feel safe and secure. He moved us from the city of Detroit to an outlying suburb, where the streets were safe to walk and no one locked their houses or cars. My mother and my new dad found another Catholic church and school for my brother and me to attend.

Church services were very ritualistic, repetitive, boring, and meaningless to me. I had the complete Mass memorized and could recite it to anyone, at any time. However, my favorite part of the Mass was listening to the readings from the Epistles and the Gospels that included the Words spoken by Jesus!

As a high school student, I started to notice the behavior of the priests, my parents, and my fellow students at school. The priests had bingo nights and Vegas nights in the basement of the church, where there was gambling, drinking, and armed police officers at the doors. My parents would leave service early to get out of the parking lot before it got all congested. My fellow students were drinking alcohol and making out with each other in the confessionals, right next to the sanctuary where a huge cross with the body of Jesus hung. And everyone, including myself, damned God and cursed Jesus' name consistently in our everyday language, thinking nothing of it.

THE REVELATION

In April of 1979, I was playing racquetball in a tournament against a born-again Christian. Our matches were always close. Since a racquetball court is a 40x20x20-foot cement room, sounds within echo loudly. Unintentionally, every time I skipped the ball, allowing it to hit the floor before it hit the front wall, I would loudly damn God or curse Jesus' name.

During our second game, my opponent stopped me from serving and asked, "Do you have to damn God or curse Jesus' name every time you skip the ball? I ask because it really offends me and makes me cringe during our matches."

I answered him, saying, "No, I do not have to damn God or curse Jesus' name every time I skip the ball." I sincerely didn't realize I was doing that. I now knew that this man was a born-again Christian—everyone knew that about him. However, he was a really nice guy and I liked him.

After our match, he asked me what I was doing on Sunday morning. I told him it would depend on how much I had to drink on Saturday night. "Why?" I asked.

"Well, I'd like you to come visit my church this Sunday."

I said, "Okay," thinking, *What could it hurt?* I'll pacify the guy. So he gave me the address. After thinking about it, I felt a little uncomfortable about going alone, so I called my closest Catholic friend, Chris Kerr, and asked him to go with me. He obliged.

Sunday came, and we pulled up into the St. Clair Shores Assembly of God Church parking lot. It was packed. We found a seat. The praise and worship music was loud, and everyone stood and sang with their hands and arms raised. We were definitely not used to that. However, you could feel the sincerity in the voices.

The pastor captured my undivided attention as he described Jesus' work on the cross and how Jesus is the only bridge between God and sinful man. He described God's unfathomable love for us through His Son Jesus. At the end of the service, he said that if anyone would like to develop a personal relationship with Jesus and get to know Him intimately, they should come to the altar.

Both my friend Chris and I left our seats and walked up to the altar. My mouth got dry and my hands got sweaty as I walked up with many other people, not knowing what to expect. I knelt, and the pastor laid his hand on my shoulder, praying for me. I had never heard anyone pray like he did. I repeated his words, asking and confessing Jesus as my Savior. I was overwhelmed by the Holy Spirit and wept on the spot.

From that moment forward to this day (46 years later), I have never used God's name in vain or cursed Jesus' name. I became hungry for God's Word and eager to develop my relationship with Him through it. I've been a follower of Jesus since then and have never turned back.

If you declare with your mouth, "Jesus is Lord," and believe in your heart that God raised Him from the dead, you will be saved (Romans 10:9-10 NIV).

LOVE AND HEARTBREAK

At the age of 28, I married the most beautiful woman I had ever seen. She turned heads everywhere we went. She was not a follower of Jesus, however; my spirit battled with my flesh, and my flesh won.

For I know that good itself does not dwell in me, that is, in my sinful nature (Romans 7:18 NIV).

Six months after I married her, she had a nervous breakdown and was diagnosed as bipolar and schizophrenic. I was crushed and scared. She experienced psychotic episodes that were not real and heard voices telling her what and who to fear, including me. I had to have her hospitalized.

I began praying for her constantly, along with my new Christian friends. We would lay hands on her every week, praying without ceasing. Within the next six months, she stopped hearing the voices and no longer hallucinated. Her doctors were astonished. My wife was healed.

*But He was pierced for our transgressions, He was
crushed for our iniquities; the punishment that brought
us peace was on Him, and by His wounds we are healed
(Isaiah 53:5 NIV).*

Being cautious, I waited one year after her healing to start a family. Miraculously, after a whole year, she had not experienced any bipolar or schizophrenic symptoms. She was truly healed! Three months later, she was pregnant. In March 1988, she gave birth to a beautiful boy. I was thrilled! We named him Alexander.

THE DARKNESS RETURNS

After my wife and I brought Alex home, I noticed she was different. Her energy level was low, and she lost the excitement of being a new mother. I would get up in the middle of the night to feed and burp Alex while my wife ignored his crying. I was told that was normal, that many new mothers suffer from postpartum depression. Those words frightened me.

During the next six months, my wife dove into a deep depression—so deep that I feared for Alex's and my safety. She said the voices told her to watch out for me, that I was a threat to her life. I had to have her hospitalized again, and I immediately notified social services.

I decided it was best that Alex and I leave the situation. I filed for divorce and for custody of my son. My divorce was granted, but joint custody was all the court would give me without proof that she was an unfit mother. When I went to pick up Alex, she would hide him in the dryer and tell me he wasn't home. I had to bring the police to her house every week to force her to let us in to get Alex.

I pleaded with the judge to grant me full custody, as my ex-wife repeatedly denied me time with my son. I also continuously prayed for full custody. After five years of attempting to prove that Alex's mother was unfit, the court finally agreed with me. I was granted full custody of my son and took him home with me for good. God answered my prayers!

I took Alex to church regularly. He joined the children's group and was introduced to Jesus. At the age of 6, he was water baptized. I enrolled him in swimming, hockey, and art classes—he loved to draw, and I got him a pager and a house key. We were both happy. I took him to visit his mother only when another adult was there to supervise.

When Alex was in high school, unbeknownst to me, he became intimidated by some rich kids in his class who ridiculed him about his shoes, car, and the home we lived in. So he started a business selling Xanax to his friends and their parents. His business grew quickly. He had a source in the medical field who was supplying him and taking a cut.

One day after school, Alex called to tell me that someone had broken into our home and stolen the safe from his room. Then, I started receiving early morning calls from business owners in the surrounding area telling me to come and get my son, as he was wandering around the streets and parking lots. Alex had started taking the drugs he was selling. I was devastated. He assured me he was okay and was not addicted.

Then I received a call from the local police department telling me my son had been arrested and was awaiting a court date. I drove around to ten different police departments trying to find my son, but not one department would admit if they had him.

The next time I saw Alex was in a courtroom. They brought him into the room in an orange jumpsuit, shackled and chained at his hands and feet; he had been severely beaten. A deep pain ran through my mind and body. I found out that one of Alex's customers set him up in a sting operation, and four undercover detectives had beaten and tased him.

After his hearing, I posted bond and took Alex home. While he was there detoxing, out of nowhere, he would have a seizure, flopping around the living room uncontrollably. A few times, I called an ambulance and rode in the back with him to the nearest hospital. Those were terrifying experiences.

THE BREAKING POINT

Months later, on a cloudy, rainy Saturday morning, I received a call from our local police telling me to come get my son. They said he had been involved in a very serious car accident and was in the back of their squad car. When I arrived, I saw that Alex was so numb and relaxed that he was uninjured despite the accident. He had been driving 45 mph when, without braking, he ran into a car stopped at a red light.

I took him to the hospital for an examination. They kept Alex for several days, continuously running different tests on him. During my daily visits, I always laid hands on Alex, prayed for him, and encouraged him that he would be going home soon.

Hearing me pray, one of the nurses came up to me and said, "Mr. Coury, with all due respect, sir, none of the patients on this floor ever go home, sir."

I looked at her and said, "Well, my son is going to be the first one to!"

I will not die but live, and will proclaim what the Lord has done (Psalm 118:17 NIV).

I brought my son home two days later. At the hearing for the ticket, Alex's license was restricted to driving only to work, and even then, he had to submit to a breathalyzer test. He also had to go to counseling for a year, was put on probation, and was randomly called for urine testing.

This was the final straw for me. My nerves and patience were exhausted. My money was too! My faith was not, though.

THE HARDEST DECISION OF MY LIFE

I needed some tools to deal with this problem. I searched around and learned about Families Anonymous, a 12-step program giving the loved ones of addicts the tools required to deal with this disease; this helped me understand and cope with my son's addiction. Many of the family members involved in this program had lost their children to overdosing.

I decided it was time for me to step out of the way and let God deal with Alex, and let Alex deal with God. So I told Alex he had 45 days to find a place to live. I took an 8 ½ x 11 piece of paper and, with a black magic marker, wrote the number 45 on it, circled the number, and taped the paper to the cupboard where we kept our drinking glasses. Every day, I took down the piece of paper and put up a new one: 44 days. 43 days. 42 days. And so on.

As the days counted down, I would ask Alex if he had found a place to live yet. He would answer no, and that I was making him nervous.

Then, on Friday, July 2, 2010, I woke Alex up and told him that the day had come; the hour had arrived; my home was no longer his home. "Please get up and shower. This gym bag is for you to pack your clothes. These two police officers are here to protect me and these two other gentlemen while they empty everything in your room into the U-Haul truck you see outside. Here is the key to the storage unit I rented for your belongings. This other gentleman here is a locksmith who will now change the locks on the doors."

That was the hardest thing I had ever chosen to do as a parent. But I did it in faith, trusting God that He would save Alex. It was a very BIG step of faith.

When I am afraid, I put my trust in you. In God,
whose word I praise—in God I trust and am not afraid
(Psalm 56:3-4) NIV).

Trust in the Lord with all your heart and lean not on your understanding; in all your ways submit to him, and he will make your paths straight (Proverbs 3:5-6 NIV).

A couple of hours later, everyone was gone: Alex, the U-Haul truck, the mover, the locksmith, and the two undercover police officers. I was relieved and scared at the same time. A week later, Alex left a suicide note on my door. Now all I had was my faith. I let go and let God.

GOD'S MIRACLE UNFOLDS

Alex ended up in jail, then was transferred to a rehab facility. He completed the rehab training and graduated with honors, giving a speech to the other patients on his way out, which they framed for us to take with us. Alex then attended my Families Anonymous meeting with me, where he spoke to all of the families there coping with loved ones with addiction. My emotions were too complex to contain while listening to him. The members there were awestruck.

Alex was then awarded his full driving privileges back from the Secretary of State. By the grace of God, Alex was able to secure a lease on an apartment despite having a low credit score and only two weeks on the job. He is still in that apartment today! And after 10 years of living clean, the felony on his record was expunged. My son was spared, saved, and healed by the grace of God. I witnessed a miracle!

Alex taught himself to cut hair by taking a self-study course, and then he obtained his barber license by passing the state exam on his first attempt. Now, he's using his artistic gift from God to earn a clean living. He runs his own barber shop—a boutique shop that stands out from average shops. And it is growing every year.

In August of 2023, Alex married the woman God had saved for him.

Amanda is the kind of woman Alex always dreamed of marrying. They were both 35 years old, never married, and had no children out of wedlock. They are expecting their first child in December 2025—my first grandchild, a baby girl they plan to name Elianna, which means, "God answered." I'm thrilled!

When I visit Alex and Amanda, they love to break open God's Word with me and soak up the wisdom of the Scriptures. What a blessing!

I said at the beginning that Jesus came to give us life to the full; He has certainly done that for me. From the beginning of my brokenness at age 8, when my dad went to prison, until now, God has never left my side despite many trials. I am indeed blessed. If you are a child of God, you are blessed, too. If you've not yet said yes to a relationship with Him, now is the perfect moment.

Nick Reyes

Nick Reyes, born and raised in Cleveland, Ohio, is a proud husband and father of three. As the Broker/Owner of Acclaimed Realty, Nick leads with integrity, passion, and a deep commitment to elevating the standard of service in the real estate industry. His mission extends beyond buying and selling homes—he is devoted to mentoring agents and creating a positive impact within the industry by fostering a culture of Excellence, Integrity, and Communication.

With a natural passion for helping people, Nick has built a career rooted in trust, relationships, and a genuine desire to serve. His faith and family are at the core of everything he does, shaping both his leadership and approach to business.

Outside of real estate, Nick enjoys working on cars, lifting weights, and spending quality time with his wife and children. Whether he's in the garage or the office, Nick is driven by the opportunity to make a difference and leave a lasting legacy in both his community and his profession.

Discovering Whose You Are

By Nick Reyes

When someone asked if I wanted to share my story, I had to take a moment to think, *What is my story?* It's remarkable how easily we can forget how God is at work in our lives. As I sat and thought about all the experiences I've been through, a beautiful testimony began to unfold. I'm grateful I have the opportunity to share it with so many people, as I know we all struggle with many of the same things.

As a young man, I didn't understand my identity. *Who is Nicholas Angel Reyes, and what am I supposed to do with my life?* This pressure broke me and turned me into a person I never imagined I could be. But God.

I grew up in inner city Cleveland, Ohio. I'm the oldest of three brothers. My parents divorced when we were young. We spent most of our time with our father and would see our mother on weekends.

My mom has such a beautiful heart. She tried everything she could to better her life for us. Today, she has a degree in nursing and continues her career in the medical field. She worked hard and started from the bottom to achieve her current position. I'm incredibly proud of her.

My dad worked in a steel factory for many years. He was a hard worker and taught us early on the importance of a strong work ethic. He would tell us to complete a chore or task, saying, "Take pride in what you are doing! Do it right or don't do it at all!" Whether I was washing dishes, mopping the floor, or cleaning my room, I always strived to make it perfect. My dad is the most important man in my life, and I have always wanted to make him happy.

I was academically successful—an A/B student from first grade through the last day I attended school. I excelled in "gifted classes," and took pride in everything I put my hands to.

> Whatever you do, work at it with all your heart,
> as working for the Lord, not for human masters
> (Colossians 3:23 NIV).

Even before I knew God personally, He was already shaping my character through my father's teachings.

THE UNRAVELING

My life became overly complicated during high school, as I attended five different schools in three and a half years. I started ninth grade living with my dad, and then we moved multiple times. I ended up in Florida for 10th grade, but I didn't enjoy it at all. I decided to have a tough conversation with my dad and told him I wanted to move back to Ohio and live with my mom.

When my mom went to enroll me in the new school, they said I was behind on the credits needed to complete high school on time and suggested a vocational school. I'd always had a passion for cars and wanted to join the automotive program, but it was full. I wasn't happy, but I chose to pursue a career in culinary arts.

I began to excel in the culinary arts program and developed a passion for cooking. Chef O, who taught the program, recognized my potential and began to push me to improve, becoming another important man in my life. I started competing with my classmates in culinary competitions; we did so well that we had an article published about us. Chef O was setting up interviews for me with well-known chefs in the area; he believed the sky was the limit for me.

Twelfth grade started, bringing with it many problems. Teachers and counselors began asking, "Where are you going to college?" "What career are you going to pursue?" Then I started hearing these questions from my friends. Then from my parents. Then from my brother. I had no clue what the answers to these questions were. I was simply enjoying where my life was for a 12th grader. I had a job, a car, and a girlfriend; I was doing well in school, and was at the top of my culinary program.

When I didn't know the answers to the questions about my future, however, I began to question if what I was doing was the right thing. *Am I where I'm supposed to be?* Is this the person I was meant to become? I didn't like the fact that I didn't have an answer, and I began smoking marijuana—a lot. I wanted to numb my mind to those thoughts and questions.

I had a friend in the culinary arts program who worked at the same restaurant I did, and we made it our mission to stay high all the time: during school, at work, on weekends, and anytime in between. I just could not handle the pressure and wanted to do anything I could to forget about it and not think about it.

The path I was on led me to places I never imagined I would be. I developed an addiction to a dangerous drug, and it became my identity. All I wanted to do was get more, and I would do whatever it took to make that happen. As with most addictions, my income could not support it. I started to run out of money, and I began to steal from my mother. I started missing work, skipping classes, and hanging out in parts of town that I had no business being in. Looking back, I'm surprised I even made it out of those parts of town alive.

Even though I was going on this path of self-destruction, I was still on track to graduate high school on time. Then, about three months before graduation,

I hit rock bottom. An incident occurred at school that resulted in a 10-day suspension, with a recommendation for expulsion pending a hearing with the superintendent. I lost my after-school job, and since I could not pay the monthly car payment, my mom took it over.

My stepdad accompanied me to the superintendent's hearing and pleaded that I was a good kid who had just made some bad decisions. The superintendent was impressed with the number of violations listed in this recommendation for expulsion. In fact, she was so impressed that she gave me a 365-day expulsion.

A few days later, my mom noticed the missing money from her accounts, and she confronted me. She was shocked that I would do anything like this, and, like any mother, she had serious concerns about me and what I was really doing. She had no idea about the dark life I was living in secret. I was so ashamed that I couldn't even look her in the face, so I left.

THE WILDERNESS

Within a matter of two weeks, I was expelled from school, lost my job, lost my car, lost my girlfriend, and was living on the streets at 17 years old. I bounced around from house to house. Eventually, I found a job detailing cars. The owner of the business had a home that he rented. All the guys living in the house also worked for him, but I was glad to have somewhere to go every night. I made enough money to cover the rent and buy groceries...it stunk.

After a few months of living like that, I called my dad in Florida and told him I needed to come back and start over. I planned to pick up my check and head straight to the airport. When my boss handed me my check, I opened it and saw that the upcoming rent had already been deducted. I was furious and confronted him immediately. He explained, "You didn't give me a 30-day notice. That's not how this works. Welcome to the real world!" I walked out of there and cried like a baby! My dad graciously covered the plane ticket and told me to get to the airport right away.

The Lord is close to the brokenhearted and saves those who are crushed in spirit (Psalm 34:18 NIV). Though I didn't know it then, God was near to me even in my darkest hour.

From the age of 17 to 29, I suffered an identity crisis. I had many jobs and tried different things to figure out who I was and what career to pursue. I never stayed at a job longer than two years. I was doing better, but I was a lost kid trying to find my way in this world.

Often, I would be driving on the highway and hear a voice telling me to drive off the bridge coming up. Or I would be walking somewhere high up, and the voice would say, "Just jump. It would be easier." I would tell it to SHUT UP! It wasn't my voice; I had no idea why this was happening to me.

Some nights, I would wake up paralyzed, like something was sitting on top of me. I would get this feeling of just evil around me.

These voices and these nights went on for years. I kept fighting them off. I just had no idea why this was happening to me. I later discerned that the enemy was trying to destroy me before I could discover my true identity in God.

> Be alert and of sober mind. Your enemy the devil prowls
> around like a roaring lion looking for someone to devour
> (1 Peter 5:8 NIV).

DIVINE FREEDOM

At 29 years old, I had my first son. My girlfriend and I were filled with joy. He was born healthy, and we were out of the hospital in three days. We were ready for this! Or so I thought...

On our first day at home, I began to suffer from extreme anxiety attacks to the point where I could not move, think, or talk. I had no idea what was going on. I called my dad and asked him, "Is this normal? Did you go through this when I was born?"

His response shocked me. He said, "Son, you just need to pray."

I laughed and replied, "Dad, I need some real advice!" My dad prayed for me right there, and just like that, the anxiety was gone! I was shocked and curious at the same time. I thought to myself, *Maybe there is something to this Jesus guy.*

I spoke with my girlfriend, and we started attending church to learn more. We began to study the Bible with another couple and the pastors from the church we were attending. I learned a great deal about myself in the coming months and started making some substantial changes in the way I lived my life.

The first thing I needed to do was propose to Nela, my girlfriend. We had a son and were living together, and we both felt it just wasn't right. We invited our family over for dinner one night and announced that I was going to move out. They all looked at us like we were nuts! But we knew that the way we were living wasn't right, and we just wanted to do the right thing for God.

On September 28th, 2018, Nela and I were baptized. When I emerged from that water, I felt new life taking over my body. It was amazing; I felt the power of God now living inside of me. The next weekend, Nela and I were driving past a local retail store and had the idea to go in and tell someone about Jesus. We were so nervous, but we did it. We were on fire for God and wanted to do everything we could to share His message with everyone.

Therefore, if anyone is in Christ, the new creation has come: The old has gone, the new is here! (2 Corinthians 5:17 NIV). This verse became my reality that day. I was literally a new person!

On October 20th, 2018, Nela and I got married. I moved back in, and life was finally moving in a positive direction. The more I sought God and worked on my relationship with Him, the more I came to understand who He is and who I am.

In 2021, He called me to begin a journey working for myself. It was a battle my wife and I prayed through for months. I felt uneasy about leaving a paycheck every week without knowing when or how I would pay the light bill. One morning, I was crying out to God, and I heard Him say to me, "Just trust Me."

I immediately told Nela what happened. Her response was, "If God said it, then you need to give them your resignation notice today!"

April 1st, 2022, was my last day, and God showed me that I could indeed trust Him. In the real estate industry, many people wash out after 2-3 years. In fact, I was told not to expect to make any money for the first two years... but my God had other plans for me. I began to grow in ways I never imagined. There were times I wasn't sure how the bills would get paid, but He always came through. We have been truly blessed.

I know God is shaping me into the man He created me to be. Every day, I lean on Him more. I'm grateful for how many people God has placed in my path who needed to hear His Word, needed prayer, or just needed someone to listen. I began to seek God in everything I did and said; that is when I began to experience true freedom!

SHARING GOD'S LOVE

And whatever you do, whether in word or deed, do it all in the name of the Lord Jesus, giving thanks to God the Father through him (Colossians 3:17 NIV).

It doesn't matter what career we choose or which college we go to. The only thing that matters is that we bring God with us everywhere we go. He calls us to be the light of the world. And THAT is what truly matters.

*"You are the light of the world. A town built on a hill cannot
be hidden. ... In the same way, let your light shine before
others, that they may see your good deeds and glorify
your Father in heaven"* (Matthew 5:14, 16 NIV).

In August of 2024, I had the requirements to test for a Real Estate Broker's License. I submitted the application, took the exam, and today I am a licensed Broker in the state of Ohio. God continues to stretch my imagination and bless everything I put my hands on. I'm now opening my own Real Estate Brokerage. Many people in the industry ask me what the key to my early and fast success is. I always point them back to God. Some people don't understand that answer, so I begin to pour my heart out in hopes they will see His love in me.

Following and trusting God over the past few years has created in me a burning desire to share His love with everyone I can. I have made it my life's mission to tell the world how amazing my Father is. After over a decade of suffering through an identity crisis, today I know exactly who I am: A CHILD OF GOD CREATED TO BUILD HIS KINGDOM! NOTHING CAN STOP ME!

*"For I know the plans I have for you," declares the Lord,
"plans to prosper you and not to harm you, to give you
hope and a future"* (Jeremiah 29:11 NIV).

God had a plan for my life even when I was at my lowest point, stealing from my mother and living on the streets. He saw past my failures to the man He created me to be.

The identity crisis that tormented me for over a decade wasn't just about career choices or college decisions. It was about not knowing who I was.

Unstoppable Leaders: Pressing Forward with Power

Once I discovered that I belong to God—that I'm His beloved son with a divine purpose—every other question found its answer. The voices that once whispered death and destruction have been silenced by the voice of my heavenly Father declaring His love over me.

To every man reading this who feels lost, confused, or overwhelmed by the pressure to have it all figured out, hear me clearly: Your identity isn't found in your job title, education, relationships, or achievements. Your identity is found in Whose you are. You are a child of the Most High God, created with purpose, and destined for greatness in His kingdom.

Don't let the enemy convince you that your past disqualifies you from your future. God specializes in turning our messes into messages, our trials into testimonies. The very things that brought me shame—addiction, theft, expulsion, homelessness—God has transformed into platforms to reach others who are walking the same dark paths I once traveled.

Whether you're 17 and living on the streets, 29 and battling anxiety, or feeling lost and purposeless at any age, know this: God is not finished with your story. He's the author of comeback stories, the specialist in impossible transformations, and the God who makes all things new.

True unstoppable leadership does not begin with knowing what you want to do; it begins with knowing Whose you are. When you discover your identity as a child of God, every other aspect of life falls into divine alignment, and nothing—absolutely nothing—can stop the plans He has for your life.

I love you all, and I pray that my testimony encourages you to seek the One who has the answers to every question your heart is asking. He's waiting for you with open arms, ready to transform your identity crisis into your greatest victory.

AN UNSTOPPABLE LEADER IS...
AUTHENTIC

Leading with Genuine Purpose
Instead of Fabricated Perfection

By Brett Dabe

*A simple man believes everything, but the
prudent man carefully considers his ways*
(Proverbs 14:15 WEB).

In a world obsessed with image and reputation, the most powerful leaders I know are the ones who dare to be real. They understand that people don't follow perfect leaders; they follow authentic ones.

King David gives us a great example of authentic leadership. This guy didn't try to hide his struggles or pretend he had it all together. Read the Psalms—they're full of raw, honest emotions. David wrote about feeling abandoned by God, being afraid of his enemies, and struggling with guilt over his mistakes.

But here's what made David "a man after God's own heart" (from Acts 13:22): he was genuine about his relationship with God. When David finally came to grips with the sin he committed with Bathsheba, he cried out to God, writing Psalm 51: *Have mercy on me, God, according to your loving kindness...Against you, and you only, I have sinned* (Psalm 51:1,4 WEB).

That's authentic leadership—owning your failures and working to make them right.

Barnabas shows us what authentic encouragement looks like. This guy's real name was Joseph, but the apostles nicknamed him Barnabas, which means "son of encouragement." He didn't just say nice things to make people feel better. He saw potential in people that others missed and invested in their development.

When everyone was afraid of the newly converted Paul, Barnabas vouched for him. When John Mark quit during their first missionary journey and Paul refused to give him a second chance, Barnabas took Mark under his wing. Barnabas was authentic about seeing the best in people, even when they'd failed.

Often, men think they need to project an image of having everything figured out. They wear masks at work, at church, even at home. They believe that showing weakness will undermine their authority, but the opposite is true. People connect with leaders who are real, not perfect.

The apostle Paul took this approach throughout his ministry. He could have impressed people with his credentials: educated under the best teachers, a former Pharisee, and a Roman citizen. Instead, Paul called himself the chief of sinners (1 Timothy 1:15) and shared openly about his "thorn in the flesh" (2 Corinthians 12:7-10).

Paul didn't let his past mistakes disqualify him from leadership. He used them to demonstrate God's grace, writing, *By the grace of God I am what I am* (1 Corinthians 15:10 WEB). His transparency about his weaknesses made his message about God's strength more, not less, powerful.

Jacob had to wrestle with God all night before he received a new name and destiny. That wrestling match left him with a permanent limp, but it also gave him the blessing he'd been seeking his whole life. Sometimes God has to break us before He can use us authentically.

Authentic leadership starts with knowing who you are, including your strengths and weaknesses. Jacob was a schemer and deceiver for most of his life. But when he finally wrestled with God and surrendered, he became Israel, the father of God's chosen people.

Thomas gets a bad reputation for doubting Jesus' resurrection, but his skepticism was authentic. When the other disciples told him they'd seen Jesus alive, Thomas said, *"Unless I see in his hands the print of the nails, put my finger into the print of the nails, and put my hand into his side, I will not believe"* (John 20:25 WEB).

When Jesus appeared to Thomas and invited him to touch His wounds, Thomas responded with one of the most powerful declarations of faith in the gospels: *"My Lord and my God!"* (John 20:28 WEB). Thomas's authentic doubt led to authentic faith.

Authentic leaders don't pretend to have all the answers. When Joshua was taking over from Moses, God didn't tell him to act confidently; He told him to be strong and courageous. There's a difference. Strength comes from knowing God is with you, not from pretending you're not afraid.

Stephen demonstrated authentic courage when he stood before the religious leaders who were about to stone him. He didn't try to save his life by softening his message. He spoke truth with love, even knowing it would cost him everything. His authentic witness converted a persecutor named Saul, who became the apostle Paul.

Being authentic doesn't mean oversharing or making every conversation about your problems. Authentic leadership is strategic vulnerability, sharing your genuine self in ways that serve your mission and help others, not just to meet your own emotional needs. It means admitting when you don't know something instead of bluffing your way through, apologizing when you make mistakes instead of deflecting blame, and asking for help when you need it instead of pretending you can handle everything alone.

Judah shows us what authentic repentance looks like. When his father Jacob asked him to guarantee Benjamin's safety on their trip to Egypt, Judah didn't just make empty promises. He said, *"I myself will guarantee his safety; you can hold me personally responsible for him"* (Genesis 43:9 NIV).

This was the same Judah who had suggested selling his brother Joseph into slavery years earlier. But Judah had learned from his mistakes. His authentic change of heart positioned him to become the leader of his brothers, the Israelites, and an ancestor of the Messiah.

The world is hungry for authentic leadership. People are tired of leaders who say one thing and do another, who present perfect images while their personal lives are falling apart. They want leaders they can trust. Not because those leaders are perfect, but because they're genuine.

Your authenticity permits others to be real, too. When you're honest about your struggles, others feel safe sharing theirs. When you admit your mistakes, you foster an environment where others don't need to hide their mistakes, but can learn from them.

The choice is clear: you can spend your energy trying to maintain a perfect image, or you can invest that energy in becoming the leader God designed you to be. Authentic leaders choose truth over image, substance over style, and genuine growth over fake perfection.

The world doesn't need another leader who acts as if he is perfect. We need authentic leaders who point to our perfect God.

George Mercado

George "Child" Mercado is a gentleman who wears his heart on his sleeve. He is an artist, adventurer, and designer who specializes in themed decor and urban street art. His art pieces are showcased in various venues, homes, and within the interior and exteriors of established businesses.

George's passion for creation is second to his love for God and family. He is a devoted follower of Christ, husband, and father who shares the Word of God every chance he can.

George strongly believes that every success story begins with risks and failures, and that faking it before you make it is never an option. He believes that every experience, whether good or bad, is part of the process of spiritual growth, and unless you are willing to take leaps of faith, you will never truly know how far you can fly.

George can be contacted via Georgemercado.com, Graphicola.com, or Child357.com

THE SEARCH FOR SERENITY

By George Mercado

I look to the past and the life I lived. I recall my mistakes, regrets, and moments that haunt me. I was nothing more than a simple man trying to be relevant in a world that often portrayed men as irrelevant. A knight in shining armor in a world where no castles existed, no dragons needed to be slayed, and no maidens were to be rescued.

I felt that nothing I contributed was good enough, and no one saw my value. I, like many men, travelled on a path of brokenness. Every day felt as if the darkness was choking me, its fingers gripping my throat, as it whispered in my ear. I was consumed by it, for it transformed the man I was within. Like a wounded beast that lashed out at everyone and everything, the emotional pain I carried was unbearable.

This, my friends, is a state of mind that no person should ever experience. It is a state of loneliness, where you ponder whether you want to live or die. A season where your emotions balance on a rusted razor's edge; where one step in either direction would cause you to lose your soul or save it.

The decades of disappointment became the catalyst that isolated me within the cage of my mind. Oh, I recall the nights of loneliness, and how I would scream and cry. I begged the Lord for someone to set me free. But no one did; no one ever came. Then, one day, I chose to escape and found healing within the wilderness. Nature became my refuge, my sacred place, my one-on-one time with God.

THE GREAT ESCAPE

Early one morning, after a restless night of anguish, I called my best friend, Fahad Asmat, and spoke with him about leaving on a week-long adventure to hike in Colorado and Utah. Fahad, who lives in Pakistan, agreed to accompany me. Just two best friends from worlds apart, braving the wilderness, in search of inner peace. Little did we know that this trip would be different, that what we sought, we would find.

I was excited about this trip, as it took my mind off my problems. I finally found something to be happy about. But then death came knocking, and with it came an unexpected loss. I lost a friend, a protégé, a young lady named Alisa. When I met her, she was a lost, rebellious soul like me, always getting into trouble. I took her under my wing and mentored her for almost a decade. In turn, she evolved from being a crazy girl into an educated mother and powerful woman. Her death was beyond unexpected; she was not supposed to die before me. Even though we had never met in person, I mourned this wonderful soul, who had previously won a battle with cancer. I repeat, she was not supposed to die; she had her whole life in front of her.

Two days after the news of her death, Fahad called and informed me that we had to reschedule our trip. The United Kingdom had instilled a travel ban on citizens from Eastern Asia, due to the lingering COVID-19 scare. We would have to push our travel arrangements back another week, which was a thorn in our sides.

I contacted James Bennett in Colorado, a close friend, adventurer, and owner of Lost Creek Tattoo. James informed me he was unavailable to host us that weekend, but would arrange an Airbnb for us and provide a vehicle. James is a great guy who we are blessed to call a friend.

ALMOST THERE!

The day of our trip arrived, I grabbed my bags, and rushed out the door. En route to the airport, my wife and I experienced a delay, which caused me to miss my flight. I called Fahad, who was wondering why I wasn't on the flight with him. I told him I would meet him in Colorado; little did we expect it to be eight hours later.

When I finally arrived in Colorado, we had already lost half the day and barely made it to the Airbnb that night. Thankfully, James arranged for his friend Josh to pick us up and drop us off. The following morning, after a restless night, we prepared ourselves to hit the road.

Fahad sat in the driver's seat of James's truck and asked me for a destination. I said Utah! However, I did not want to drive. I said I just wanted to merely enjoy the scenery and collect my thoughts. Fahad smiled and said, "Sit back and relax, buddy, I got you!" He never pressed me once on what I was going through. He knew that in due time I would tell him.

On the drive, we discussed God and family, and we reminisced about trips we had taken. I couldn't help but think to myself, *Here is my brother, a man who lives half a world away, but loves me like his own.* This was someone I trusted with my family, business, and life. I am ever so grateful to experience life with him.

I recall closing my eyes and pondering all the people I loved and lost, those who lost their lives at such an early stage. Many of my friends couldn't understand why I would leave my family to hike these desolate terrains. Yet, my response to them was clear as day: I needed to find my burning bush; I needed to walk the desert to face my demons. Just as Jesus had walked the desert, I explained to them that this was my spiritual journey to discover if God was listening. I needed validation; I needed to know if God was truly with me.

MOAB

We arrived in Moab at 5:00 p.m. The weather was brisk, the temperature in the high 60s. Heavy wind gusts were blowing, and an eerie red hue shrouded the area. Dust storms and dirt devils danced frantically about, affecting our visibility.

Fahad and I exited the vehicle and looked at the trail before us. He said to me, "George, I think it is too late in the day for us to make this hike; the conditions are inadequate, and we do not have enough water. I do not think we will return before dark; we have no flashlights."

I looked at him and emphasized that we had to do this hike, we had to reach the arch. This hike represented everything we'd been through up to this point. This was no longer a mere hike, but a battle waging in my heart and head. God was calling me, even though the darkness wanted me to turn around, run away, and give up. God had other plans; he wanted me to trust Him and push on. The words "Push on and have no fear for I am with you," echoed in the farthest reaches of my mind.

Seeing how much this meant to me, Fahad grabbed his backpack and the last water bottle we had. He said, "Let's go," as we hiked the unfamiliar path forward through barren lands and rocky trails. A sense of excitement gave us purpose as we hiked, mindful of every step we took. The beauty we encountered was hypnotic, as we found ourselves in awe. We had come so far, we had lost so much, yet there we were.

As we hiked, the darkness whispered to be fearful, to turn back; that nothing good would come from this. "Go back, do it another day." Excuses filled my head. However, we were at the point of no return; we could not turn around, for my soul was at stake. In my heart, I knew that God would give me a sign; I felt Him here.

As we proceeded forward, the trail quickly transformed from a low-terrain hike to an upward forty-five-degree ascension. We found that the water in our bottle was diminishing quickly as we continued the hike upwards. What started off as an enjoyable hike quickly became a strenuous battle of mind, body, and spirit. A war of will that reached an elevation of 4,606 feet (1,404 meters).

Unprepared, I found that the combined altitude and pressure made it difficult to grasp my breath. I became winded, and every step became unmanageable. I had to stop on the trail numerous times to rest and catch my breath; I was not a spring chicken anymore.

What was I thinking? I thought to myself as fear sank in and doubtful questions flooded my mind. What if I have a heart attack here? Who would rescue me? Who would administer life-saving medical assistance? I would never see my family again. I felt my blood pressure building as anxiety got the best of me.

I stopped and told Fahad to proceed without me, to go reach the top and take photographs, as I could go no further. I had sadly given in to the fear and the doubts created by the darkness; I was determined to give up. Fahad, in turn, pleaded with me that we should turn back, but I told him he had to go on without me. He needed to experience the arch as it was a once-in-a-lifetime opportunity in these conditions. He refused to leave my side, even to the point of arguing. But I became agitated and told him to go on and that I would wait for him where I was. Not wanting to upset me, Fahad reluctantly agreed and took the remaining water with him as I sat back and rested upon a boulder.

ALONE ON THE PATH

So many thoughts ran through my head, so many reasons for me to quit. But a part of me wasn't through fighting; I found myself standing up, hiking for a few yards, then resting again. I did this numerous times over, only managing to traverse a few hundred feet before becoming winded again. Finally, when all hope was lost and I could go no further. I found myself sobbing like a child uncontrollably. I felt like a loser, like a failure, like everything I had gone through was all in vain. At that moment, a young couple hiked past me and tried to encourage me to get up, but I declined any assistance.

As I sat there sobbing alone, I noticed a beautiful, fair-skinned, red-haired woman descending the path toward me. She stopped in front of me and asked me what I was doing. So unashamed of my weakness and in tears, I told her that I could not proceed forward as much as I wanted to.

She smiled and firmly responded with a strong Irish accent, "Get off your ass; you are only a few hundred yards away from the top. I do not know what you are going through, nor where you have been. But, you are here for a reason, so get off your ass and move forward."

I gave her so many excuses, I was tired, parched, had no water, and didn't have the strength to go on. She replied, "The Lord will provide; He always provides." Then, she smiled, reached out, and softly rested her hand on mine before walking away. I lowered my head, wiped my tears, and looked up, but she was gone. I could see down the trail, but she was not there. Bewildered, I pondered to myself, was she real, or was she an angel? She, alas, was nowhere to be seen.

Nevertheless, her words and touch were the spark I needed. I stood up and started the ascent again. *A few hundred yards,* I thought to myself, *I got this.* But in truth, each step felt like I had concrete shoes; I felt as if I couldn't lift my feet. The darkness raged with every step I took. Yet, I continued onward up the steep incline until I reached a small cliff passage. The scene reminded me of Moses and the Ten Commandments. My back was against the wall as I stared at the heavens, my eyes ignoring the sheer drop to the abyss below.

That is when I heard the echoes of distant voices nearby. I quickly rose off the wall, hiked up the passage, and around a turn. There before me was the summit, as my eyes grew wide and my heart rejoiced. *I made it. I actually made it,* I thought to myself. Fahad was there along with the young couple whom I met on the trail. They cheered and yelled out happily, "You made it!"

As I stood there, I felt disappointed by the view; it was not what I expected. There was no burning bush, no sign from God, nothing that had me in awe. Perhaps I expected too much; maybe I should have stayed home. I could feel the darkness laughing from within as I cried out silently to God.

Then, in that instance, I felt the distinctive soft touch of a woman's hand on my right cheek. I turned my head quickly to see who was there, but there was no one in view. Instead, the clouds in the heavens above me split open vertically, as a solid ray of light came down and illuminated the arch in a bright glow.

It was like a scene from a movie, as the glow blanketed the landscape in a surreal reddish hue. I was in awe at what I had experienced. Tears streamed down my cheeks as I pulled out my camera to snap a photo. *Wow,* I thought, *I found my burning bush.* The drizzling rain had stopped, the stormy weather faded, and all was silently at peace. I knew at that moment that God was ever present. That no other condition could reproduce this beautiful moment.

As I stared into the heavens, I heard the voice of the young couple calling me over to see the view. I jogged over, no longer out of breath or tired, as I proceeded to climb a perch behind them. I stared at the glowing arch before me and smiled. The young man turned to me and said, "Turn around, George, look behind you, this is what we came for." As I turned to see what he was referring to, my eyes swelled up in tears, for before me formed a double rainbow.

Here was my sign, the Lord heard my cries. My whole body was overcome by a sense of peace and happiness. No pain, no despair, no darkness, in that instant, I was being embraced by God. Fahad came behind me and put his hand on my shoulder. I was weeping as I looked at him and said, "You may think I am crazy, brother, but God spoke to me."

"What did God say?" Fahad asked.

I replied, "God said, 'No matter what you go through in life, no matter the obstacles and heartaches you endure, if you go the extra distance, I will show you beauty like you have never seen before.'"

Fahad smiled at me, hugged me, and said, "Amen, brother!"

With that, dusk arrived, as we prepared for our descent. Feeling parched and thirsty, I asked Fahad for the bottle of water. He told me that he had left it with a young lady with red flowing hair, as he motioned to where she was sitting.

I walked over, our empty bottle wasn't there; instead, I found an unopened filled water bottle. "The Lord will provide," echoed in my head. This is what the red-headed girl said to me. "The Lord will provide". That night, we descended the mountain under a moonlit glow, no fear in our hearts, for the darkness was no more. On that day, God granted me the serenity I had sought after and desperately yearned for.

THE UNSTOPPABLE LEADER EMERGES

That experience changed everything for me. The depression that had held me captive for so long lost its grip, the darkness lost its voice, and the will to die had no power over me. God had been with me all along, even when I felt alone. I was a new man; I was no longer broken. I had found that what I was searching for was not just serenity, but the unshakeable knowledge that God sees us, hears us, and will never abandon us.

Now, when I encounter men who are struggling as I once did, I share my story. I tell them that their pain is real and their feelings are valid; their story doesn't end in that dark place. I've learned that sometimes the most powerful thing a leader can do is show others the scars of wars waged and say, "I've been where you are, and there's a way through."

The woman with the red hair, whether she was an angel or simply God's instrument, delivered exactly the message I needed to hear. Her words, "The Lord will provide," proved prophetic in ways I couldn't have imagined. I learned that true leadership isn't about being strong all the time. It's about being willing to take the next step even when you feel weak, broken, and defeated. It's about refusing to quit when everything in you wants to give up.

I say to those who are reading this: Do not quit, do not give up, and do not let the whispers of the darkness make you falter. God loves you and believes in you; He is waiting to meet you halfway. Your burning bush moment is waiting, your double rainbow is coming. You just have to be willing to take that next step in faith, even when you can't see the path ahead.

The serenity we found on that mountain wasn't just for us; the story was meant to be shared. Every man who feels irrelevant, every person who believes they're alone, needs to know that God has a purpose for them. You just need to be willing to believe, surrender, and fully commit to following Him.

STANLEY VANHORN

Stanley VanHorn is from Port Orange, Florida, and is a proud father of four and grandfather of nine. Though he never imagined he would become an author, his recent experiences have shown him that with God, nothing is impossible!

After working two jobs for most of his life—40 years as a city worker and 36 years as a Walmart employee—Stanley is now retired and focuses on sharing his story and doing as much good as he can to help others. He attended a Band of Brothers bootcamp, where he was inspired to get more involved in ministry and find his own purpose and true calling. Stanley is grateful for the opportunity to inspire others through his story.

Stanley's favorite scripture is, *So in everything, do to others what you would have them do to you* (Matthew 7:12 NIV). This is a verse his mother instilled in him at a very young age and has shaped him into the man he is today. He looks forward to seeing how God continues to work in his life and those around him.

FINDING THE WARRIOR IN ME

By Stanley VanHorn

For God so loved the world that he gave his one and only
Son, that whoever believes in him shall not perish
but have eternal life (John 3:16 NIV).

Could God love a man like me? To be honest, I'm not sure what I'm doing here within the pages of this book. Recently, I attended a Band of Brothers Boot Camp event, which my daughter had invited me to several times over the years.

At first, I was unsure of my purpose there. Then I heard a very impactful statement that struck me. During one of the sessions, the gentleman speaking said words that will stick with me forever: "You have a warrior inside of you, and that's God's purpose for you. You can do anything if you let the warrior out."

For once, I felt I could fight all the pain I had dealt with in my life. I've wanted to find that warrior inside of me for many years. The warrior my children could be proud of, and who would achieve something for God. Most importantly, I wanted to find the warrior who could stand up to the very thing that's been holding me back from my purpose: depression.

A SHAKY FOUNDATION

When I was a young boy, my family lived in poverty. My parents were older by the time I came along as the youngest of six children. My dad was in his 40s, and he was tired and less active. He was a war veteran who had fought in the Normandy landings during World War II. My dad's experience there had a significant impact on how he felt mentally and physically when I was born in 1959.

My mother was always busy taking care of everything and managing the children, the grandchildren, and the household. She was the daughter of an elementary school principal and grew up under very strict parenting. As a parent, she chose to lean in the opposite direction of her strict upbringing, but she was tough when she needed to be. I was the baby and very close to her.

Being the youngest, I was left to fend for myself as my siblings pursued their own lives. I learned the art of being independent and adopted a strong work ethic from my father. I became very resilient and resourceful. School wasn't enjoyable for me, and I was labeled "not very intelligent," mainly due to a profound stutter and the insecurities of our living situation.

We barely had enough money for food. I remember eating mayonnaise or ketchup sandwiches many days; having meat was a luxury. Even though money was tight, my mother always managed to provide for us and teach us valuable life lessons through church groups.

When I was younger, I attended the Royal Rangers church group. We learned about Jesus and memorized scripture. I enjoyed it and can look back now and see that those were seeds of faith being planted. In the Royal Rangers, I learned one verse that always stuck with me. It was about treating others the way you want to be treated. I've held that verse close all my life.

So in everything, do to others what you would have them do to you, for this sums up the Law and the Prophets (Matthew 7:12 NIV).

I left school in my early teen years, around junior high, to start working. I believe the stress of facing real-life stuff at a young age contributed to the depression I would later battle.

When I was around 16 years old, I met a girl about my age, and we quickly rushed into marriage. She was trying to escape her own home life, and I was eager to leave mine as well. I wanted to build my own family to escape the voids and feel validated. Before I knew it, we had four kids, and I was working two blue-collar jobs to support us. This placed a heavy strain on me as a young man, and it also took a toll on our family because I wasn't able to be around as much as I would have liked.

By the time we turned 21, drinking and partying had become a big part of our lives. We longed for the youth we'd missed. Life spiraled out of control—I was rarely home, and when I wasn't working, I was either partying or chasing my wife out of bars. We were both making mistakes, unintentionally hurting our four small children.

FACING BATTLES

It was during this time that my mother came to me and asked if she should undergo a life-saving surgery for her heart—the same surgery that had recently claimed the life of someone we knew. I told her that the decision was ultimately hers to make; I was afraid that something might happen to her. She chose not to have the surgery, and before I knew it, she was gone.

The last moment I shared with my mom was a moment that will hurt me forever. When I arrived at her home, she had already passed, and I just held her in my arms. Losing her felt like a crushing blow from a bulletless gun. I felt responsible. I think this was the moment when my struggle with depression got bad. It became a permanent part of me, something I would fight against daily.

I had already experienced the pain of losing one of my brothers in a tragic accident, which had nearly destroyed my mother. Years later, my other brother was hit by a drunk driver. He was severely injured and became disabled, only to later in life take His own life from the physical pain he endured.

The weight of these losses haunted me. This was a big part of my hole digging. My mom had been the glue that held our entire family together. She was a Christian woman and loved God with all her heart. She constantly taught all her kids about the Lord. To this day, I wear a cross around my neck as a reminder of what she taught me about Jesus.

Our home was filled with pictures of Jesus and crosses on every wall. But even with all these reminders, I went the wrong way and struggled to find my own relationship with Him. As a little boy, my mom would take me to revival meetings, where I witnessed people passionately praising the Lord. Those experiences planted seeds of hope in me. It was in those moments that I thought, *Okay, this God must be real.*

However, it would take many more years for me to have an intimate relationship with God and truly surrender my life to Him. But I never stopped believing in Him. I always knew that He was real, but He seemed so far away.

After my mom passed away, my life spiraled further into chaos. The drinking, partying, smoking, and fighting with my wife only intensified, and our children began to suffer as a result. It was a series of poor decisions that led to my incarceration, the loss of my driver's license, and eventually, my family. My wife filed for divorce and took our children to another state, leaving me feeling alone and lost.

That was the turning point in my life. It was my rock bottom—a painful realization of how far I had fallen and the impact my choices had on those I loved. I came to a decision: I would no longer allow alcohol and unhealthy habits to take away anything that was mine. This decision marked the beginning of a new journey, but I still didn't see a warrior in me.

FIGHTING SHADOWS

For the next several years, I threw myself into my work, and that became my life. I was juggling two jobs seven days a week. It was the best and easiest thing I could do. I was earning enough to cover my bills and child support while sending my kids extra money for things they needed and spoiling them during the holidays. Staying busy at work helped keep my depression hidden, even though it was still a part of me.

Looking back, I wish I had given more thought to what my children were going through. I regret not playing catch with my son or encouraging my daughters in sports. I didn't know how to do those things because I had never experienced them myself, and I was preoccupied with my own struggles. I carry enormous guilt for that part of my life, which only worsened the darkness inside me.

I had fought hard to overcome my addiction, confront my anger, and change myself. However, the thing that had the tightest grip on me was depression. The darkness became tangled up with every part of me. Depression was who I was and what I would fight daily in secret.

Even as I tried to heal in other areas, I found it incredibly hard to shake off this weight. It was as if I were carrying a shadow with me, a constant reminder of my past struggles and losses that I felt responsible for, and now my wife and children were part of that—buried in my big hole of people that I lost.

I would be lying if I said I didn't put a gun to my head at times. But I was uncertain that if I were to end my life, I would find myself in heaven. The thought of not being reunited with my mother and loved ones again was an even more crippling burden than the depression itself. And the thought of my children having to clean up my mess and being left alone also kept me from pulling the trigger.

So there I was... Depressed and alone without a purpose.

THE IMPACTS OF TRAUMA

Around that time, my girlfriend and her children moved into my house, which caused a lot of issues with my other kids. They couldn't understand why I allowed them to live with me, and they saw my girlfriend as a threat. She was very strict with all the children, and her rules were firm. Since I was always working, I just ignored it all and the chaos of blending our families.

Still, as the years went by, my children began returning to Florida to live with me, one by one. My oldest daughter was the first to come back, and she struggled with frequent bouts of trouble and time in detention centers. At the time, we all viewed her as just a troubled teenager, but now I realize she was a hurt teenager, struggling with the trauma of her childhood. Trauma I was partly to blame for. She is currently serving 12 years in prison on drug-related charges.

Not long after, another daughter joined us, also carrying her own hurt and brokenness, though her struggle did not revolve around drugs. Eventually, my youngest daughter and my son also made their way to Florida. They, too, came with heavy burdens of trauma; my youngest daughter especially struggled to function in the world and make the right choices.

Everyone labeled my children as "bad kids" who were disobedient and troublemakers. However, in reality, they were simply fighting their inner battles to survive. The weight of knowing that I bear some responsibility for their struggles is crushing. I buried those feelings deep inside, attempting to cover them up by drowning myself in work, but I just found myself more depressed and avoiding everything.

As the children grew older and I went through a couple of different relationships, my youngest daughter stayed with me the longest. Unfortunately, she was a full-blown drug addict. I'll spare the details of those hard years, but I can tell you now that I deeply regret how I handled her addiction and my reaction to it.

During one of her drug episodes, she was found foaming at the mouth and rushed to the hospital. Doctors discovered collapsed lungs and said she probably wouldn't survive. Miraculously, she recovered fully, and we hoped she would turn her life around.

One day, I called her in the morning to see if she needed anything from the store, but she didn't answer. When I got home, I banged on the door, still receiving no response. I assumed she was sleeping. After about an hour or two, I went back to her door and began banging on it again. Her boyfriend was supposed to be over, so I warned him that he had better open the door or I was going to force it open. When I finally kicked the door in, I found her lying there in a fetal position, stiff as a board.

I remember thinking, *Oh my God, please no!* I quickly grabbed her and started to carry her into the bathroom, where I ran cold water over her. I had done this before to bring her back from being unconscious, and I hoped it would work again, but that time was different. Her body felt different, so I stopped in the living room and lay her on the floor. I was shaking her and screaming, begging her to wake up. I had never felt her body in such a stiff state before. Her teeth were clenched tightly, and her hands were in fists. I knew this was serious, so I called 911 immediately.

When the paramedics arrived, they pronounced her dead. My daughter was gone. Just like my mom, she died close to my arms. Thoughts swirled in my head: *I could have prevented this. Why didn't I do something? Why didn't I help her? This is my fault.*

I will spare the details of what this loss did to me physically, emotionally, and spiritually; I felt dead inside and completely hopeless. My depression threatened to overtake me.

Around this exact time, I lost two of my sisters—my only two sisters who were still living. They passed away within months of each other. And then my nephew died in a tragic motorcycle accident. These were all people I was very close to, and they lived just minutes away from me. In what seemed like an instant, I lost all of them.

How could this happen? Where is my God? I can't survive this. Does God even love me?

The weight of loss was unbearable. My youngest daughter was gone, and I wanted to trade places with her. I spent many days and nights in my bedroom alone, visualizing that same old gun to my head. I didn't want to live; there seemed to be no purpose for my life, and I felt like the furthest thing from a leader. I was lost and broken, and I had hurt those I loved. The pain of losing so many people at once was overwhelming.

HEAVENLY VOICE

But suddenly, something changed. A voice began telling me that everything was going to be okay. "Just go one more day." It constantly reminded me of the good things I still had in my life.

> *"The Lord your God is with you, the Mighty Warrior who saves. He will take great delight in you; in his love he will no longer rebuke you, but will rejoice over you with singing"* (Zephaniah 3:17 NIV).

Even though my life has been painful and hard, and I've made so many mistakes, I heard that same voice saying, "I forgive you."

I realized that if God in heaven can forgive me, and my children can forgive me, maybe I could forgive myself. And maybe forgiving myself would allow the depression to loosen its grip on me and help me climb out of my hole to live my life.

WARRIOR AWAKENING

Not too long after that, I was baptized and surrendered my life to Jesus. The small voice that had been buried by darkness continued to get louder. I would be lying if I said that climbing out of that hole has been easy; it hasn't. It's been hard, and I'm still climbing.

> *"Have I not commanded you? Be strong and courageous.*
> *Do not be afraid; do not be discouraged, for the Lord your*
> *God will be with you wherever you go"* (Joshua 1:9 NIV).

Every single day, no matter how tough things are, I see a little light. And every day, I hear that voice constantly telling me that there is a warrior inside me. If I can find a way to let that warrior out, I can live an unstoppable life that honors God and leads others to Him.

A warrior isn't someone who never falls down. A warrior is someone who gets back up, fights through the darkness, and chooses to trust God even when everything feels hopeless. That's the warrior God has been developing in me through every painful experience, every loss, every moment I wanted to give up.

> *"But those who hope in the Lord will renew their strength.*
> *They will soar on wings like eagles; they will run*
> *and not grow weary, they will walk and not be faint"*
> (Isaiah 40:31 NIV).

So, can God love a man like me? Absolutely.

And if He can change a man like me, He can do that for you, too.

Our God is a loving Father. No matter what you are going through or have done in your life, He loves you and wants to set you free.

We all have a warrior inside us waiting to be set free! I hope you find yours and never lose hope.

I know that my daughter Amanda is in heaven; her voice joins with God's as she reminds me not to give up, so we can be together one day. The warrior in me fights on, not just for myself, but for everyone who needs to know that God's love never gives up on us.

An Unstoppable Leader Is...
PURPOSEFUL

Driven by Meaning Beyond
Money and Status

By Ken A. Hobbs II

"For I know the plans I have for you," declares the Lord,
"plans to prosper you and not to harm you, plans to give
you hope and a future" (Jeremiah 29:11 NIV).

In a world obsessed with metrics—net worth, social media followers, job performance—purpose can easily become confused with prestige. But the Christian unstoppable leader walks a different path. Their compass is not popularity or profit, but divine purpose. They are driven by meaning that transcends money and status, rooted in a calling that echoes through eternity.

A Christian leader doesn't wait for a title to begin leading. Their purpose is not confined to a corner office or a pulpit. It's a mission etched into their soul by God Himself. Whether a CEO, a teacher, a parent, or a volunteer, they understand that leadership is influence, and influence begins with intention.

Purposeful leaders ask, "What does God want to do through me?" rather than "What can I gain from this?" Their decisions are shaped by a desire to serve, not to be seen. They know that true success is measured not by what they accumulate, but by what they contribute to God's kingdom.

Purpose ignites passion. When a leader is aligned with God's calling, their work becomes worship. They don't just clock in—they show up with fire in their bones. Their energy doesn't come from caffeine or applause, but from a deep conviction that they are part of something eternal.

This kind of passion is contagious. It inspires teams, transforms communities, and challenges the status quo. People follow purposeful leaders not only because they're charismatic, but because they're consistent. Their lives preach louder than their words.

In seasons of uncertainty, purposeful leaders remain anchored in their God-given calling. While others chase trends or panic over profits, they stay the course. Why? Because they know why they're doing what they're doing. Their purpose gives them clarity in chaos.

Jesus modeled this perfectly. Amid pressure from crowds, criticism from religious leaders, and the looming shadow of the cross, Jesus never lost sight of His mission. *"I must be about my Father's business,"* He said (Luke 2:49 KJV). That same clarity is available to every Christian leader who seeks God's will above their own.

Following God's purpose often means being misunderstood. Christian leaders may be called to make unpopular decisions, speak hard truths, or walk away from lucrative opportunities. But they do so with courage, because their aim is obedience, not applause.

Consider Nehemiah. When rebuilding the walls of Jerusalem, he faced opposition, distraction, and threats. Yet he famously declared, *"I am doing a great work and am unable to come down"* (Nehemiah 6:3 NASB). That's the voice of a purposeful leader—focused, firm, and faithful.

Purposeful leaders think generationally. They're not building empires—

they're planting seeds. Their goal is not to be remembered for their wealth, but for their witness. They invest in people, not just profits. They mentor, disciple, and empower others to carry the torch.

Paul wrote these words to Timothy: *And the things you have heard me say... entrust to reliable people who will also be qualified to teach others* (2 Timothy 2:2 NIV). That's legacy—leadership that multiplies and purpose that outlives the leader.

Ultimately, purpose is not discovered in a strategy session—it's revealed in the secret place. Christian leaders find their true calling not by chasing ambition, but by seeking God. In prayer, in Scripture, and in surrender, they hear the whisper of heaven showing them the path to walk.

Purpose is not a product of hustle—it's a fruit of intimacy. The more time a leader spends with God, the clearer their mission becomes. And the more they walk in that mission, the more unstoppable they become.

An unstoppable leader is purposeful. They are not swayed by trends or tempted by trophies, but are driven by a divine assignment that gives meaning to every moment. For them, leadership is not about climbing ladders; it's about carrying crosses. They know that money fades, status shifts, and applause dies down. But purpose—God-given, Spirit-led, Christ-centered purpose—endures. It's the heartbeat of heaven pulsing through our lives.

If you want to be unstoppable, don't chase success; seek significance. Don't build a brand; build the kingdom. And don't ask, "What's in it for me?"; ask, "Lord, what do You want to do through me?"

That's the kind of leader the world needs. That's the kind of leader God is raising up. That's the kind of leader you were born to be. Be an unstoppable leader today!

Tyler Carroll

Tyler Carroll is a young entrepreneur and servant of the Lord. He grew up in Ohio with his eight siblings and moved to Tennessee with his immediate family when he was young. There, he started his first business in landscaping. When he turned 18, Tyler moved back to Ohio, where he now continues his landscaping and is also building a financial services career with his soon-to-be fiancée, Madison.

Tyler is currently involved in a men's Bible study group and is also a committed member of his local church. Additionally, he serves on the leadership team of the Great Lakes Band of Brothers bootcamp in northeast Ohio.

Tyler's mission is to be an evangelist, spreading the gospel wherever he goes. He knows that God has truly anointed him with the gifts and resources to lead people to the Lord. By God's grace, Tyler also plans to start his own ministry with the purpose to help people live their healthiest lives — physically, mentally, emotionally, financially, and relationally— through biblical principles.

God's Perfect Plan

By Tyler Carroll

She likes to say she was the reason I decided to move back, and although she was a part of it, that wasn't the main reason. I knew I wanted to grow closer to God. If this was the girl God had for me, I wanted to know more about God and the Bible so that I could lead her spiritually.

> *He who finds a wife finds a good thing, and obtains favor from the Lord* (Proverbs 18:22 NKJV).

CHILDHOOD

I grew up in Northeast Ohio and lived there for the bulk of my childhood. Growing up, I didn't really have faith modeled for me by either of my parents. But I remember going to Vacation Bible School as a young kid, and ever since then, I've always believed in God. My family was wealthy, and I didn't have much hardship. However, my father was dealing with wounds from his childhood, and he did not have a relationship with God. Therefore, my siblings and I experienced the negative effects of that growing up.

I can still remember getting in trouble and being sent to my room, lying on my bed, crying, and begging God that my dad would choose to use his hand this time instead of the belt. The belt hurt. Even in those moments of pain, I somehow knew to call out to God.

The Lord is close to the brokenhearted and saves those
who are crushed in spirit (Psalm 34:18 NIV).

When I was about 12 years old, my parents called the family together and told us we were moving to Tennessee. It was scary hearing that I would be moving away from the only place I'd ever known, away from all the friends and memories I'd made throughout my life. At the time, I couldn't see God's hand in this move, but now, I see this was part of His divine plan. He was orchestrating every detail for my good.

"For I know the plans I have for you," declares the Lord, "plans to prosper you and not to harm you, to give you hope and a future" (Jeremiah 29:11 NIV).

STANDING APART

Tennessee was cool. I made a lot of friends throughout the rest of middle school. At some point, I had heard the scripture about not having sex until marriage. After hearing that verse, it weighed heavily on my heart; I knew this was something I wanted to follow.

So throughout middle and high school, relationships never made sense to me; I knew there was no point in dating someone unless I planned to marry them. I didn't have access to a Bible and wasn't attending church at the time, but I had heard bits and pieces of scripture that always resonated with me. For as long as I can remember, I have had this respect for the Word of God and have always wanted to do my best to obey what I knew.

Your word I have hidden in my heart,
that I might not sin against You
(Psalm 119:11 NKJV).

This desire to live differently wasn't coming from my strength. Even the small portions of God's Word that I had heard were taking root in my heart, creating a conviction that would guide my decisions.

My freshman and sophomore years of high school had their ups and downs. I started to hear and learn more about God through friends at school, with whom I became very close. I began to enjoy living in Tennessee and made a lot of great memories. Around that time, I also joined the basketball team, and for some reason, a few of the seniors chose me as the freshman to pick on. I didn't feel like I fit in; I hadn't hit puberty like they had, and I wasn't as good a player as they were either.

One time, our whole team was sitting in the locker room when one of the seniors started picking on me. I didn't really know how to stand up for myself, and it got to the point where he said, "You should just kill yourself. Nobody would even care if you did." And wow, that hurt. Not only did it hurt, but it was also embarrassing, as it was said in front of the whole team. I don't think I will ever forget that moment.

Since then, I have forgiven him in my heart and found peace in the phrase, "Hurt people hurt people". I know he was fighting his own battles. However, at that moment, I did seriously consider taking my life.

Things were still rough with my family, and the physical abuse from my dad returned. I was also still wrestling with what my purpose was in Tennessee. I felt hatred and resentment towards my parents for robbing me of the life I could've lived in Ohio.

So I was left feeling ugly, unworthy, unloved, confused, lost, and depressed. There were too many nights when I genuinely contemplated taking my life. I would pray almost every night. I still didn't know what I was praying to or why I was praying, but I would lie in my room and look at the ceiling, crying and asking God why.

You keep track of all my sorrows. You have collected all my tears in your bottle. You have recorded each one in your book (Psalm 56:8 NLT).

Even in my darkest moments, when I felt completely alone, God was collecting my tears. But looking back, I can see the spiritual battle that was raging over my life.

"The thief comes only to steal and kill and destroy; I have come that they may have life, and have it to the full" (John 10:10 NIV).

PURSUED BY GOD

I started my own landscaping business in Tennessee. While on a job one day, I was putting in a garden bed when an HVAC technician pulled up in his van. As he was walking to the door, he just confidently asked, "Are you saved?" And there I was, frozen in my tracks, not knowing how to answer his question. I had told God I believed in Him, I had prayed and repented of my sins, but I still didn't feel confident enough to answer surely. Out of embarrassment, I said yes.

When the man came back outside, I stopped him and asked, "How do you know for sure?"

He started talking about his relationship with Jesus; he explained that the more he prays and reads the Bible, the more connected he feels.

Never having had access to a Bible, I asked him, "Where do you get a Bible?"

He answered, "Anywhere. Amazon,... Walmart,... church." But then he said,

"Will you be here at the same time tomorrow?" I said I would, and he told me he would bring me a Bible.

And the things you have heard me say in the presence of many witnesses entrust to reliable people who will also be qualified to teach others (2 Timothy 2:2 NIV).

God had orchestrated that divine appointment to get His Word into my hands.

PURSUING GOD

I began to pursue God more deeply during my junior and senior years of high school. It was around that time that I really struggled with lust and pornography, which I have since been delivered from. It was a serious problem for me and my mental health. I thought that if I was still sinning, but it wasn't with a girl, then it wasn't as big of a deal, but Jesus said, *"Anyone who looks at a woman lustfully has already committed adultery with her in his heart"* (Matthew 5:28 NIV).

God doesn't view any sin as greater than or less than any other. Every time we sin, we feel a sense of conviction. Every time I would fall into temptation, I would think about the Bible under my bed and why I was doing what I was doing.

No temptation has overtaken you except what is common to mankind. And God is faithful; he will not let you be tempted beyond what you can bear. But when you are tempted, he will also provide a way out so that you can endure it (1 Corinthians 10:13 NIV).

God was teaching me that victory was possible.

Throughout the rest of high school, I never really went to parties, drank alcohol, or did drugs because I knew I wanted to be different from most people. I also understood that those things wouldn't fulfill me anyway. I spent most of my time running my landscaping business, preparing for the future with various side hustles, working out, and spending time with my close friends.

Do not conform to the pattern of this world, but be transformed by the renewing of your mind (Romans 12:2 NIV). Even without fully understanding that verse, I was living this out.

I never really wanted to get too attached to anything in Tennessee because, ever since the day my parents told me we were moving, I always knew I wanted to move back to Ohio. There were many nights through the rest of high school when I just felt so alone and depressed, thinking that the Lord had abandoned me. I'm so thankful today that God kept me strong enough to make it through that, now knowing and further understanding the good Lord's plan all along.

> And we know that in all things God works for the good
> of those who love him, who have been called according
> to his purpose (Romans 8:28 NIV).

I learned a lot throughout my time in Tennessee. God was using every painful experience, lonely night, and moment of despair to shape me into the man He designed me to be.

Soon after I turned 18, I decided to move back to Ohio on my own. A few months before, I had been visiting Ohio, working with a friend to flip a house. During that trip, I went to the gym to work out and met a girl named Madison.

GOD'S PERFECT PLAN UNFOLDS

Things started to line up for my move back to Ohio. I even spoke with my friend about going to church with him when I returned. It was definitely hard leaving my family in Tennessee because they were a huge part of my life, and I had never lived on my own before.

After making the move, I initially worked with my friend Steven for the first week or two. I had also kept in touch with the girl I met at the gym. Our first hangout was going to church together in December 2023.

I was nervous. It was the first church service I had ever attended. I used to think that church was just a place where weird, creepy religious people gathered every Sunday—like a cult. That's what I had been told by my dad when I was growing up. But boy was he wrong.

In that service, I prayed the prayer to give my life to Jesus for the first time.

If you declare with your mouth, "Jesus is Lord," and believe in your heart that God raised him from the dead, you will be saved (Romans 10:9 NIV).

This was my spiritual birthday, the day I truly became a son of God.

Madison and I continued to go on dates and get closer. On February 17, 2024, after being in Ohio for only about two months, we started dating. Looking back, God's timing has been nothing but perfect throughout my entire life. I feel very grateful that God has trusted me to love one of His daughters.

When we met, we were in a very similar spot in our faith, and we have been growing rapidly together, becoming more and more on fire for the Lord. Since we started dating, we have attended church regularly every Sunday, begun reading the Bible more, and surrounded ourselves with godly people.

We have also been blessed to be part of young adult groups and Bible studies.

> As iron sharpens iron, so one person sharpens another
> (Proverbs 27:17 NIV).

God brought Madison into my life, not just as a romantic partner, but as someone who would challenge me to grow in my faith.

As I write this, we have been dating for about a year and four months, chasing after the Lord every day. She has helped bring my smile and joy back to my life. It definitely hasn't been perfect, but we both know that there was no coincidence in our meeting, and we are committed to doing whatever is necessary to stay together.

We agreed to make God the center of our relationship. Though one may be overpowered, two can defend themselves. *A cord of three strands is not quickly broken* (Ecclesiastes 4:12). We understand that without God, our relationship would fall apart.

We have plans to get engaged and married within a year or so.

Madison and I now run a business together, teaching people about how money works and helping them manage their finances. I'm also a part of several different ministries, one of which is Band of Brothers. I helped open a new men's ministry location in the Great Lakes area, and I currently serve on the leadership team for that location.

GOD'S ANOINTING REVEALED

Looking back over my journey, I can see God's anointing on my life in ways I never understood before. Every painful experience, every moment of despair, and every time I felt abandoned, God was preparing me for something greater. He was developing in me a heart of compassion for others who are struggling, feel worthless, and are battling depression and thoughts of suicide.

> *Praise be to the God and Father of our Lord Jesus Christ,*
> *the Father of compassion and the God of all comfort, who*
> *comforts us in all our troubles, so that we can comfort those*
> *in any trouble with the comfort we ourselves receive from God*
> (2 Corinthians 1:3-4 NIV).

The anointing on my life isn't just for my benefit—it's so I can reach other young men who are exactly where I was. The pain I endured hasn't been wasted. The depression I fought through wasn't meaningless.

When I stand before a group of men in Band of Brothers and share my story, I see recognition in their eyes. They see someone who has walked through the valley of the shadow of death and come out the other side. That's the anointing—God using our greatest struggles to transform them into our greatest strengths in ministry.

> *And he said to me, "My grace is sufficient for you,*
> *for My strength is made perfect in weakness"*
> (2 Corinthians 12:9 NKJV).

God's anointing isn't about perfection; it's about His power working through our weaknesses to accomplish His purposes.

Today, I'm not just a survivor of depression and suicidal thoughts; I'm a warrior equipped to help other men win their battles. I'm not just someone who has struggled with purity; I'm someone who can show others the path to freedom. I'm not just a guy who felt abandoned growing up; I'm a man who has found his identity in his heavenly Father.

The anointing of God on my life is evident in every area—in my relationship with Madison, in my business, in my ministry leadership, and in my daily walk with Christ. What the enemy meant for destruction, God has turned into my greatest testimony and my most powerful tool for ministry.

This is what it means to be an unstoppable leader: Not being perfect, but learning to let God's anointing flow through our imperfections to impact the lives of others.

The God who carried me through my darkest moments is the same God who has equipped me to be a light for others as they walk through their own darkness.

BRETT DABE

Brett Dabe is an accomplished entrepreneur, author, and visionary founder of Godfident. com, a platform that guides men toward biblical success in an unbiblical world. He also works alongside his wife, Maria, in a ministry that prepares Christians for covenant marriages.

Brett's journey to success was paved with decades of adversity and numerous trials. Through these challenging experiences, he discovered profound spiritual truths that would reshape his entire worldview. He uncovered the essential elements for living an abundant life through perseverance and faith. Empowered by God's grace, Brett has developed transformative tools and resources that have not only changed his life but also inspired and uplifted many others.

As a dynamic speaker, mentor, and leader, Brett's work has a profound impact. He not only excels as a business professional in the payments processing industry but also as a dedicated ministry leader. His and Maria's story reflects their commitment to spreading hope and encouragement, a mission they continue to pursue with unwavering dedication and passionate purpose.

He can be reached via Brett@Godfident.com

FROM FEAR TO LOVE

By Brett Dabe

There is no fear in love; but perfect love casts out fear,
because fear has punishment. He who fears is not
made perfect in love (1 John 4:18 WEB).

Let me tell you about fear. Not the kind that makes you jump when someone sneaks up behind you. I'm talking about the deep, soul-crushing fear that drives every decision you make in relationships. The fear of being rejected. The fear of not being enough. The fear of being truly known and found wanting.

That fear controlled my life for 50 years.

I want to be honest with you about my story because I've learned that unstoppable leaders don't hide their failures—they use them. And if my mess can help prevent a mess in your life or give you hope that God can rebuild what you've destroyed, then it's worth my vulnerability.

CRACKS IN MY FOUNDATION

Growing up in a Christian home, I was enrolled in a small Christian day school, attended church faithfully, and even had "all the right verses" memorized. That all should have been an advantage. But somehow, I never learned how to relate to people, especially women. I was an awkward kid who knew Bible verses but couldn't figure out how to have a conversation.

When I hit public high school in ninth grade, the bubble that had always protected me burst, and I got bullied hard. Really hard. The kind of bullying that makes you question everything about yourself. I was mediocre at most sports. I wasn't cool. And I wasn't confident. I just tried to survive each day without getting humiliated again.

Looking back, that is when my fear really took root: Fear of not measuring up, of being exposed as inadequate, of being rejected by people whose opinions I thought mattered.

Scripture tells us that *God didn't give us a spirit of fear, but of power, love, and self-control* (2 Timothy 1:7 WEB); however, I was living from a completely different spirit. Every relationship decision I made was driven by fear, not faith.

During my junior year, I transferred to a Catholic high school where I finally found some success. I was a decent tennis player and even became a coach for the girls' tennis team. For the first time, I felt like maybe I could actually talk to women without completely embarrassing myself.

That's when I entered my first real relationship, which I handled exactly how you'd expect a fear-driven teenager to. When I no longer wanted to be in the relationship, instead of being honest and having a difficult conversation, I did what cowards do—I started ghosting her, making it awkward and avoiding the hard stuff.

I hurt a really sweet girl because I was too afraid to be honest. That was my introduction to how *not* to be a man in relationships.

In my next relationship, I thought I'd found love. We became sexually active, and I convinced myself she was the one. But when she went away to college, the relationship fell apart. She basically did to me what I'd done to the previous girl. And man, that hurt.

But pain can be dangerous when you're operating from fear. Instead of learning from what happened, I made a vow: I would never be hurt like that again. I would find someone who was "safe." Someone who met all the religious criteria. Someone my family would approve of. Someone who couldn't possibly reject me because we were "equally yoked."

The Bible does talk about being equally yoked: *Don't be unequally yoked with unbelievers, for what fellowship have righteousness and iniquity? Or what communion has light with darkness?* (2 Corinthians 6:14 WEB). But I twisted this truth into a formula for avoiding pain rather than pursuing God's best.

THE PERFECT CHRISTIAN FAÇADE

Then I found her—a pastor's daughter from my conservative Lutheran denomination. My mother was thrilled. Everyone thought we were the perfect Christian couple. We went to church every Sunday, looked the part, and acted like we had it all figured out.

But we were living a lie.

We were practically living together, having sex, and doing everything married couples do. We, however, didn't commit to marriage, but instead wrapped our sin in religious language. We looked holy on Sundays, but lived unholy Monday through Saturday. Our relationship, on my part, was produced due to fear. I sought performance instead of intimacy, was more concerned with managing my image instead of establishing an authentic connection, and wanted to look the part religiously instead of developing spiritual intimacy.

We kept up appearances, getting married right after college graduation. However, from day one, something was off. I'd hoped marriage would solve my struggle with lust and masturbation, but it didn't. When high-speed internet became available and I got my first computer, within a month, pornography became a regular part of my life.

By my mid-twenties, we were expecting our first child, but the doctors told us our daughter probably wouldn't survive birth. We actually made funeral arrangements. By God's grace, our daughter did live, but she had profound special needs that put enormous pressure on our marriage, which, of course, was already built on shaky ground.

Over the next several years, we had three more children, and I was still living a double life. I was earning good money, but spent more than I made. And I was in constant survival mode—financially, emotionally, and spiritually; yet I maintained my holy façade by being an elder in our church.

He who conceals his sins doesn't prosper, but whoever confesses and renounces them finds mercy
(Proverbs 28:13 WEB).

I was concealing everything, and it was destroying me from the inside out.

THE SPECTACULAR COLLAPSE

By my late thirties, my house of cards came tumbling down. I went through what you'd call a midlife crisis from age 38 to 43. It included a long list of moral, professional, and spiritual failures that I'm not proud of but won't hide from.

First, I got divorced. Then, I began a relationship I should never have been in. Next, I was divorced again within a year. I lived like a vagabond, moving between about ten different places in those five years, getting evicted from half of them.

By the time I was 43, I was broke and broken. I lived with my parents and felt I'd failed in every area that mattered. I'd been charged with felony child support violations and was facing 33 months in state prison. Because it was my first offense, I got a chance to get my life together, but I was starting over from nothing.

I'd hurt my children deeply, damaged relationships with two women who deserved so much better, and ruined my reputation and my finances. Most significantly, I nearly destroyed my relationship with God.

But here's what I learned about God during the darkest season of my life: He doesn't abandon you when you abandon Him. David wrote, *Yahweh is near to those who have a broken heart, and saves those who have a crushed spirit* (Psalm 34:18 WEB).

That was me. Broken-hearted and crushed in spirit. And that's exactly where God met me.

THE LONG ROAD TO BECOMING A MAN

At 43, with no clue what I was going to do with my life, I relocated to Florida when someone offered me a chance to earn the income I desperately needed. I didn't understand that this was God's plan to place men in my life who didn't judge me. They loved me and discipled me, teaching me what being a real man actually looks like.

Growing wasn't quick or easy. From about 44 to 50, I slowly learned what authentic manhood meant. But even during that season, I was in two more relationships where I was still trying to fill the God-sized hole in my heart with another person.

I was still operating from fear, which reared its ugly head in so many ways. I feared being alone, being unwanted, and not being enough. Fear-driven relationships end up hurting everyone involved, so it is no surprise that I hurt myself and two more women who just wanted what I wanted: a blessed relationship that would last. I was still trying to get from others what only God could give me.

Trust in Yahweh with all your heart, and don't lean on your
own understanding. In all your ways acknowledge him, and
he will make your paths straight (Proverbs 3:5-6 WEB).

I knew this verse, but I wasn't living it. I was still leaning on my own understanding, still trying to manage outcomes through my own efforts.

By the time I was 51, something had shifted. Through the patient discipleship of godly men and years of slowly learning to surrender control to Jesus, I finally understood what being in a covenant relationship actually meant: being deeply committed to each other in good and bad times, with mutual love, a shared purpose, and a sacrificial stance willing to put the other person first.

I also realized that to be healthy going into any relationship, Jesus Christ needed to be on the throne of my heart—not just in theory, but in practice. And not just on Sundays, but every day. I knew that the woman I would eventually marry would need to have the same foundation. It wasn't about finding someone from the right denomination or someone who checked all my boxes, but about finding someone who genuinely loved Jesus and was surrendered to Him. For the first time in my life, I was actually seeking God's kingdom rather than my own comfort.

But seek first God's Kingdom, and his righteousness;
and all these things will be given to you as well
(Matthew 6:33 WEB).

LOVE REPLACES FEAR

In the spring of 2022, I went hiking in Utah for the first time. After an incredible day in God's creation, I was driving back to my Airbnb and had a conversation with God. I told Him I didn't know who He had for me in the future, but I would be patient. I also told Him that whenever His timing was right, I was ready, but she'd have to love hiking, because I was definitely going to want to do more of it.

Within 48 hours, I was introduced to Maria, who lived in New York City and loved hiking. She'd had almost the exact same conversation with God just two weeks before, telling Him she was looking for someone who "really loves Jesus."

Our relationship was different from day one than any other I'd had. For the first time, I kept Jesus at the center. Maria and I prayed intentionally about whether God was bringing us together rather than just following our emotions and desires.

We were engaged within six months and married a few months after that. The difference in this relationship is hard to put into words, but the biggest change was the absence of fear. I had gone from fear, which had driven my whole existence, into love rooted in Christ's love for us.

> We love him, because he first loved us
> (1 John 4:19 WEB).

I finally understood that I couldn't love properly until I truly received God's love for me. All my previous relationships had been attempts to receive love from someone else, rather than expressions of the love I'd already received from Christ.

When you know you're completely loved by God, you stop trying to manipulate others into loving you. When you're secure in Christ, you can actually serve someone else instead of just using them to meet your needs.

Solomon wrote, *Whoever finds a wife finds a good thing, and obtains favor of Yahweh* (Proverbs 18:22 WEB). This has absolutely been true in my life, but only after I learned to find my identity in Christ first.

LEADERSHIP LESSONS

So what does all this have to do with being an unstoppable leader? Everything.

Leadership isn't just about vision, strategy, and making tough decisions. Leadership is about relationships. And you can't lead others to places you haven't been yourself. You can't give what you don't have.

For 51 years, I operated from a place of fear in my relationships, and it produced nothing but destruction. Fear makes you selfish and manipulative. It makes you try to control outcomes instead of trusting God's process.

But love changes everything. When you're rooted in God's love, you can actually serve others instead of using them. You can be vulnerable instead of hiding behind masks and have difficult conversations instead of avoiding conflict.

Here's what I wish I'd learned decades earlier: Unstoppable leaders in relationships don't try to find the perfect person; they *become* the right person. They don't focus on meeting their own needs; they focus on meeting others' needs. They don't avoid difficult conversations; they initiate them.

Most importantly, unstoppable leaders understand that every relationship is ultimately about pointing people toward Jesus, not toward themselves.

When you get relationships right, everything else improves. My relationship with my children, which had been devastated by my failures, began to heal as I learned to love like Jesus loves. My business relationships improved because I stopped operating from a place of scarcity and fear. My leadership became more effective because people could sense authenticity instead of performance.

Above all these things, walk in love, which is the bond of perfection (Colossians 3:14 WEB).

When love becomes your operating system instead of fear, every area of your life is affected.

So, here's my challenge to you, especially if you're a man reading this: Stop trying to manage your relationships through fear and control. Stop avoiding the hard conversations. Stop trying to find someone to complete you instead of becoming complete in Christ.

If you're single, use this season to become the man God designed you to be. Get discipled by older, wiser men. Learn to serve others without expecting anything in return. Deal with your areas of bondage and brokenness now, before you drag someone else into your mess.

If you're married, stop trying to change your wife and start focusing on becoming the husband God calls you to be. *Husbands, love your wives, even as Christ also loved the assembly, and gave himself up for her* (Ephesians 5:25 WEB). Christ's love is sacrificial, not selfish.

If you're divorced like I was, don't rush into the next relationship while trying to heal from the last one. Let God heal you first. Let Him transform your motivations. Let Him teach you what love actually looks like.

Perhaps you're reading this and thinking your relationship history is too messy for God to work with. Maybe you've hurt people, have been hurt, or are afraid it's too late to experience something real and lasting. Let me tell you something: God specializes in redemption stories. He takes broken pieces and creates something beautiful. He takes fear-driven failures and transforms them into love-driven successes.

Therefore if anyone is in Christ, he is a new creation. The old things have passed away. Behold, all things have become new (2 Corinthians 5:17 WEB).

Becoming a new creation in Christ is not just a theological theory; it's a living reality for anyone willing to surrender their relational patterns to Jesus. The same God who walked on water wants to walk through your relationship storms with you. The same Jesus who turned water into wine longs to transform your relational disappointments into something beautiful.

But your transformation must begin with surrender. So, surrender your need to control, your fear-based patterns, and even your timeline and your preferences. Completely surrender to the One who loved you enough to die for you.

Unstoppable leaders understand that relationships are about two complete people choosing to build something together that honors God and serves others. They don't enter relationships from neediness but from abundance. They don't hide their struggles but use them to help others. They don't avoid difficult seasons but walk through them with faith.

Most importantly, unstoppable leaders understand that every relationship is a stewardship from God. Whether in marriage, friendship, parenting, or leadership, we're called to love others the way Christ has loved us. That kind of love casts out fear, creates safety for vulnerability, builds trust through consistency, and produces fruit that lasts generations.

God's love changes everything. It is the foundation that allows relationships to go the distance and will transform broken men into unstoppable leaders.

The journey from fear to love isn't easy, but it's worth it. Take it from someone who spent decades getting it wrong before God taught me to get it right.

Your story doesn't have to end with the mistakes you've made. With God's help, your most daunting failures can become your most powerful testimonies. Your deepest pain can become an unending source of compassion for others.

That's the hope I want to leave you with. No matter where you've been, no matter what you've done, no matter how many times you've failed at relationships, God isn't finished with your story.

He's still writing. And if you'll let Him, He'll help you write a love story that reflects His heart for the world.

From fear to love. It's possible. I'm living proof.

AFTERWORD

As you've seen over and over in this book, unstoppable leadership is not about having the correct title or filling the highest position; it is about influence, resilience, and inspiring others toward a shared vision. Unstoppable leaders are not born; they are forged by God in the fires of adversity, refined by purpose, and propelled by a relentless commitment to growth. Whether you are looking to grow in your own leadership or mentoring others to do so, the journey to becoming unstoppable begins with intentionality, courage, faith, perseverance, and leaning on brothers who will see you through. Unstoppable leaders know where they are going—they have a compelling vision that transcends personal ambition and sees adversity as an opportunity. Their vision becomes a spiritual GPS, guiding decisions and allowing them to energize other leaders.

We pray that you've been able to understand and relate to the Men of Honor who stepped up to transparently share the obstacles they've faced, offering you a glimpse of how God can work victoriously. We hope their words and experiences have illuminated the adversities that may be ahead of you, preparing you to seek God's guidance as you recognize and admit that we all need His strength. Revisit these accounts and teachings as you keep pressing forward with power...

As an unstoppable leader, seize the opportunity to build resilience through adversity. We all face setbacks, but an unstoppable leader rises from the chaos stronger. They do not avoid adversity, but rather transform it into opportunity. They reframe challenges—instead of asking, "Why is this happening to me, God?" they ask, "What is this teaching me, Lord?" And they help others do the same. When someone is struggling, an unstoppable leader does not just offer solutions or try to fix it, but instead, offers their presence, guidance, and wisdom, highlighting what God is developing through the struggles. An unstoppable leader helps others see the strength within their faith.

To be the leader God has called you to be, live your values. Do not just talk about them, embody them. Let your actions reflect your faith, beliefs, and principles. Create a values-driven culture. And help others define and live by their values, building trust and unity with your brothers, family, and those you are called to lead. Inspire action through passion. Passion is contagious. When leaders are lit with the Holy Spirit from within, they ignite others.

Unstoppable leaders do more than manage others; they mobilize, inspire, and empower. So lead with energy. Show up with enthusiasm. Your passion and faith can be the spark that lights someone else's fire and gives them hope. Make it your goal to fan others' flames. Recognize what excites and motivates those around you and help them pursue what sets their soul on fire. And share your story; others can use it as a survival guide to help them find their advertunity, perhaps even becoming an unstoppable leader themselves.

Leadership is not a solo sport; it is a relay. As you grow, prepare to pass the baton. Help others rise by leading and coaching intentionally, sharing your wisdom and wounds so others can learn from your journey, and acknowledging small wins. Recognize that encouragement fuels momentum and choose to challenge with love, compassionately pushing others to grow. Believe in the God-given potential of those you lead, even when they doubt it. Create opportunities that offer room to lead. Encourage risk-taking, decision-making, and learning through experience.

The stories you have read were not written by men who are fearless; they were written by men who chose to be faithful to the promises of God and never lost hope as they looked to Him for strength. These authors have shared their stories to empower you to be faithful to God and His purpose, people, and principles. They want you to know that when you lead with heart, humility, and hope, you will not just become unstoppable, you will help others become unstoppable, too. We have learned through our adversities to love God, love people, and keep pressing forward no matter what.

I press on toward the goal to win the prize for which
God has called me heavenward in Christ Jesus
(Philippians 3:14 NIV).

In this verse, Paul uses the analogy of a runner who focuses on the goal ahead of him, guarding him from distractions and preventing him from stumbling. Paul plainly states his spiritual goal: Christ Jesus!

So, rise. Lead boldly. And lift others as you fight through adversity. Choose to be unstoppable every day. Tomorrow might be your greatest chance to stand up and be called an *Unstoppable Leader* who Presses Forward with Power... God's Power, which lives in you!

Be Unstoppable. Be the Leader that God has called you to be!

MORE WPP ANTHOLOGIES!

Faith Unchained: Climbing to Freedom by God's Grace is more than a book; it's a lifeline for weary hearts ready to rise. On these pages, you'll discover powerful testimonies from women who have walked through fire and found freedom. The words within don't present a quick fix; they offer hope and healing.

The stories and teachings in *Restoration* will fill you with hope as you witness God's steady and sure hand at work. Although we may feel like we've lost everything, we can stand strong, knowing God will bring beauty from the ashes of our lives. There is no need to despair—God's restoration will begin the moment you give your heart and circumstances to Him.

Men, families, communities, and countries must be on guard as courageous and battle-ready warriors. Men of God are each commissioned to be vigilant conquerors, prepared to lead the fight to overcome evil. The valiant authors in *Fit 2 Fight* share how they have overcome using the weapons that ensure victory no matter what we face.

God longs for you to have ferocious faith grounded in His unwavering love. Get ready to be encouraged as you open the pages of *Unshakable: God Will Sustain You*. Through true stories written by faithful and resilient women, you will witness God's sustaining power available to those who rely on Him.

The authors of *Unseen: You Are Not Alone* share their struggles of feeling isolated and unnoticed and detail how our awesome God helped them overcome every obstacle to find what truly matters: Him. These stories and devotional teachings shed light on the truth of your significance and value. You are never alone!

Despite all the adversities we face throughout our lives, God is the source of our hope. As you read the pages of this book, you will see firsthand how God brings *Hope Alive* to every person who is yearning for a reason to go on. Like a broken tree in a dark place is primed for new growth, God can use the rich soil of your dark place to prepare a new life to sprout in you.

The authors of *Miracle Mindset: Finding Hope in the Chaos,* have experienced the wonders of God's provision, protection, and guidance. These stories and teachings will ignite a spark within you, propelling you to encounter the marvel of God's miracles, even in the chaos.

Life is full of storms and rough waters. The stories in *Navigating Your Storm: By United Men of Honor* will give you the ability to see the light of God and navigate your storm victoriously.

With *Joy Unspeakable: Regardless of Your Circumstances,* you will learn how joy and sorrow can dance together during adversity. The words in this book will encourage, inspire, motivate, and give you hope, joy, and peace.

Surrendered: Yielded With Purpose will help you recognize with awe that surrendering to God is far more effective than striving alone. When we let go of our own attempts to earn God's favor and rely on Jesus Christ, we receive a deeper intimacy with Him and a greater power to serve Him.

United Men of Honor: Overcoming Adversity Through Faith will help you armor up, become fit to fight, and move forward with what it takes to be an honorable leader. Over twenty authors in this book share their accounts of God's provision, care, and power as they proclaim His Word.

Embrace the Journey: Your Path to Spiritual Growth will strengthen and empower you to step boldly in faith. These stories, along with expertly placed expositional teachings will remind you that no matter what we encounter, we can always look to God, trusting HIS provision, strength, and direction.

Victories: Claiming Freedom in Christ presents expository teaching coupled with individual stories that testify to battles conquered victoriously through the power of Jesus Christ. The words in this book will motivate and inspire you and give you hope as God awakens you to your victory!

WPP'S MISSION

World Publishing and Productions was birthed in obedience to God's call. Our mission is to empower writers to walk in their God-given purpose as they share their God story with the world. We offer one-on-one coaching and a complete publishing experience. To find out more about how we can help you become a published author or to purchase books written to share God's glory, please visit: **worldpublishingandproductions.com**

From the award-winning, bestselling *I'm Sober... So Now What?* series, comes *Unity in Recovery*—a powerful next step for anyone seeking deeper healing after addiction. This book goes beyond staying sober and explores what it means to live in true connection—with ourselves and with others.

This phenomenal story of rescue, restoration, hope, healing, and forgiveness will captivate you. *Who Is Able? The Dana Louise Cryer Story* is an incredible journey of tremendous pain, pierced by tumultuous circumstances and filled with twists and turns. God's incredible love transforms this true-life survival account into a miraculous outcome of total freedom. This book will leave you breathless and in tears at what only God can do.

At seventeen, Audrey Marie experienced a sudden and relentless excruciating firestorm of pain. *Chronically Unstoppable* tells of her true-life journey as she faced pain, developed strength, and battled forward with hope.

The world has become a place where we don't have a millisecond to think for ourselves, often leaving us feeling lost or overwhelmed. That is why Max Gold wrote *Planestorming!*—a straightforward guide to help you evaluate and change your life for the better. It's time to get to work and make the rest of your life the BEST of your life.

Riley Rossey is not your everyday bullied student, but one who discovers how to utilize his talents to assist other shy and picked-on individuals. Journey with Riley as he meets bullying head-on and becomes a God-given blessing to so many in *The Bullied Student Who Changed All the Rules* by Robert M. Fishbein.

www.ingramcontent.com/pod-product-compliance
Lightning Source LLC
Chambersburg PA
CBHW071708120626
46550CB00001B/150

* 9 7 8 1 9 5 7 1 1 1 5 1 3 *